THE OHIO RIVER VALLEY SERIES

Rita Kohn and William Lynwood Montell
Series Editors

D1566503

THE
KENTUCKY
RIVER

William E. Ellis

THE UNIVERSITY PRESS OF KENTUCKY

Publication of this volume was made possible in part by a grant from Cinergy, the parent company of ULH&P, and a grant from the National Endowment for the Humanities.

Editorial and Sales Offices: The University Press of Kentucky
663 South Limestone Street, Lexington, Kentucky 40508-4008

07 06 05 04 03   5 4 3 2 1

Library of Congress Cataloging-in-Publication Data

Ellis, William E. (William Elliott), 1940-
    The Kentucky River / William E. Ellis.
        p. cm. — (The Ohio River Valley series)
    Includes bibliographical references and index.
  ISBN 0-8131-2152-3 (acid-free paper)
  ISBN 0-8131-9063-0 (pbk: alk. paper)
    1. Kentucky River (Ky.)—History. 2. Kentucky River (Ky.)—Bibliography. 3. Interviews—Kentucky—Kentucky River. 4. Oral history. I. Title. II. Series.

F457.K3 E45 2000
976.9'3—dc21   99-048254

Manufactured in the United States of America

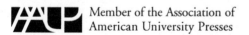 Member of the Association of
American University Presses

Hill and valley, mountain and plain, gorge, meander, sandbar and riffle—all are but passing local features in the ceaseless change of a great river.

—Willard Rouse Jillson, *The Kentucky River*, 1945.

CONTENTS

ILLUSTRATIONS

MAPS

SERIES FOREWORD

The Ohio River Valley Series, conceived and published by the University Press of Kentucky, is an ongoing series of books that examine and illuminate the Ohio River and its tributaries, the lands drained by these streams, and the peoples who made this fertile and desirable area their place of residence, of refuge, of commerce and industry, of cultural development, and ultimately, of engagement with American democracy. In doing this, the series builds upon an earlier project, "Always a River: The Ohio River and the American Experience," which was sponsored by the National Endowment for the Humanities and the humanities councils of Illinois, Indiana, Kentucky, Ohio, Pennsylvania, and West Virginia, with a mix of private and public organizations.

The Always a River project directed widespread public attention to the place of the Ohio River in the context of the larger American story. This series expands on this significant role of the river in the growth of the American nation by presenting the varied history and folklife of the region. Each book's story is told through men and women acting within their particular place and time. Each reveals the rich resources for records, papers, and oral stories preserved by families and institutions. Each traces the impact the river and the land have had on the individuals and cultures and, conversely, the changes these individuals and cultures have wrought on the valley with the passage of years.

As a force of nature and as a waterway into the American heartland, the Ohio and its tributaries have touched us individually and collectively. This series celebrates the story of that river and its valley through multiple voices and visions.

From the epoch of Archaic people building a sophisticated culture, to the era of Native Americans encountered by Europeans, to the time of Euroamerican settlement, to the present, the Kentucky River has been a highway for trade and a provider of goods and power. The Kentucky continues to touch the lives and fortunes of about one-sixth of its namesake state. Meandering northwestward through four distinct geological regions from its origins in the southeastern highlands, the Kentucky River enters the Ohio between Carrollton and Prestonville, about a half-mile below the Little Kentucky River.

William E. Ellis, in his new history of the river, merges extant scholarship with first-person narratives, collected from 1989 to 1998, to provide new insights to a valley intimately entwined with the American story. Major figures such as naturalist James Audubon, frontiersman Daniel Boone, and the industrious Shakers are synonymous with the Kentucky River Valley. However, though rich in history, literature, and prestige—it hosts the state capital, Frankfort—proponents for Kentucky River improvements have had a hard time being heard. Ellis's intimate knowledge of details and personalities illuminates two centuries of realities of politics in an economically challenged area. Within the scope of eight chapters, Ellis examines the past to direct attention to the future. Thomas D. Clark, in his foreword for *The Kentucky River,* places it in the context of his own benchmark lifelong scholarship on both the river and the state named Kentucky.

Rita Kohn
William Lynwood Montell

FOREWORD

Early in the Depression-ridden 1930s, that romanticist, Constance Lindsey Skinner, promulgated the concept that the rivers of North America were in fact streams of poetry and folk history. The rivers were the living cords which bonded the course and mores of American life. It is doubtful that she knew much about the Kentucky River. Throughout untold centuries rains have fallen on its drainage basin, and the waters have gnawed deep channels and up-hollow coves across the face of the land. The Kentucky has conquered great stone barriers and deep-seated loess levels with unrelenting force. Physiographically the Kentucky River Valley has ever been a broad natural laboratory of ecological, geological, and environmental forces.

Before the end of this century there will have appeared three books relating to the Kentucky River. Fortunately these books complement each other. The United States Corps of Engineers has in publication a study which describes the Kentucky River basin in terms of its physical being, and man's longtime efforts to harness and utilize its flood. The river is viewed in terms of its physiological being, its behavior in times of floods, and in stinging droughts.

For years Mary Verhoeff searched diligently and patiently for data detailing the history of the Kentucky River Basin in terms of its human population, trade, and political past. She delineated the history of the region in terms of its impact upon the ways of human life, and upon the economy of Kentucky. There is not a single fork, creek, or spring branch in the Kentucky River drainage system that has not produced some kind of physical or human history. In recognition of this fact William Ellis has woven a deep-hued tapestry of the ways of life, or memories, and myths of life along the forks, the creeks, and the main stream of the Kentucky.

The history of the Kentucky River and its drainage area has been inextricably interwoven with geology, environment, economics, and the politics of Kentucky. From the outset of penetration of the great trans-Appalachian littoral by adventurers and pioneering settlers the Kentucky River has been a benchmark in the history of the sprawl of Anglo-American civilization. It had a fundamental bearing on the centralizing of the political Commonwealth of Kentucky.

In plain down-to-earth terms of reality no one knows how many thousands of land deeds bear the locational legend, "on the waters of the Kentucky" or on those of one of its branches. By the same token the bottomlands or shoulders of the river have generated a wide diversity of cultural, economic, and political conditions of human lives. In the upper reaches headstreams of the Kentucky historically led human settlers inland to become culturally and economically locked behind isolative land barriers. In these areas time and folkways stood still for more than a century.

Standing in sharp contrast the downstream Kentucky basin produced lavish field crops and great meadows populated by livestock with more impressive pedigrees than those of their owners. The produce of the fields could be moved only by flatboats down the Kentucky and ultimately to the markets in Natchez and New Orleans. This annual flotilla of flatboats not only bore away the abundant resources of Kentucky fields and meadows, it stamped the impress of personalities and images in the annals of American history. In a broader sense the Kentucky River was a decisive factor in the location of the capitol of Kentucky, a place where both virtue and violence sprang up in equal measure.

Spring and fall tides, which occurred on the Kentucky with calendrical regularity, were moments when farmer-log raftsmen drifted millions of board feet of virginal timber to the downstream sawmills. In time the highlands about the three forks of the river were stripped of the finest hardwood timber to be found on North America. How many times in this era could one have found men in the flesh who equaled, perhaps exceeded, Mike Fink, Paul Bunyan, John Henry, and all the rest as half horses-half alligators. Every bend, eddy, suck, and rocky shoal in the river was a challenge to manly courage and venture.

Fortunately William Ellis has been able to sift the final tailings of the river's early history. There still linger memories of the log runs, the long, labor-intensive polings of johnboats, and shootouts with bank-squatting ruffians. Embedded in the silt-ladened bowels of the river are untold thousands of feet of sunken logs that are as sound now as they were the day of their harvest. There prevails in spots tangible relics of the rafting days. Chain dogs have remained driven into trees along the ancient anchorages. Long-barreled "hog rifles" and 45-caliber pistols were as much standard log man equipment as were axes, pike poles, cant hooks, and chain dogs.

Over two centuries men have pawed out ferry landings, built bridges, and choked the river with locks and dams. They have defiled it with silt from their strip mines, emptied their sewerage into its current, and cluttered its banks and channel with their cast-off garbage and worn out machines. They have raped its forested hinterlands, and poisoned its waters with chemicals. The Kentucky flows on, wielding a mighty influence upon the lives of its admirers and its defilers with a stubborn will. It holds within its banks and current the fate of towns, industries, and even state and federal governments. In a surly mood it can destroy human life, property, with unruly flood tides. In drought the Kentucky is still the mistress of the region, choking the land in a crisis drought constrictions.

William Ellis has tramped the river's banks and neighboring roads, engaged men and women in reminiscent conversations about the river and its place in their lives. The people he interviewed are as indigenous to the river basin as the line of trees which cast their long shadows on the bosom of the river tide. I have read this book with a deep tinge of nostalgia. What a help a tape recorder and more textual book space would have been in 1938-1941. The author of this book has filled in many a niche with rich historical and nostalgic mortar, and given an impressive new dimension to the river, its valley, and folklife. This book presents a strong historical lacing between the river, the environment, and the course of human life well removed from the sinuous course of its channel and flood plain.

Thomas D. Clark

PREFACE

Three fine books have been written about the Kentucky River: Thomas D. Clark's *The Kentucky*, Willard Rouse Jillson's *The Kentucky River*, and Mary Verhoeff's *The Kentucky River Navigation*. Each used a specific method that will not be duplicated in this book. Clark's approach was cultural and historical; Jillson adhered strictly to geology; Verhoeff used economic analysis. My purpose is synthesis, building on these books and using information not available to these authors. I have no proprietary claim on the river or its history but intend to use a unique approach to understanding the history of Kentucky's namesake river.

In one sense this is a book of history, of factual information, quite conventional in style and approach. But it is also a book of ideas—the idea of the river, in this case the Kentucky, in the minds of those who have lived, worked, played, and grown up on it. Much of the book is based on oral histories collected in the late 1980s and early 1990s, a crucial time for interviewing, because the "old-timers" had begun to die out. When possible the recollections of Kentucky River people have been checked with other sources; this is not always possible, however, because their experiences were often out of the realm of the written record. In many places these common people, the nonelite, speak quite eloquently in their own idiom about the Kentucky.

Each chapter of *The Kentucky River* examines a particular crisis that the people of the valley have faced. The crises of transportation and the economy, ecology and the environment have often clashed with political reality and other forces in the valley. Can the Kentucky political climate of the late twentieth and early twenty-first centuries save the river?

I am forever indebted to all those people who, during interviews, opened their homes and, quite often, their hearts to me. Most spoke lovingly of their time on the river. I can only hope that this book does justice to their candor and to their concern for the Kentucky River. This book is dedicated to them and to all who keep a watchful eye on the Kentucky, cleaning up its trash, encouraging improved water quality, and forcing political attention on the river. May their efforts one day return the river to its rightful place as a centerpiece of Kentucky life. If never again pristine and recognizable to the likes of Daniel Boone, the Kentucky River can, and should, once again become a place of playful, joyous experience for the youth of the Commonwealth of Kentucky.

Todd Moberly deserves a special thanks for his help in interviewing many of the subjects in the "Living and Working on the Kentucky River Oral History Project."

Thanks also to Garland R. Dever Jr., who proofed my most difficult chapter, "Folds, Faults, and Uplifts," and saved me from many geological blunders.

Former Eastern Kentucky University Department of History secretary Pauletta Perkins and former Oral History Center secretary Opal Horn helped in many ways on this project.

The Oral History Commission of the Kentucky Historical Society, directed by Kim L. Smith, deserves special thanks for funding the "Living and Working on the Kentucky River Oral History Project." Over 170 interviews from this project are on file with the commission and in the Special Collections of Eastern Kentucky University. The commission also funded transcriptions of a substantial number of interviews which have been invaluable in writing this book.

Archivists of special collections and librarians at Eastern Kentucky University, The Filson Club, Berea College, the University of Kentucky, the Inland Rivers Library of the Hamilton County Library, Cincinnati, Ohio, the Kentucky Historical Society, and the National Archives, Southeast Region, Atlanta, helped in numerous ways to bring important materials to my attention.

I am grateful for sabbatical leaves granted by Eastern Kentucky University in 1990 and 1998, without which it would have been impossible to research and write this book.

Finally, the life and work of Thomas D. Clark has been an inspiration to me and to several generations of Kentuckians. No person or state could have a better mentor. If we heed his words, his gentle admonitions, and his good-natured advice, the Commonwealth of Kentucky will be a better place, finally fulfilling its promise after over two hundred years of bitter frustration. Thanking me for sending greetings upon his ninety-fifth birthday, Tom replied: "I hope your life flows as freely as does the Kentucky." I am sure he would wish the same for all the people in the Kentucky River Valley.

CHAPTER ONE

The Kentucky

Time and the River

Kentucky—the very name is mysterious. Wrongly believed by many people to mean "dark and bloody ground" or a combination of "cane" and "turkey," the name is still clouded in controversy. Could it mean "land of tomorrow" in Wyandot, or "place of meadows" in Iroquois, or the name of a river bottom in Algonquin? Part of the continuing romance of the state is that we do not know the precise origin of "Kentucke." Contrary to a widely accepted view, native Americans such as the Cherokee, Shawnee, and Choctaw frequented the region for many generations. They left surprisingly little trace of their habitations before Euroamericans came to what Daniel Boone described as "the beautiful level of Kentucke."[1]

Kentucky is also the name of a river, a river being, according to an old definition, a stream at least 100 miles in length. Nearly 255 miles long, the Kentucky flows from the confluence of the North and South Forks at Beattyville on a generally northwesterly course to the Ohio River at Carrollton. The headwaters of the Three Forks of the river, the North, Middle, and South, rise in the eastern Kentucky mountains near Pine Mountain. Covering a drainage of nearly 7,000 square miles, or about one-sixth of the total for the Commonwealth of Kentucky, the river drops 226 feet from Beattyville to Carrollton.[2]

The geological formation of the river basin came over a period of millions of years. The Cincinnati Arch, which crests at Camp Nelson, caused the land to rise from the Pliocene epoch 10 million years ago into the Pleistocene, which began nearly 600,000 years ago. At one time the mouth of the Kentucky flowed into the ancestral Ohio River, the ancient Teays system, far north of the present-day site of Carrollton. Glaciation and constant weathering have added to the character of the river.[3]

The river flows through four regions: the Cumberland Plateau,

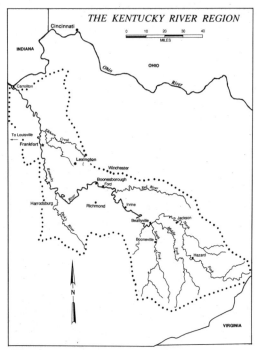

THE KENTUCKY RIVER REGION

The Kentucky River Region. (William G. Adams, Richmond)

the Knobs, the Lexington Plain, and the Outer Bluegrass. For eons ancient shallow seas deposited sediments that formed the region's limestone. The oldest of the state's rock formations, the Ordovician, dates back a half billion years and is found in the Bluegrass area. In several areas old river channels are found, long cut off by flooding and the shifting of the earth. Major faults slash across the river, with two particularly dangerous ones in the Clay's Ferry area of Madison, Clark, and Fayette Counties.[4]

In the upper reaches of the river region massive coal seams were laid down from decaying swamps of the Pennsylvanian period. Later the Appalachian Mountains began to rise. In the region of modern day Lexington, an *anticline*, or dome shape, began to appear. Erosion of the weaker rock in central Kentucky formed a somewhat flat area called the Lexington Peneplain. The river cut deeply into the limestone. Over eons it scoured out the Palisades, an entrenched meander 400 to 500 feet deep from Frankfort up the river for 100 miles to Boonesborough. A region of nearly impermeable rock, the Eden Shale, encircles the Bluegrass region, but it could not keep the Kentucky River from eventually breaching it and returning to its northwesterly course.[5]

The geology of the region also dictates subterranean features. Wherever limestone is in such great profusion, there is a *karst* region, a system of sinkholes and caves that could be as extensive as that of Mammoth Cave or as small as the numerous cliff overhangs in eastern Kentucky. Much of the water in central Kentucky lies beneath the soil in underground streams and is subject to extensive pollution from agricultural, industrial, and human wastes.[6]

The first humans in the region faced not our modern problems but those of a more primitive, natural world. Though there is still great debate over where the first Asians appeared in the New World, there is little doubt that people had made their way into the Ohio Valley by 12,000 B.C. Early man was drawn to the region by the bountiful wildlife, and, from the eastern part of the state, where they lived under sandstone cliffs, to the well-known mounds at Wickliffe in far western Kentucky, the imprint of native peoples was made on the region long before Europeans arrived.[7]

Prehistoric Native American cultures have been divided by archaeologists and anthropologists into four distinct groups: Paleoindian, from 12,000 B.C. to 8000 B.C.; Archaic, from 8000 B.C. to 1000 B.C.; Woodland, 1000 B.C. to A.D. 1000; and late pre-historic, often called Fort Ancient for a site just north of present-day Cincinnati, from A.D. 1000 to the advent of Euroamerican exploitation of the west, about 1750.[8]

During the time of the Paleoindians, the climate was much cooler and wetter than at present as it changed from the Pleistocene, the last of the ice ages, to the earliest Holocene, the most recent epoch of geologic time. The weather would have been much like that of upper Canada today as the last of the ice ages retreated northward. Paleoindians lived in small groups, hunting and gathering across the evergreen forested landscape. They stalked large animals with heavy lances tipped with fluted spearpoints. Both climatic change—the warming of the region and the final retreat of the southernmost glaciers— and hunting led to the extermination of mammoth, mastodon, giant bison, and other Pleistocene animals much larger than today's North American mammals. The remains of such creatures have been found in profusion at Big Bone Lick in northern Kentucky and at other bone-yielding sites.[9]

As the weather warmed around 8000 B.C., Archaic peoples hunted animals and gathered plants much like those of today. White-tailed deer and buffalo became staples in their diets, as well as elk, turkey, and the occasional bear. When the forests changed in many places to dense groves of oak and hickory, these people collected hordes of nuts, called *mast*. Living in semi-permanent camps they roamed river valleys, such as the Kentucky, which was now thoroughly entrenched throughout much of its course. They worked the river, catching fish in low water pools and collecting shellfish of several varieties. The rising of floodwaters obliterated most traces of their habitations long ago.[10]

Archaic Indians are differentiated from their predecessors by the type of projectiles that predominated in their hunting repertoire. They tipped their spears with notched and stemmed stone spearpoints and used a wooden stick, an extension of the arm called an *atlatl*, to provide greater force and accuracy. They began living longer in one place and slowly developed agriculture. Perhaps squash was the first plant domesticated, and, although we do not know its origin, it probably came from the south as corn, or maize, did. Stone mortar and pestles were used for grinding nutmeats and plant material into palatable food.[11]

By about 1000 B.C. climate patterns were similar to those of today, and the Woodland Native Americans developed new living skills in their environment. They made the first clay pottery. They continued a lifestyle much like that of the Archaic peoples; however, they began to depend more on gardening, and grasses, sunflowers, and squash were among the most important staples in their diets.[12]

Woodland peoples developed trade relationships with other Native Americans, exchanging their wares for shells from the seacoast and copper from the north. More specific cultures, such as the Adena and Hopewell, appeared across the region. Their craftsmen made translucent mica into intricate flat objects that can only be described as works of art, undoubtedly of religious significance. Often known as the Mound builders, the Woodland people built circular burial mounds all over the Kentucky River region. Large mounds in Madison and Clark Counties testify to their intricate social and political organization. Along the river bottoms these people began to live a more sedentary lifestyle, depending more and more on agriculture while breaking up into smaller familial groups in the harsher months of winter. Long before the settlements of Euroamericans in the Kentucky River region in the mid-1770s, native Americans were already feeling the impact of European diseases for which they had no immunity passed on by the continual flow of migrants across the frontier.[13]

Euroamericans began to make inroads into the western regions in the seventeenth century. For generations the Native Americans had used the land well, often employing fire to control the underbrush to make a better hunting environment. By 1750 Native Americans of the Fort Ancient era had melded into the well-known tribes of the historic period, such as the Choctaw, Cherokee, and Shawnee. They had adopted the bow and arrow for hunting, developed large villages, and warred with each other over the bounty in Kentucky. Eastern tribes were pushed westward and entered the ancestral grounds of other tribes. The river valley was poised on the brink of momentous change.[14]

Contrary to the old story that a squirrel could have jumped from one tree to another all the way from the Virginia coast to the Mississippi River, Kentucky in the late eighteenth century was dotted with open savanna land. Herds of buffalo in the thousands, as well as other big browsing animals, kept large areas nearly treeless, with only grasses and low shrubs surviving the onslaught. Open savanna land still can be found in isolated places in the Inner Bluegrass. Land like this captivated early settlers, who dreamed of herding cattle, sheep, and horses on the sweet bluegrass. Buffalo traces existed all over the Kentucky River region. Large herds, seeking the line of least resistance to their travels, crossed the river many times. Native Americans and white pioneers also used these more-or-less natural trails as their roadways.[15]

Gabriel Arthur, in 1674, may have been the first white man to see the Kentucky River. By the time Daniel Boone and the famous long hunters made their trek into the wilderness in the 1770s, the outline of much of the area had been mapped. The Kentucky River was a well-known feature to Boone and others long before actual white settlement.[16]

When Boone sighted the river for the first time, it looked much different than it does today. The river has been canalized by dams into a series of lakes, but when the first pioneers saw the Kentucky, stretches of pooled water, varying from a quarter mile in length to more than 5 miles, were separated by rocky shoals, called ripples or riffles, that provided fording places for man and beast. The shoals were sometimes nearly dry, while the pools contained only a few feet of water. The many tributaries spilled large quantities of sand and gravel into the river, creating sometimes impassable bars. Periodically a major flood would wash them away, or at least redeposit them. However, no major barrier to transportation could compare to the Falls of the Ohio at present-day Louisville, which in early pioneer days required a portage for much of the year. The Kentucky would flood occasionally but not nearly as often or as greatly as it did after the Euroamericans brought their extensive agricultural methods to the area. Mining and timbering only added to the denuding of hillsides that soaked up rainfall before 1775 and the advent of white settlements in Kentucky.[17]

Boone also would have seen hundreds of buffalo grazing on canebrakes, which covered dozens of acres of Kentucky River bottomland. Now difficult to find because of the extensive agricultural use of the river bottoms by white settlers, cane grew to heights of 20 feet in pioneer days. There could have been no more beautiful sight to Boone and other Euroamerican pioneers than these plentiful buffalo, at home with their environment and offering a seemingly endless source of meat and hides. By the early part of the nineteenth century, the woodland buffalo had disappeared from the Kentucky River Valley.[18]

The first attempts at permanent settlements converged on the

Kentucky River. In 1774, James Harrod brought his pilgrims down the Ohio River by flatboat and then up the Kentucky to a spot near present-day Shaker Landing in Mercer County before taking off across country to what is now known as Harrodsburg. A year later, Boone led his group through Cumberland Gap, up the Wilderness Road to a site on the Kentucky. Hence, Kentucky's origin as the first of the western territories depended on the river for transportation, food, water, and safety.[19]

The earliest Euroamerican fur trappers used Indian-style dugout canoes on the river, while the first white settlers used both canoes and flatboats to work their way down the Ohio and up the Kentucky. As early as 1790, three crude barges carrying coal, often called *stone coal* to differentiate it from charcoal, floated down the Kentucky from the highlands near Beattyville to Cleveland's Ferry, now called Clay's Ferry. However, for many years, the plentiful hardwood forests made coal usage mostly unnecessary. Wood made into charcoal fired the first iron furnaces that dotted the landscape near the Kentucky River in such places as Estill County and the Red River country.[20]

The settlements at Boonesborough and Harrodstown weathered the depredations of attacks by the British and their native allies during the Revolutionary War. Indeed, after the brief abandonment of Harrodstown, only the continuous success of the Boonesborough experiment, along with the heroic efforts of General George Rogers Clark and his men in the Ohio Valley, gave the Americans an uncontested claim to control Kentucky. Kentucky continued as a county of Virginia throughout the war, eventually splitting into three counties afterward.[21]

As Kentucky neared statehood (1792), the burgeoning white population used the Kentucky River as a daily highway in and out of the region. Daniel Boone and others traveled the banks of the river, hunting, trapping, and fishing. The river abounded with sturgeon as big as a full-grown man, and paddlefish, a type of catfish, were almost as large. Naturalist John James Audubon once remarked about a hunting trip he took with Boone along the Kentucky that the squirrels were so plentiful they could be easily shot out of the trees. Boone, however, showed Audubon a way that did the least damage to the animal's flesh. From a distance Audubon estimated as fifty paces, Boone calmly raised his long rifle and "barked" a squirrel, splintering the wood beneath the animal and killing it with the concussion of the lead ball.[22]

By the time of statehood, numerous settlements had been made up and down the Kentucky. In 1775, Leestown, named for Capt. Hancock Lee, became an early English settlement on the banks of the

Kentucky near the distillery in present-day Frankfort. Frank's Ford, a sandy crossing on the Kentucky named for Stephen Frank, who was killed during an Indian attack one evening in 1780, became a more populous settlement and thus Kentucky's capital. From the mouth of the Kentucky at Carrollton, originally called Port William, upriver to Beattyville, settlements sprang up in the valley.[23]

These communities attempted some control over the Kentucky. Where the river could not be forded during periods of high water, ferries appeared by the score. Richard Callaway received the first ferry authorization at Boonesborough in 1779. The next year Indians attacked workers constructing a ferryboat on the banks of the Kentucky at Boonesborough, killing two whites and abducting two slaves. The oldest continuous business in the state still exists in the very viable Valley View Ferry, authorized in 1785, where Madison, Jessamine, and Fayette Counties meet. Most ferries were small wooden flatboats capable of carrying a wagon or two as well as a few human and animal passengers. The earliest ferries were pulled across the river hand over hand by a rope or wire suspended over the water. A hindrance to navigation of the river, ferries were the only reasonable crossing points long before any bridges were built over the river. Names like "Old Landing" in Lee County exemplify the importance of such places in the ordinary lives of nearly everyone in the region. Other entrepreneurs built fish dams and grist mills on the river as well as along the many creeks that emptied into the Kentucky.[24]

From the earliest days, local and state officials understood the importance of river transportation for the future of the region. In 1787, Gen. James Wilkinson, a powerful figure in the early history of the Commonwealth, sent a flotilla of flatboats down the Kentucky, the Ohio, and the Mississippi to New Orleans. The Spanish had denied the "right of deposit" for American citizens, but Wilkinson received a concession. Wilkinson, whom Kentucky's historian laureate Thomas D. Clark cogently identified as "a man of fine address, sound talent, exceedingly industrious, and wholly unscrupulous," had designs for separating Kentucky from the United States if he could not totally control the fate of the region. He tried to monopolize the river traffic, grossing $100,000 for his river ventures until 1791, but ended in spurring others to develop the natural and agricultural resources of the region. Kentucky whiskey, flour, butter, and pork, as well as wide poplar wood planks from the flatboats, enriched the "Crescent City" of New Orleans and its citizens. Iron from Franklin County was smelted on what is now called Old Ironworks Pike in Fayette County, then used locally or shipped down the Kentucky in the western trade. Wilkinson and others built wharves on the river in Frankfort and throughout the river region to supply the outside world with other Kentucky products such as hemp, salt pork, and tobacco. Kentucky would never be the same, and as part of the western movement, would continue to expand American influence.[25]

Before the canalization of the Kentucky, flatboats and keelboats lined the banks in late winter waiting for the "spring tide," a rising flooded river, in order to begin their journey toward New Orleans. Many carried tobacco, a crop encouraged by Wilkinson's lucrative trips downriver. In early 1806 John Stuart, a flatboat crewman, noted in his diary at least one hundred such craft lining the banks of the river at Frankfort. Flatboats were usually from 12 to 25 feet wide by 20 to 60 feet long. Most had a modest cabin for the crew. Plentiful poplar wood was a favorite among boatmakers because of the wide boards that could be sawn with relative ease. A long oar called a *gouger* was used at the stern for control, and side oars known as *side horns* or *sweeps* were part of the navigation system. Between 1805 and 1807, more flatboats arrived in New Orleans from the interior of Kentucky than from any other western stream. Indeed, these boats were called "Kentucky Boats" in the Crescent City, where the poplar planks from such craft went into constructing houses. While flatboats might be more easily constructed, keelboats, with a pointed prow were needed for trips upriver. Elijah Craig, often given credit for inventing the process for making bourbon whiskey, developed a fleet of keelboats operating as far upriver as the mouth of Dix River. The manifest of one such large craft, the *Sophia*, listed 2 tons of tarred cordage, 50 barrels of flour, 70 gallons of peach brandy, 28 barrels of saltpeter, 650 gallons of whiskey, 900 pounds of bacon, as well as other products. Warehouses were built along the river at Boonesborough, Dick's River, Cleveland's Ferry, Jack's Creek, and numerous other places extending the length of the river. After trade on the river ballooned, the state legislature began to license official inspection stations and warehouses, eventually creating thirty-eight, in order to ensure quality control over the goods produced and shipped from Kentucky. By 1802 trade valued at over $1 million a year made its way from Kentucky to New Orleans by flatboat.[26]

But even if the trade could be controlled to some extent, such as by refusing substandard tobacco to be transhipped downriver, there was little that could be done to rein in the behavior of the river men. Mathew Carey noted in 1828 that Kentucky River men, while not as wild as pictured, did "pride themselves on the roughness and rudeness

of their manners . . . the half-horse, half-alligator" way of life perpetu-
ated in the tales of Mike Fink and his cohorts. At least in the eyes of the
middle class, the section of the Frankfort waterfront known as the
"Craw" became synonymous with lawlessness and immorality. This
community originated in the makeshift homes of people who came to
Frankfort to be near family incarcerated in the nearby state penitentiary. According to historian Thomas D. Clark, travelers could find
"all the drunken wickedness of the Biblical twin cities in concentrated
form" in the Craw. The bordellos, gambling dens, and "blind tigers," a
name given to unlicensed drinking establishments, emptied the pockets of many a hard-working, and unfortunately hard-living, river workman. A raftsman often returned to his highland home carrying the chains
used to tie the logs together and little else. But such an experience with
city life gave him another reason to return soon to Frankfort.[27]

In sharp contrast with the bawdy denizens of the Craw, the industrious Shakers were another important river community. The Cane
Ridge Revival, often called the Great Revival, was the most obvious of
the roiling religiosity sweeping the Kentucky frontier at the turn of the
nineteenth century. The Shakers, or the United Society of Believers in
Christ's Second Appearing, abstained from sex in the belief that the
imminent second coming of Christ precluded the need for such sins of
the flesh and "the world," as they called the outside. By late 1806 the
Shakers had established their presence in Kentucky at Pleasant Hill,
overlooking the Kentucky River in Mercer County.[28]

Shaker Landing soon became one of the busiest ports and ferry
sites on the Kentucky. Eventually controlling over 4,000 acres, the
Shakers built their western utopia on a strong agricultural base. Although celibate themselves, their animals and plants proliferated boun-
tifully. Naturally the Shakers, like other more worldly Kentuckians,
turned to the Kentucky River as their highway. They built a state-of-
the-art gristmill on Shawnee Run Creek, which even contained a me-
chanical elevator, shucker, and sheller. But something had to be done
with their bounty.[29]

Before the advent of steamboats, the Shakers built their own flatboats and operated a ferry at the site of the present boat ride at Shaker
Landing. Their flat brooms and garden seeds became some of the most
sought-after and profitable of their goods. They also bred some of the
best livestock in the West. Hardwoods along the river became the substance of their fine furniture, which is still highly prized today. Their
simplistic streamlined designs fit not only their ethos but the spirit of
the times as well. The buildings at Pleasant Hill today testify to people

at once seeking the simple life while living better than the vast majority of Americans in the early nineteenth century.[30]

The Kentucky River played an important role in the release of tensions, sexual and otherwise, in the Shaker community. The rugged gorge below the settlement offered an opportunity for healthful walks, and viewing spring wildflowers and other wonders alleviated some of their drudgery. The river offered them the joy of fishing in abundant waters. They picnicked on the river in large groups in another form of "releasement" that one dour diarist described as a waste of the energies of such a religious community. The Civil War disrupted most of the trade on the Kentucky River and ominously encouraged a sea change in Shaker industry that would eventually lead to the end of the settlement. After the war, construction of the Southern Railroad's High Bridge, literally within sight of the Shaker enclave, foreshadowed the arrival of modern transportation and technology to the Kentucky River Valley. The Shakers were no longer as isolated as before, even taking in borders and serving meals to outsiders, who visited the magnificent palisades and the new iron bridge.[31]

Early Kentuckians looked hard at improvements on the Kentucky. Depending as it did on the whims of the river's tides to provide the depth necessary for shallow-draft craft, Kentuckians interested in regularized transportation on the Kentucky often called upon the legislature to do something about their plight. As early as 1792, the year of statehood, the state legislature discussed improvements. In December 1801 the legislature chartered the Kentucky River Company, for the purpose of clearing obstructions to navigation, but it accomplished nothing.[32]

In 1811 the state legislature authorized a lottery to raise $10,000 to finance improvements on the Kentucky with the ambition of clearing impediments from the South Fork down to Carrollton. The saltworks of Gov. James Garrard on Goose Creek in Clay County and other business ventures would have prospered with better transportation down the Kentucky. Unfortunately the necessary funds could not be raised, as investors looked for more lucrative investments elsewhere.[33]

The race was on to apply the steam engine to propelling a boat. Several Kentuckians tinkered with the new form of power. Edward West, a Lexington watchmaker and inventor, designed a simple single piston engine, tested as early as 1793 on a model boat. Although his machine ran ten years before Robert Fulton's, he was relegated to anonymity by the New Yorker's fame and fortune. Stephen H. Long built a steamboat at Hickman Creek at Camp Nelson on the Kentucky. Possibly using a steam engine shipped in from outside the area, this craft made an exploratory trip up the Missouri River in 1816. Others became interested in the new technology, including Richard M. Johnson, the hero of the Battle of the Thames during the War of 1812 and later a vice president of the United States, who financed another steamboat. Another Kentuckian, John Fitch, built working steamboats in the Bardstown area. Frustrations with patents and the legal system ended in his untimely death caused by substance abuse. Only New Yorker Robert Fulton reaped the financial rewards for his patented steam conveyance and the appearance of his steamboat *New Orleans* on the western waters in 1811.[34]

One area in Frankfort, owing to the industriousness of local businessmen and artisans, became known as Steamboat Hollow. Though small by Ohio and Mississippi River standards, Frankfort led the state's shipbuilding. The *Calhoun, Frankfort, Kentucky, Lexington, Providence,* and *Plough Boy*, all shallow-draft vessels drawing less than 2½ feet and ranging in tonnage from 112 to 450, were built in Kentucky River boatyards between 1818 and 1825. By 1820 at least seven boats were in regular service on the Kentucky.[35]

Although steamboats now plied the Kentucky, only during a few short months of the year during the tides could boats operate with any regularity. The State Board of Internal Improvements, created by the General Assembly, obtained federal surveys of the river in 1828 and 1829. These surveys, made by the War Department, recommended a slackwater system of locks and dams and the removal of mill and fish dams from Boonesborough to the mouth of the river. Two army engineers suggested construction of an experimental dam at Frankfort. Because the Kentucky River was entirely within the boundaries of the state, any plans for federal construction aid got caught in the conflict between Kentucky's Sen. Henry Clay and President Andrew Jackson. The president vetoed Clay's Maysville Bill, which provided for a road connecting that town on the Ohio with Lexington. "Old Hickory" argued that the road would only help the citizens of one state, being intrastate, and therefore did not fit his interstate dictum for internal improvements. No federal money would be forthcoming for improvement of the Kentucky River either.[36]

As river trade increased, dozens of steamboats appeared on the Kentucky. Though hampered by the months of low water, Frankfort continued as the center for much of the trade. In 1834 the *Argo* carried the engine for the Lexington and Ohio Railway locomotive that employed an incline plane to move in and out of Frankfort. Plying the waters of the Kentucky, steamboats also made the lengthy trip to Louisville. Other boats on the Kentucky included *Nick of the Woods, Ocean, Arena,* and *Blue Wing.* They carried everything from coffee to nails, mackerel to wine. Like many other steamboats, the *Blue Wing,* originally the *Fannie Freeze,* went through frequent name changes as it moved from river to river. For anyone "who has ever been on a steamboat in the wintertime," marine architect Alan L. Bates humorously recalled, "that name is appropriate. They were bought and sold like jackknives."[37]

Steamboat accidents, the most violent of which were boiler explosions, became such a problem that in 1836 the state legislature passed an act "to protect lives and property on board steamboats." In one incident in 1828, the *Sylph* burned, killing three people. The year of the law's passage, three men were scalded to death when the *Star* blew up. Like most riverine states, Kentucky also outlawed boat racing, which often contributed to accidents and explosions.[38]

In the days before the Civil War, there were few railroad connections in the region of the Kentucky River. Steamboats provided an important role in transportation and communication. For example, in 1832 a young Mercer County entrepreneur took a shipment of 200 sacks of corn to New Orleans and expected to make a good profit. However, there was always the danger of accidents on the western rivers and the uncertainty of fluctuating commodity prices. To ship goods from Cincinnati to Frankfort cost twenty-five cents per 100 pounds on the *Arena* in 1846. These boats carried downriver central Kentucky products such as tobacco, flour, whiskey, and hempen goods. The Kentucky River Mills opened in Frankfort, leased waterpower, and produced hempen goods, such as carpet backing and binder twine, well into the twentieth century. The river provided not only waterpower for that business but a transportation route as well.[39]

If the state could not depend on federal aid in the Jacksonian era for developing the Kentucky River, it would find other ways to finance the venture. In the 1820s and 1830s many states developed their transportation resources, New York's Erie Canal being the most famous of the revolutionary changes taking place in water transportation throughout the country. A series of Whig governors began to push for a Kentucky version of Henry Clay's American System of internal improvements. The Kentucky State Board of Internal Improvements, created at the behest of Gov. James Turner Morehead by the state legislature, recommended canalization in a landmark 1836 report. Kentucky was ready to join the race for commerce.[40]

R.P. Baker, chief engineer of the state of Kentucky, presented a forty-six-page report. Because of the Kentucky's length and periods of low flow, he suggested a series of dams just past Frankfort, or 100 miles from Carrollton, creating a slackwater section. He admitted that a series of locks and dams could not be guaranteed to stand up to the ravages of floods and that constant vigil would be needed to keep them operational and free of sediment. The four or five locks (two plans were presented) connected to the side of the dam would have inside measurements of 170 feet in length and 36 feet in width, and would provide a lift of 15 feet. Baker estimated that vessels up to 250 tons could use the waterway for most of the year. Waterpower could be tied into each dam such as had been accomplished on streams in Ohio and Pennsylvania. To allay fears that the purity of the river would be harmed by the dams, he suggested that the regular opening and closing of the locks would alleviate that problem. The stream would be widened and deepened by the dams, aiming at a minimum depth of 5 to 6 feet at all times. Furthermore, he predicted that the pools, the stretches of water between the dams, would appear nearly motionless most of the time. Baker's report even suggested, rather grandiosely, tying together the Kentucky and the Cumberland Rivers with a canal. Barbourville citizens, isolated as they were at this time in eastern Kentucky, applauded this part of the report. The estimated total cost of the project, if built all the way to Beattyville, would be $669,503.[41]

The Kentucky project was the most extensive of its kind on western waters, and although experimental, it appeared to have a good chance of success, according to engineer Baker. The state also planned to build projects on the Green River and proceeded to sell bonds. Although the legislature approved a $2 million expenditure, investors purchased only $350,000, making it necessary to borrow more funds. After more problems, eventually contracts were written for five dams.[42]

Like many such projects, construction of the navigation system was not completed on time and ran considerably over cost estimates. Each structure averaged $220,000 to build. Upon completion in 1842, five stone-masonry locks, had been constructed with clearances of 38 by 145 feet and with wooden-lock doors. The locks would last much better over time than the rock-filled timber crib dams, which were being covered with wooden planks. Though back-filled with rock, the dams constantly leaked. One cheap method of filling these leaks, used into the twentieth century, consisted of floating hay and coal dust into the rifts, thereby offering a temporary cure that would soon be breached again by turbulent waters. The system provided 95 miles of slackwater to 30 miles upstream of Frankfort at Oregon. The depth of low water on the lower miter sill of each lock was expected to be 6 feet, leaving a pool of at least that depth to the next dam.[43]

Leaders of the state expected an immediate return on their investment when toll collection began. Cabin passengers paid six-and-a-quarter cents per mile, with servants, children, and deck passengers being charged half that price. With only a railroad connection between Lexington and Frankfort, commerce from eastern as well as central Kentucky flowed up and down the river. New boats appeared on the river, such as the *Isaac Shelby, Kentucky, Monticello, Sea Gull, Buckeye,* and the famous *Blue Wing II.* Many of the boats, like the *Medium,* were shallow-draft packets drawing less than 3 feet. An 8 March 1847, manifest for that vessel indicated an "ascending ton freight" of only 8 to 10 tons, from Carrollton halfway to Frankfort. *Medium* often carried hemp from the Kentucky Penitentiary in Frankfort to Cincinnati, or whiskey to Rockford, Indiana. On one trip the Methodist Book Concern shipped books to Frankfort, while more worldly businesses shipped coffee, liquor, and wine. Other shallow-draft steamboats, usually needing less than three feet of water, could push as far as Beattyville during high water periods from winter and spring tides. When the water was even shallower, pushboats, or poleboats, propelled by the muscles of mountain men, plied the waters of the upper valley in Troublesome Creek and up the forks to Hazard and Oneida.[44]

But if the state thought it would make money from the project, it was mistaken. Toll collections and river travel disappointed the state, and in 1852 a new company, The Kentucky River Navigation, chartered by the state, took over the project. Toll receipts did not increase; the company collected only $2,078.57 in February 1852. By the time of the Civil War, costly maintenance and other problems allowed only a 1 percent return on the capital investment. There would be no new state money to extend the slackwater system to Beattyville.[45]

Nevertheless, Kentuckians used the river when possible. Trade on the river included flour, salt, whiskey, soap, and tobacco. Human cargo also included slaves "sold down the river." Many a transplanted slave must have lamented for "my old Kentucky home, far, far away," in the steamy Mississippi Delta in the 1840s and 1850s.[46]

The Civil War, ultimately fought over the "peculiar institution," devastated Kentucky in many ways. Thousands of her native sons joined the contending armies. On a hot October day in 1862, one quarter of the Union and Confederate forces engaged in battle at Perryville suffered casualties. Moreover, the economy of the state suffered nearly irreparable harm. The Kentucky River navigational system also came under duress. Another boat by the name of *Blue Wing*, this one the *Blue Wing II*, plied the Kentucky during the war. On 10 December 1862, *Blue Wing II* was seized by a Union gunboat. Taken to the Arkansas River, she was burned a few weeks later by Confederate forces. Such was the fate of many a steamboat during the Civil War. The Union Army stronghold at Camp Nelson became a bastion that the Confederates could not penetrate. To keep the lower river functioning, Union engineers placed three-foot timber walls on the five dams to maintain larger pools. The resulting rush of water over the dams smashed the wood decking and washed out the rock in the timber cribs. Confederate guerrillas added to the woes of the navigational system by wrecking the locking mechanism at Dam Number 1 in August 1864. After the war the Kentucky River Navigation Company tried to return the dams to their pre-war condition. However, floods had already undermined the dams, making the pools unusable. The dams were breached in places and collapsed in others. The whole system became a hindrance to navigation except in times of high water, when boats and rafts could safely slide over the dams.[47]

Even with the river navigation system in disarray, the river still served the commerce of the state. Salt could be found at the surface, in places known as licks, or at springs in central Kentucky where massive herds of buffalo and other grazing animals found in abundance this much needed nutrient. Used for the preservation of meat, salt was in great demand, and an early industry developed. Brine from wells in Clay and Perry Counties was heated in copper kettles over large fires, boiling off the water and leaving concentrated salt. The salt industry became so large it quickly consumed hundreds of acres of surrounding timber. Eventually coal fueled the massive fires needed to maintain the boiling kettles. Like most industries, the eastern Kentucky saltworks depended on the vagaries of the marketplace and transportation networks. One year when there was no tide, the salt could not be shipped down the North and South Forks to the Ohio and had to be sold locally. But when the river was at its highest, during the winter and spring tides, salt barges, 60 feet long by 14 feet wide, floated down the Kentucky for the southern trade. During the Civil War, Secretary of War Edwin Stanton considered the Clay County saltworks so strategic he ordered Union forces to destroy the salt on hand. Enterprising soldiers dropped cannonballs down the brine well casings. The industry had barely recovered when the exploitation of large salt domes in Louisiana undercut salt prices and ended this native Kentucky industry.[48]

Iron also became a major industry in eastern Kentucky in the an-

Work underway at refurbishing Lock and Dam 4 at Frankfort in mid-1883. The hempen goods factory is on the opposite bank. (National Archives)

tebellum period and lasted in some places to the turn of the twentieth century. With local iron ore, limestone, and charcoal from the abundant forests, a sizeable trade opened in Estill, Powell, and Lee Counties. Coal from the Three Forks near Beattyville was barged downriver to the iron smelter. The largest of all the ironworks, the Red River Iron Manufacturing Company, capitalized in 1865 at the then astounding sum of $1 million, produced until the early 1880s. In 1871 the Red River Furnace at Fitchburg, produced 10,000 tons of pig iron valued at $600,000, but went cold for the last time in 1874. If the slackwater had extended far enough during this period, the industry might have been saved. However, without the extensive iron ore deposits found around Lake Superior and in Alabama, the old Kentucky iron industry died, not to be revived until its rebirth at Ashland's Armco plant in 1920.[49]

Another industry—logging—used the Kentucky River to great advantage. From 1870 into the 1920s lumber companies purchased large quantities of eastern Kentucky hardwoods. Huge stands of poplar, walnut, chestnut, oak, hickory, and other species offered the opportunity for mountain men to earn cash. High in the mountains they built splash dams to back up small streams that emptied into the Three Forks and the main river. During the winter months they felled trees, where oxen pulled them to a streamside. There the logs were stripped of bark and made into rafts. Most logs were purchased by sawmill buyers before their voyage down the river. Individual brands, made by striking the wood with a metal hammer, identified the owner. The rafts were made up of sixty to eighty logs held together with either hickory pins or metal spikes connected by chains called *chain dogs*. The crew consisted of five to seven men, with the steersman at the end of the raft acting as commander of the venture. At each end of the craft large oars made of poplar were used to guide the raft in the river's often swift current.[50]

The rafts served another purpose as well. A Frankfort citizen remembered that as a young boy he and his friends would "get out on those big rafts and dive from one, under another, and come up on the outside of a raft in the middle of the river. We used to play hide-and-seek that way." Far ahead of her time, one Frankfort woman joined the men rafters and made regular trips from Beattyville to Frankfort for about twenty years.[51]

At first, most of the logs went to the mills in Frankfort or on to Louisville or other ports on the Ohio. Then entrepreneurs moved mills upriver to Valley View in Madison County, Ford in Clark County, Irvine, Beattyville, and finally to Jackson on the North Fork. Companies like Burt and Babb in Ford, although incorporated in other states, operated company towns like the coal company towns of eastern Kentucky. Shipping lumber to places as far away as Great Britain, Burt and Babb prospered in the pre–World War I years.[52]

After the Civil War, Kentucky struggled to return to its antebellum prosperity. Railroads began to push farther into eastern Kentucky, obviating the need for locks and dams on the Kentucky. At the same time, landmark pork barrel rivers and harbors legislation made it possible to repair and complete the early nineteenth century plans to build a more extensive system. More money was appropriated for improving navigation of the western rivers in a ten-year span than ever before. First, the Kentucky General Assembly and then the United States Congress in 1878, appropriated money for a study of the Kentucky by the Army Corps of Engineers. The General Assembly passed an act ceding control of the river to Washington, and federal ownership became a fact in March 1880. Plans were now underway for a major change in the Kentucky River's history.[53]

Capt. R.H. Fitzhugh, a former Confederate engineer, estimated

Above, The Beartrap under construction at Beattyville. (National Archives). *Below*, A pushboat, or poleboat, on the Kentucky River. (J. Winston Coleman Collection, Transylvania University)

it would cost just over $1 million to repair the "dilapidated condition" of the five old locks and dams and to build twelve more to the headwaters. Although the old stone locks were still in good condition, the rock-filled timber cribs that passed for dams were, for the most part, "rotten from comb to foundation." He suggested continuing the slackwater system up the North, South, and Middle Forks, building an extensive system of stone locks and rock-filled timber crib dams at a cost of over $3 million. The Corps report touted the fine quality coal, timber, iron ore, and other resources that only needed an efficient slackwater for exploitation. Political and business leaders in the valley, like Kentucky congressman Thomas Turner and *Kentucky Yeoman* editor Josiah Stoddard Johnston of Frankfort, could not have desired a more favorable report from the Corps of Engineers. Their pressure in Washington had been felt.[54]

Congress appropriated $100,000, and contracts were drawn up in 1880. First came the reconstruction of the original five locks and dams. Owing to pressure from Frankfort, Capt. James W. Cuyler, placed in charge of the Kentucky River project, pushed ahead with plans to repair the slackwater to Frankfort. As is still true today, projects approved by Congress had to be granted annual appropriations for completion, and many projects competed for federal money.[55]

Although there were innumerable problems because of poor weather, floods, breached works, and the continual shortfall of appropriations from Washington, these did not deter the Corps from completing the slackwater to Tyrone in Woodford County in 1886. These problems took a human toll as well; Fitzhugh retired after a breach at Dam Number 1 and Cuyler possibly took his own life. While the new captain of engineers in charge of the Kentucky, James C. Post, could claim a reduction in freight rates in his annual report, he also reported the sinking of the *Hibernia* at Lock Number 1 and the drownings of two workmen on the river. With rejuvenation of the Kentucky River navigation, log rafts made up much of the traffic flow, terminating in Frankfort. The question remained: Would the expenditure of funds justify building such works, particularly all the way up the river to Beattyville?[56]

While the lower half of the river now had a navigation system, the upper section did not. Upper Kentucky River businessmen, still without a nearby rail source, pressured Congress and the Corps of Engineers for a quicker solution to their navigation needs rather than waiting for the slow progress of locks and dams up the Kentucky. Their pleas were answered with an experimental lock and dam called a *beartrap*. Officially known as Lock and Dam Number 6, this type of structure had been used in Europe but never before in America. With cost over-runs already far above original estimates for the reconditioning of Locks and Dams 1–5, the beartrap appeared to be a quick fix that would give coal and timber men a way to get their products down the river during the low water season.[57]

With a $75,000 appropriation from Congress, the Corps reluctantly agreed to locate the project at Beattyville because of local political pressure. With heavy lobbying from eastern Kentuckians, Congress directly fixed the site. Army engineers insisted the dam would silt over quickly but followed orders and built it anyway. Many of the supplies for the construction had to be brought in by pushboats, small flatbottom boats pushed upstream by a crew of six to eight men. The dam at Beattyville would be of similar construction as the others, a rock-filled wood crib with plank sheeting to protect the dam from the flow of water over it. Twin 300-foot-long lock chambers, or guidewalls, would be constructed. In each would be a moveable wooden weir, 60 feet wide, backing up water to a 12-foot depth behind the dam. These gates would be held up by water pressure, and when the water had built up to a sufficient height behind the dam, the gates would be collapsed by opening a valve. Then boats, barges, and timber rafts would float through the opening on the tide into the lower river. After the water level had flushed into the river below, the moveable dam gates, the beartraps, would be raised again.[58]

Unfortunately, the Beattyville beartraps did not work. When the gates were dropped, the water rushed through with such great velocity that rafts and boats broke up. Crewmen, panicked by the speed of the water, jumped from their crafts. They refused to make the journey again. With faint hope for success, the beartraps were abandoned and the plan changed to constructing regular lock gates. Then a flood destroyed five thousand barrels of cement brought in for the new project and washed debris 5 miles downstream to the stone quarry. Moreover, by this time the Kentucky Union Railroad, crossing the North Fork, had pushed within 6 miles of Beattyville, demonstrating that there had been no need for the beartrap dam in the first place. Already the Corps of Engineers reported a "notable decrease in total tonnage" moving on the Kentucky, particularly grain now being shipped by other methods than the river to the numerous distilleries on the Kentucky.[59]

As the twentieth century began, Kentucky had not yet fully recovered from the economic devastation of the Civil War. Nevertheless, the Commonwealth had the highest average income in the South and led the region in many manufacturing areas. Among southern cit-

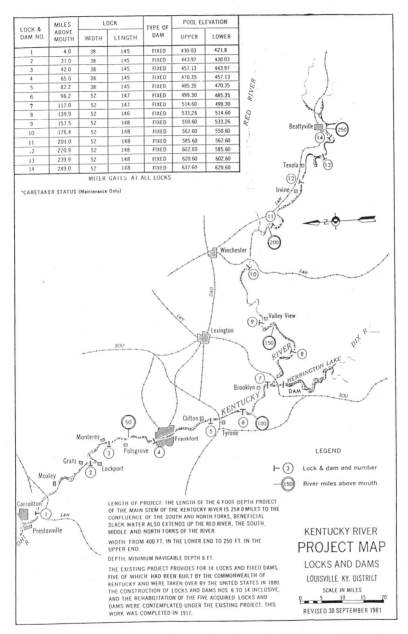

LOCK & DAM NO.	MILES ABOVE MOUTH	LOCK		TYPE OF DAM	POOL ELEVATION	
		WIDTH	LENGTH		UPPER	LOWER
1	4.0	38	145	FIXED	430.03	421.8
2	31.0	38	145	FIXED	443.97	430.03
3	42.0	38	145	FIXED	457.13	443.97
4	65.0	38	145	FIXED	470.35	457.13
5	82.2	38	145	FIXED	485.35	470.35
6	96.2	52	147	FIXED	499.30	485.35
7	117.0	52	147	FIXED	514.60	499.30
8	139.9	52	146	FIXED	533.26	514.60
9	157.5	52	148	FIXED	550.60	533.26
10	176.4	52	148	FIXED	567.60	550.60
11	201.0	52	148	FIXED	585.60	567.60
12	220.9	52	148	FIXED	602.60	585.60
13	239.9	52	148	FIXED	620.60	602.60
14	249.0	52	148	FIXED	637.60	620.60

MITER GATES AT ALL LOCKS

*CARETAKER STATUS (Maintenance Only)

Beattyville

Texola

Irvine

Winchester

Valley View

Lexington

Brooklyn

HERRINGTON LAKE

DAM

Clifton

Tyrone

Monterey

Polsgrove

Frankfort

Gratz

Lockport

Moxley

Carrollton

Prestonville

RED RIVER

KENTUCKY RIVER

DIX R

LEGEND

Lock & dam and number

River miles above mouth

LENGTH OF PROJECT: THE LENGTH OF THE 6 FOOT DEPTH PROJECT OF THE MAIN STEM OF THE KENTUCKY RIVER IS 258.0 MILES TO THE CONFLUENCE OF THE SOUTH AND NORTH FORKS. BENEFICIAL SLACK WATER ALSO EXTENDS UP THE RED RIVER, THE SOUTH, MIDDLE AND NORTH FORKS OF THE RIVER.

WIDTH: FROM 400 FT. IN THE LOWER END TO 250 FT. IN THE UPPER END.

DEPTH: MINIMUM NAVIGABLE DEPTH 6 FT.

THE EXISTING PROJECT PROVIDES FOR 14 LOCKS AND FIXED DAMS, FIVE OF WHICH HAD BEEN BUILT BY THE COMMONWEALTH OF KENTUCKY AND WERE TAKEN OVER BY THE UNITED STATES IN 1880. THE CONSTRUCTION OF LOCKS AND DAMS NOS. 6 TO 14 INCLUSIVE, AND THE REHABILITATION OF THE FIVE ACQUIRED LOCKS AND DAMS WERE CONTEMPLATED UNDER THE EXISTING PROJECT. THIS WORK WAS COMPLETED IN 1917.

KENTUCKY RIVER
PROJECT MAP
LOCKS AND DAMS
LOUISVILLE. KY. DISTRICT

SCALE IN MILES
0   5   10   15   20

REVISED 30 SEPTEMBER 1981

Kentucky River Project Map, showing location, size of locks, and elevations. (United States Army Corps of Engineers, Louisville District)

Kentucky River Trip promotional picture advertising "The Hudson of the West."
(Kraemer Collection, Kentucky Historical Society)

ies, Louisville ranked second only to New Orleans in population. But these statistics were deceptive, for Kentucky was to decline even in relation to her southern neighbors in the first two decades of the new century. The history of the Kentucky River in the new century would also be one of unrealized dreams.[60]

After the Beattyville beartrap debacle, the steady march of unneeded locks and dams progressed upstream. There were always unforeseen problems. Flood waters in 1905 washed out areas around Dams 9 and 10 at Boonesborough and Valley View, necessitating substantial expenditures for auxiliary dams. Nevertheless, Kentucky lawmakers in Washington and local boosters kept up the pressure on Congress and cut pork barrel deals of the "you scratch my back and I'll scratch yours" variety with other members of the nation's legislature in order to get continued appropriations to build the remaining lock and dam at Heidelberg, 6 miles below Beattyville. Ironically, by 1902 coal shipments represented the biggest upriver rather than downriver traffic while timber, either as freefloating logs or rafts, was the largest downriver traffic. Rafts, of course, did not need lockages in the first place. Traffic on the Ohio River and some other inland rivers also declined during this period as railroads appeared to have won the day.[61]

Even before the completion of Lock and Dam Number 14 in 1917,

The *Falls City II* docked at Frankfort. (Kentucky Historical Society)

some Corps of Engineers leaders honestly admitted that the whole enterprise had been little more than throwing good money after bad. In 1905 the chief of the Kentucky operation flatly declared, "It can be stated that the project for the improvement of the Kentucky has had, so far, no effect on freight rates." This same message would be repeated time and again in Corps of Engineers reports and for other rivers as well. Meanwhile, the system had to be kept operational because it was part of the federal system. Loose logs in particular continually damaged the dams, as they pierced the old plank decking. Concreting over the old dams added some measure of protection, but this procedure was more cosmetic than anything, as water soon penetrated the new facing.[62]

The upper dams were more modern, Numbers 9–14 being entirely built of connected concrete "monoliths," and the locks were larger—52 feet wide by 147 feet long. An appropriation from the Rivers and Harbors Act of 1911 allowed for completion of the Kentucky River system; but even this improvement did not allow for rapid lockages, and only small boats could navigate the Kentucky. "Moveable

Bryant's Showboat at Gratz pushed by the *Valley Belle*, ca. 1920. (Kentucky Historical Society)

crests," were added to the dams at Numbers 11 and 12 when the pools there did not average sufficient depth. Steel gates replaced the old wooden ones in all the locks. The Corps built a workboat for the river, the *Kentucky*, a 244-ton steam vessel, 148 feet long. This boat had to turn sideways in the shorter locks in order to make its way up the river. Its 5.6-foot draft scraped the bottom in places, hence one of its major duties included dredging the river and snagging drift.[63]

Finally, 21 January 1917, the chief engineer reported "the whole project is completed," but only after the government itself took over completion of Lock and Dam Number 14 when the construction company could not finish its task. A "permanent indefinite appropriation" of $2,946,264.50, nearly three times the original estimate, had been needed from 1884 through 1917 to complete the system by rebuilding 1–5 and constructing the new works at 6–14. In between had been the construction and dismantling of the ill-fated Beattyville beartrap.[64]

In the early twentieth century, with trade on the upper Kentucky declining, the greatest competition for trade took place in the lower part of the river below Frankfort. Well into the twenties, highways had

The *Revonah* (Hanover spelled backwards) docking at Frankfort. (Bob Rowe, Frankfort)

not yet penetrated the riverine areas of Henry and Owen Counties. Moreover, railroad transportation could only be found in Frankfort. From the mouth of the river at Carrollton, to Moxley, Gratz, Lockport, Monterey, and Polsgrove, past the 50-mile marker on the river, small and large boats competed for the river trade. Boats like the *Falls City II*, a steamer that could only fit into the lower locks by turning sideways, was owned by the Louisville and Kentucky River Packet and Towboat Company. A *packet* was the common name given for a small steamboat with an open main deck used primarily for freight, but such boats would carry passengers as well. A group of wealthy farmers created the People's Packet Company in order to give farmers on the lower river competitive transport prices. People's Packet operated the steamer *Rescue*.[65]

Madison, Indiana, and Cincinnati competed with Louisville for the Kentucky River trade. The Committee of Industrial and Commercial Improvement of the Louisville Board of Trade pushed for that city's share. The gasoline boat *White Dove* made tri-weekly roundtrips between Madison and Monterey at Lock 3. Competition was keen for

Kentucky River wheat, corn, livestock, and tobacco. For example, in 1908 the *Park City* charged one customer $3.80 to transport eleven hogs from Monterey to Louisville for sale at the Bourbon Stockyards. Entrepreneurs scoured the river valley drumming up trade for their boats and processing plants. *Pinhookers*, independent tobacco buyers, often bid at the farmer's barns rather than at a tobacco warehouse in one of the larger towns. Upriver went Ballard and Ballard flour and other provisions from the large Ohio River cities. Steamboats often raced, illegally, and not just for sport. On one occasion when *Rescue* beat its rival through the locks at Monterey, the enterprising captain of the *Falls City II* dispatched his deck hands over land to tobacco warehouses at Gratz. When the *Rescue* arrived at Gratz, the *Falls City II*'s workmen had commandeered the town and were already emptying the warehouse in anticipation of their boat's arrival.[66]

The river not only transported commerce but it provided entertainment as well throughout the length of the valley. "Did You Ever See a Whale!" a broadside blared about a display of a 65-foot-long creature of the deep to be put on display on a steamboat at Gratz. The cost—fifteen cents for adults and ten cents for children. Excursions to "The Rhine of America," as the Palisades were called, could be taken on the *Park City* from Louisville to Camp Nelson for only eight dollars including meals. Boats like the *Hibernia* took revelers on voyages, on one occasion "half fare, dancing free" on Christmas day with "plenty of good music."[67]

The *Falls City II* was the premier boat on the Kentucky at the turn of the century, operating regularly from Valley View to Louisville from 1898 to 1908. The boat measured 132 by 32.6 feet with a six-foot draft. The craft boasted an elevator to carry ninety hogsheads of tobacco to the hold with the ability to haul more than one hundred more on deck. On Sundays and holidays the boat also carried passengers on excursions. The crew consisted of a captain, Tom Leitch being the most famous, two pilots, two engineers, a chief clerk, and an assistant called the "mud clerk." Cooks, maids, and "roustabouts," almost always African Americans, filled out the crew. An overnight trip from Frankfort to Louisville cost six to seven dollars, meals included, with children and deck passengers paying half price. Most steamboats ended their days either wrecking or burning, or being sold off for scrap. After being shifted to the Mississippi River in 1915, the *Falls City II* fell victim to the latter. The packets *Royal* and *Richard Roe* were the last old-fashioned steamboats to run on the Kentucky, ending their service in 1920. Small gasoline boats like the *Hanover* and her sister ship, the *Revonah*

(*Hanover* spelled backwards) made the run from Frankfort to the Ohio River into the 1920s.[68]

Many people marveled at the wonders of the Kentucky, including the famous Mayo brothers, who made annual trips up the Kentucky on their private steamboat, the *Minnesota*, well into the 1920s. They always carried an automobile on board for touring the Bluegrass. The showboat *Princess*, owned and operated by Capt. Billy Bryant, provided entertainment into the twenties, ranging from plays to the new-fangled motion picture. In the warmer months the boat would often make a roundtrip run up the river as far as Irvine. On the downriver excursion the show might change from *Ten Nights in a Bar Room* to something like *Mrs. Wiggs of the Cabbage Patch*. Other showboats traveled the Kentucky before better highways reached the valley, allowing residents to easily reach the growing towns and cities. Until destroyed by fire in 1924, Irvine's Estill Springs resort touted five separate waters for improving the health of its guests.[69]

The river could be dangerous at any time of the year and continued to claim lives into the twentieth century. The *Sonoma*, for example, struck a snag after being hailed to pull into the bank to take on cargo. Captains without a full cargo on board were honor bound to take on more. A captain with a full load would call "blocked off," and proceed on his way. In the case of the *Sonoma*, the 130-foot-long boat sank with a loss of four lives, including a nine-month-old baby.[70]

Bad winters on the Kentucky can cause the river to freeze over in places, but the ice gorge of 1905 was one of the worst. Beginning with a tide, the river from Beattyville to Irvine froze solid and then broke into large pieces, stacking in places thick sheets of ice 20 to 30 feet high. Logs and rafts, caught in the ice floes, were ground to pieces. Sawmills suffered heavy damage. Even large dynamite explosions could not break up the ice dams that formed. The river and the ice did as they pleased. The Kentucky River Poplar Company in Irvine tried to retrieve logs by stretching a cable across the river, but it was easily broken by the moving ice. Moreover, the dams and locks on the river proved useless once the ice began to break up. Raftsmen lost thousands of dollars, while the upper dams suffered heavy damage. During the terrible winter of 1918–1919, when more than fourteen thousand Kentuckians died from an influenza epidemic, ice closed the entire river for six weeks. When it broke up, ice floes snapped 15-inch trees along the shore as if they were matchsticks, ravaging the dams downstream.[71]

By far the most serious hazards on the Kentucky are the floods, which the older generations still refer to as "tides." The tides were useful to raftsmen floating their hard-earned log rafts downriver to a sawmill. However, as construction of the locks and dams proceeded upriver, culminating in the opening of Number 14 at Heidelberg in 1917, these structures acted as more of a hindrance than an aid to the logging industry. Rafts had to be broken apart to lock through during lower water times. During tides, water had to flow several feet over a dam before the rafts could successfully navigate without being ripped to pieces. Nevertheless, rafts floated down the Kentucky as far as Irvine and Frankfort until the mid-1920s.[72]

Floods have taken their toll on the river basin in this century. Nearly every year one or more tides strike somewhere along the river. Sometimes the flood is more localized in the headwaters region. On 4 July 1939, a literal cloudburst of monstrous proportions stuck the Frozen Creek section of Breathitt County. Many people were washed away in the darkness, fifty-two died. The water that ran into the North Fork was of such volume that it briefly flowed in both directions. After a few hours it was as if there had been no localized flood at all.[73]

At other times general floods strike the entire valley, as in 1937, 1957, and 1978. In 1957 a flood hit eastern Kentucky particularly hard. Schools in some places were closed for several weeks, and President Dwight D. Eisenhower declared the entire basin a major disaster area. The 1937 and 1978 floods proved to be particularly disastrous in Frankfort, with the 1937 flood breaking the old 1883 record. The '37 flood inundated the old state prison, exacerbating racial tensions into a riot. The evacuation of all prisoners to the hill above the basin encouraged the development of the new prison at LaGrange. The flood of 1978 hit Frankfort with a vengeance, breaking all records, with the North Frankfort floodwall protecting only a portion of the city. The Kentucky Utilities Company, fearing a washout of the Dix Dam by the rapidly rising Herrington Lake, contributed to the inundation of Frankfort by loosing even more water into the river. Over one thousand people were evacuated from the flooded areas of the "Capital on the Kentucky." This disaster spurred funding for a floodwall that protected the entire city by the 1990s.[74]

Flood protection and water usage have always been important topics for those living and working on or near the river. Over the years proposals by state officials, local boosters, and the Corps of Engineers have run the gamut from extensive projects to more modest ones. In the twenties and thirties, projects were suggested on the Kentucky as well as on the Three Forks. The Federal Power Commission approved a high dam at Jackson on the North Fork in 1925, but nothing came of

Camp Nelson covered bridge with old distillery on the left and Boone's Knoll on the right. (Kentucky Historical Society)

that idea. However, on the Dix River, a tributary near Shaker Landing, the forerunner of the Kentucky Utilities Company built "the largest rock-filled dam in the world," completed in 1925. The dam provided hydroelectric power fed into the KU grid. KU proposed building hydro sites at all fourteen Kentucky locks and dams but built only one at Lock 7, which continues to operate. The Corps pushed flood control projects at several sites on the Three Forks, including the Laurel Branch project on the North Fork, the Fincastle Reservoir on the North Fork, the Buckhorn Reservoir on the Middle Fork, the Booneville Reservoir on the South Fork, and other sites. These projects languished until after 1945 because of the financial strains of World War II. Some projects, such as Buckhorn and Carr Fork, were built after the war to alleviate large volumes of flood waters emptying into the Kentucky, but great controversy also attended these projects. The Red River furor in the 1970s brought into play for the first time in Kentucky the growing environmental concerns evident in the nation. In the end, Gov. Julian Carroll announced he found no "compelling reason to build the Red River Dam," effectively killing the project that had received the utmost support of mountain congressman Carl D. Perkins.[75]

In the early twentieth century, the river basin provided more than timber and coal for the efforts of Kentucky entrepreneurs. Fluorspar, used in making steel; calcite, an ingredient in paint preparation and as a base for talcum powder; and small amounts of barite, were mined in Mercer County. The Chinn Mineral Company operated for several years in Mercer County and used the river for shipments. In 1920 that company lost four thousand dollars when a barge sank in the river near Mundy's Landing. Zinc and lead were mined in Henry County. These deposits were small and did not last beyond the beginning of World War II. The river also carried oil and gasoline from the Lee County fields for a brief time, but after World War II, trade up and down the river dwindled to a trickle. From time to time someone would barge coal downstream, but never on a long-term basis. In the past two decades, little commercial traffic has moved on the river with any regularity. At present only one company, operating in Frankfort, tows sand and gravel from a site above Madison, Indiana, on the Ohio River.[76]

As the number of ferries had dwindled—the Valley View Ferry is the only one still operating—numerous railroad and highway bridges have spanned the river. When a new bridge replaced the 241-foot-long Camp Nelson covered bridge, at one time the longest wooden cantilever bridge in America, an old era had ended and a new one begun. Now bridges were more massive and perhaps not as beautiful. Another famous covered bridge in Frankfort at St. Clair Street was replaced by a steel structure. The "singing" bridge makes a peculiar sound as auto tires pound its steel mesh and has enthralled children for decades. Perhaps the most famous of all Kentucky River bridges today are the railroad and highway bridges at Tyrone and High Bridge, a railroad bridge near Shakertown. Finished in the 1870s, High Bridge was originally the highest cantilever railroad bridge over a navigable stream in the eastern United States. Rebuilt into its present form just after the turn of the century, not only did the bridge's massive steel girders mock the seemingly tiny river, over 300 feet below, but the rumbling of trains sounded the death knell for the simple Shakers as a new technological age overtook them.[77]

For many years there has been an ongoing debate about what to do with an antiquated system of locks and dams that serve no navigational function but continue to provide pools of water for municipal usage. In 1951, a Corps of Engineers official urged that the Kentucky's Locks and Dams 8–14 be abandoned immediately, due to a lack of commercial traffic. Businessmen and politicians in the upper river valley pounced on the report, forming the Kentucky River Development Association. For many years the Corps has tried to rid itself of a naviga-tional system that long ago Mary Verhoeff and others referred to as a "white elephant" even before its completion in 1917. However, Ken-tuckians would not allow the Corps to escape so easily.[78]

At the end of one century and the beginning of another, the four-teen locks and dams still stand, and as the debate continues, there is perhaps a final settlement in sight. The Corps of Engineers began a process of turning over control of Locks and Dams 5-14 to the state and the Kentucky River Authority in the mid-nineties. The KRA has had a rocky first few years of existence because of its controversial us-age fees for taking water from the river. The city of Danville, for ex-ample, filed a lawsuit challenging the KRA, but lost in the state courts.[79]

But if Kentuckians don't often use the river for recreation and transportation today, rarely even seeing the river, there was a grave concern highlighted by water shortages in the 1980s and late 1990s. Much historical evidence in the record supports this modern-day prob-lem. The drought of 1930 frightened central Kentuckians when the river ceased flowing over most of the dams. Richmond became so parched that water had to be taken by railroad tank car to that central Kentucky municipality. The abortive attempt to build a dam on the scenic Red River ended one attempt by central Kentuckians to ensure a continuous flow of water in times of drought. The Kentucky-Ameri-can Water Company of Fayette County continues to push for a solu-tion to its business of providing a bountiful water supply to its customers in central Kentucky, particularly the rapidly growing Lexington area. Rebuffed in seeking a high dam built on the Kentucky or on Jessamine Creek to back up a reservoir, it now pursues building a pipeline to Louisville and purchasing treated water at that source.[80]

The Kentucky has been part of the warp and woof of the history of the Commonwealth for well over two centuries. It is part of the area's folklife and has even produced its own brand of humor. Allan M. Trout, who wrote for many years for the *Courier-Journal*, told a won-derful story about the mountaineer who was making his first trip downriver as a crewman on a Corps of Engineers workboat. Several farm silos had been pointed out to him along the way. When they reached Frankfort, he woke up a companion as he viewed the state capitol for the first time. "You've just got to get up," he said excitedly, "I want you to see the biggest damn silo in the world." There is an-other, probably apocryphal, story about the mountain youth who, over-whelmed by the size of Beattyville, waved his hat, yelling "Goodbye old U.S.A., goodbye!" as he passed on a raft. Integrated into folklore, oral history interviewees relate this same story told about people on other parts of the river. There are many stories about the river's "characters," few of whom are still alive. People along one section of the river at Monterey still regale themselves with stories about Tom Bondurant, a local character of the first order. Of course, the big fish story, particularly the one about the 100-pound catfish, is told the entire length of the river. And then there are the legends about gold and silver deposits. It would be a shame to forget or fail to record these impressions of a river and its people.[81]

The history of the Kentucky River has always been personal to the people living and working on the river. Oral history can fill a gap in the public memory, particularly among people who do not ordinarily record their experiences. The river is no longer the focal point it once was. Only in times of flooding or drought does it draw the attention it deserves. Shantyboats once could have been found at many points along the river, but now there are few if any. At one time people would have journeyed on the river just to view such wonders as Chimney Rock, a natural formation near High Bridge; now there are too many other diversions. Kentuckians can watch a television documentary about a river on the other side of the world or they can travel to other places. It is only human nature to look myopically beyond what we have close at hand, to the distant horizons that appeal to us all. Someplace else seems more romantic, more exotic, more interesting. It is time to take a close look at the Kentucky River, perhaps before we lose its essence forever to the fast-paced life of the twenty-first century. First, we will explore the natural state of the river. Then we will take a closer look at the impact of the river on Kentuckians, the continuing crisis caused by abuse, misuse, pollution, and the ignoring of the river. Finally, we must search for what the future may hold for the Kentucky River Valley.[82]

CHAPTER TWO

Folds, Faults, and Uplifts
The Geology of the Kentucky

There is a stillness on the flat, featureless land. Then the clouds form. The rain begins. First only a few scattered drops stain the soil. Then harder, ever harder the rain beats. It wells in pools, small at first, spilling into larger basins. Languidly it flows, muddy brown as the tropical sun appears. It meanders, not finding an easy exit. Eons pass. The river freezes in the Great Ice Age and is then warmed again. Animals that once drank its waters fade into extinction. Eons pass. The earth shudders; there are earthquakes. The river cuts deeper. Moving downhill it gathers speed with the pull of gravity. Now more vigorous, more forceful, it erodes, digging deeper, scouring the rock below, entrenching its ancient meanders.

The Kentucky River began this way, but first came the creation of the land itself through the building and tearing down of rock. The rocks on the surface of the earth can be divided into three kinds: igneous, sedimentary, and metamorphic. Igneous rocks form with the cooling of molten lava, or magma. Sedimentary rocks form from the remains of living organisms or the eroded pieces of older rocks. Metamorphic rocks, having characteristic crystals, materialize from the baking or compressing of older rocks, igneous and sedimentary. All these are the types of rock that became the basis of Kentucky's geological history.[1]

In the rock cycle one form of rock changes to another over tens of millions of years. Erosion of rock material by wind and water provided the substance for sedimentary rock. Mud, for example, can be squeezed into shale by the weight of sediment above it. Rock is constantly, though imperceptibly, moving. The cycle moves from igneous to sedimentary to metamorphic to igneous. The heat of the sun and the earth's interior fuels the process. Over time sedimentary rock is carried downward with movement of the earth's crust, where extreme pressure and temperature turns it into metamorphic. When the cycle continues the metamorphic rock begins to melt and, being lighter, rises. It is now igneous, the stuff of volcanic flows and explosions such as at Mount St. Helens. Geological events slow and speed up the process, often leaving exposed many rock formations such as we see in Kentucky. Bedrock in Kentucky has been broken, heaved upward and downward, and displaced by numerous faults, leaving its record incomprehensible to anyone without some knowledge of geology. Folding and faulting of the earth's crust stops the process and has violently impacted Kentucky's geological record. All of these events are and continue to be part of the Kentucky River's geological history. As you read, refer to the Generalized Geologic Map of Kentucky and the Physiographic Diagram of Kentucky for clarification of this important part of the history of the Commonwealth of Kentucky and its portents for the future, socially and ecologically.[2]

Geologic time is divided into *eras*, which are the longest, *periods*, and *epochs*. The oldest era, the Precambrian, originated in a molten state as the earth cooled from its primordial origins 4 to 5 billion years ago. Land masses formed and drifted like rafts in a stream. Continents moved and split apart. North and South America separated from Africa and drifted toward their present location. Meteors, asteroids, or the remnants of comets struck what became Kentucky. Four known "cryptoexplosive structures," with distinctive circular, concentric faults, exist: Jeptha Knob in Shelby County, the mile-wide Versailles site in Woodford County, the Middlesboro Basin, and Muldraugh Dome in Meade County. The first three of these are probably the result of meteor strikes. For example, on some distant day 430 million years ago something the size of a battleship struck at 25 miles per second in the warm, shallow sea that would become Shelby County, Kentucky. It smashed a crater 2 miles wide and 900 feet deep, killing all marine life for a great distance. Meanwhile, Kentucky drifted as part of Pangea, the super-continent, at one time being on the equator.[3]

During the late Precambrian era calcareous algae and invertebrates (animals without backbones) began to lay down limestone. In the many periods of the Paleozoic era, from 600 million to 250 million years ago, newer and more complex forms of life appeared. During the Ordovician period, a shallow sea covered much of the eastern United States in a setting much like the modern Bahamas. Filter-feeding animals resembling modern corals filled the sea floor as did clam-like animals. The most famous of the Ordovician fossils embedded in limestone, the Trilobite, can be found fossilized in much of central Kentucky limestone. A hard-shelled cephalopod known as Endoceras, an ancestor of the modern squid, with one form growing to 15 feet in length, lived off the Trilobites. Over a period of millions of years these animals became embedded in the limestone, a sedimentary rock. The Ordovician period ended with a mass extinction of life and an ice age.[4]

Life progressed through the Silurian and Devonian periods; the earth folded and faulted in many areas. More land became exposed as great mountain ranges began to rise. The greatest Devonian fossil beds are found at the Falls of the Ohio at Louisville. Teeth and other fossilized parts of sharks have been found in Kentucky, testifying to the warm seas of that time. However, the land was constantly straining from the internal pressures from below as the continents drifted.[5]

Through the Mississippian period, marine life diversified in the shallow seas, differentiating and predominating. In the Pennsylvanian period, massive coal seams were laid down in the great swamps that covered much of the Earth. Trees, up to 160 feet tall with grass-like leaves, ferns, and reeds proliferated in the steamy climate. When this vegetation fell, clay, silt, and sand sealed it from oxygen, preventing decay. This process repeated many times, compressing the coal beds that have provided much of the lifeblood for Kentuckians in the boom and bust cycle of this capricious business.[6]

During the Mesozoic era, dinosaurs, the most famous of extinct animals, ruled the earth. They were annihilated after a gigantic meteor strike off the coast of Yucatan, Mexico, severely altered the climate of the Earth. No such fossils have been discovered in Kentucky, but there is a widely disputed theory that they lie buried deep in western Kentucky's Cretaceous region. About this time the earliest mammals appeared. The area of Kentucky again went through great stress as the land folded, rose, and fell, repeating the process countless times.[7]

In the Cenozoic era, in which we still live, life became much more diverse. In the era's Tertiary period, mammals became more common and dominant, indeed this is often called "The Age of Mammals." Humanlike creatures developed, with the first true men appearing in Africa during the Pliocene epoch. Great glaciers advanced from the north and out of the highest mountains as the climate changed time after time in the Pleistocene epoch, or the Ice Age. One of the most famous Pleistocene animals, the wooly mammoth, roamed Kentucky, as did its cousin, the mastodon. The most recent epoch, the Holocene, encompasses the last ten thousand years or so. Now the great glaciers have retreated far to the north, and modern industry threatens to disrupt the old natural world. Predictions today of a new ice age or a

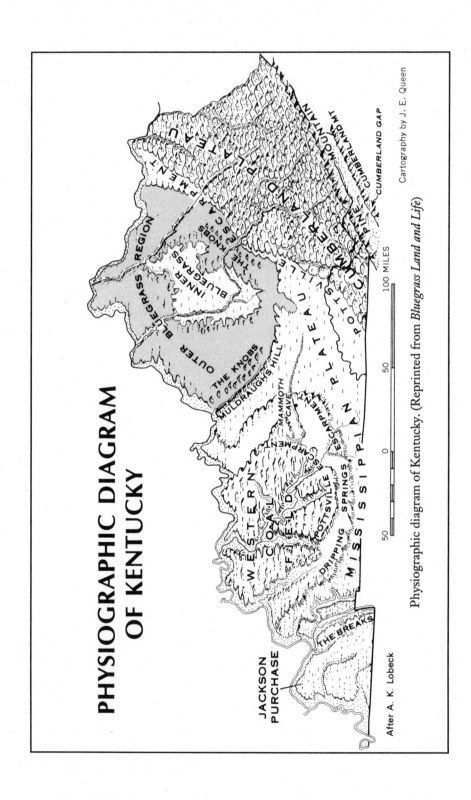

PHYSIOGRAPHIC DIAGRAM OF KENTUCKY

CUMBERLAND GAP

JACKSON PURCHASE

THE BREAKS

MISSISSIPPIAN PLATEAU

DRIPPING SPRINGS ESCARPMENT

POTTSVILLE ESCARPMENT

MAMMOTH CAVE

WESTERN COAL FIELD

MULDRAUGHS HILL

THE KNOBS

OUTER BLUEGRASS

INNER BLUEGRASS

BLUEGRASS REGION

ESCARPMENT

CUMBERLAND PLATEAU

CUMBERLAND MT

PINE MOUNTAIN

50   0   50   100 MILES

After A. K. Lobeck

Physiographic diagram of Kentucky. (Reprinted from *Bluegrass Land and Life*)

Cartography by J. E. Queen

GENERALIZED GEOLOGIC MAP OF KENTUCKY

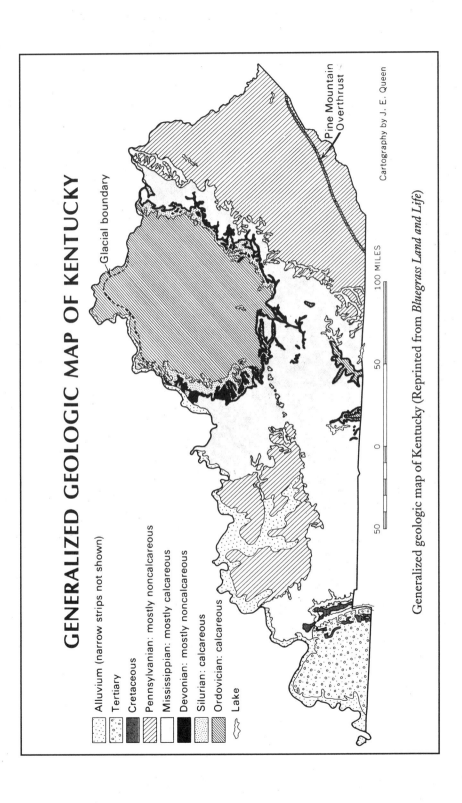

Alluvium (narrow strips not shown)
Tertiary
Cretaceous
Pennsylvanian: mostly noncalcareous
Mississippian: mostly calcareous
Devonian: mostly noncalcareous
Silurian: calcareous
Ordovician: calcareous
Lake

Glacial boundary

Pine Mountain
Overthrust

Cartography by J. E. Queen

50   0   50   100 MILES

Generalized geologic map of Kentucky (Reprinted from *Bluegrass Land and Life*) melting of the ice caps at the poles alternately frighten us about the future of our planet.[8]

What did all of this geological furor mean for the development of Kentucky and the Kentucky River? Everything. Rocks exposed at the surface determined much of the lives of the earliest inhabitants as well as our own. In eastern and upper western Kentucky, the Pennsylvanian coal seams have become both the boon and bane of the lives of many people in the twentieth century. Moreover, the geology of the entire state is of much interest. Why is there no coal in central Kentucky? Unlike the coal measures of eastern and western Kentucky, coal strata in the central part of the state have long since eroded away, once exposed, because of the uplift of the Cincinnati Arch and erosion by wind and rain.[9]

The forces that formed Kentucky were enormous. The Cumberland Mountains of eastern Kentucky are the result of folding of the earth's crust and are the highest part of the state. These mountains are geologically old—much older, in fact, than either the Rocky or Himalaya Mountains. They are worn from millions of years of weathering to their present height, and the process continues. The Pine Mountain Fault, where the Kentucky River rises, is an overthrust of lower Pennsylvanian, Mississippian, and Devonian rock, and is far different than the surrounding middle Pennsylvanian coal measures. As one moves westward toward lower elevations, an escarpment, or steep slope, announces a new land form, the Knobs. These cone-shaped hills surround the Bluegrass, from Lewis County on the Ohio River in the northeast to near the Ohio River in Jefferson and Bullitt Counties in the west. Cumberland Falls flows over a resistant sandstone and conglomerate escarpment, where rock formations change abruptly. Where shale predominates, the Knobs contain a new source of potential wealth—shale oil. No economically feasible means has yet been devised to exploit this resource. In the Bluegrass area the richest soil lies over the oldest rock in the state, the Ordovician. Moving farther west, most of south central Kentucky is in the Mississippian plateau. The western coalfields to the north, bordering the Ohio River, rise into hilly land also with a bordering escarpment, like Muldraugh Hill. Crossing the Cumberland and Tennessee Rivers, the lowest part of the state is in the Mississippi embayment.[10]

The Kentucky River begins in the eastern mountains. According to a theory of Willard Rouse Jillson, state geologist from 1919 to 1932, the Kentucky rose well into modern-day North Carolina at the beginning of the Cretaceous period, 135 million years ago. The ancestral

Ohio River ran far to the north of today's course, while the Kentucky ran in a nearly straight northwesterly course nearby present-day Lexington to a point north of Madison, Indiana.[11]

According to geologists, during these times, other ancestral rivers flowed in much different courses than the present rivers of the region. Before the major glaciations of the Pleistocene era, 600,000 to 800,000 years ago, streams like the "Old Kentucky" flowed much farther north than they do now. For example, the ancient Kentucky emptied into the Teays River in west central Ohio, far north and east of its present mouth at the Ohio River at Carrollton. Geologists have also identified other ancestral rivers, such as the Old Licking and the Manchester. They determine these old courses, streambeds, by finding sediments existing at particular levels that would have been laid by siltation over time. These samples match the sediments with known types of rock and erosional forces at work at the time. Abandoned valleys show where the rivers once flowed. The bottoms of the Manchester and Old Licking Rivers are covered with thick deposits of clay, indicating that they existed for thousands of years before being abandoned.[12]

Then the great glacier descended southward out of Canada, scouring the Great Lakes area under thousands of feet of ponderous ice and shearing off mountaintops in New York. As the glacier progressed southward, it ground over the Teays River valley, forcing its waters to pond before it. The courses of rivers moved westward, being unable to break through the glacial barrier. New streambeds cut down as erosion increased. Lake Leverett, a glacial impoundment, continued growing until the climate warmed. An abandoned high level river valley in southern Indiana has been identified as part of what was the Kentucky River at that time. When the glacier began to retreat, it left behind *erratics*, boulder-sized rocks. Some had floated on ice rafts in the cold lake far south of the glacier itself. These relics have been scattered across the Midwest and have been found in far northern Kentucky. The last major glacier did not reach Kentucky until about 130,000 ago. When it retreated, it left behind the Ohio Valley much as it is today. Another, though less dynamic, glacial period, 15,000 to 80,000 years ago, deposited in its meltwaters a glacial outwash of sand and gravel that is of great economic value.[13]

Something had to change to bring about the modern course of the Kentucky. A linear anticlinal uplift, called the Cincinnati Arch, an "arrested" rising of mountain-making proportions, halted its thrust after rising several times above the surrounding area, over hundreds of eons of geologic time. By the early Tertiary period the whole of the state had weathered, exposing Ordovician rock, the oldest in Kentucky, in what is now known as the Bluegrass. The area of central Kentucky folded upward into a dome shape, known also as the Jessamine Dome, a localized feature of the Cincinnati Arch. The area is surrounded by U-shaped valleys. Domes are folds in which the beds of rock dip outward on all sides. When beds dip inward they are called basins. Rock formations, no longer able to bend, crack under the massive pressure, forming a fault.[14]

It is faulting that has severely altered the generally northwestward flow of the Kentucky River. The fault zone across central Kentucky is on an east-west plane and intersects with the Cincinnati Arch, which runs from north to south. According to Garland R. Dever Jr., a geologist with the Kentucky Geological Survey, there is a "basic fracturing that has been reactivated many, many times, that goes all the way to the basement, four to five thousand feet deep to igneous rocks of the Precambrian. At Clay's Ferry there has been 200 feet or more of displacement." Moreover, the Mississippi River area may have been where the North American continent itself tried to break apart, but did not complete the process. Some faults in Kentucky emanate from this radius of great geological-seismic stress. The best-known faults in the United States include the San Andreas in California and the New Madrid on the Mississippi in far western Kentucky and southeast Missouri. Earthquakes along these faults are infamous. But several shallow faults, meaning those near the surface, also appear along the Kentucky River. The most important of these crosses the Kentucky at Clay's Ferry and is easily seen near the water level. This fault modified the course of the river, forcing a detour around what is now Madison County. Wearing down, entrenching itself, the river crosses the fault nine times. One fault splits off toward Lexington. At Camp Nelson the river crosses a fault once more. Although no major earthquakes from these faults have resulted in significant damage in recorded memory, it is only a matter of time until a cataclysm takes place. Could it be as disastrous as the 1811–1812 New Madrid spasms, when three 8.0 plus magnitude earthquakes ripped through the area? Only time will tell. Shocks from the New Madrid quakes were so severe that the Mississippi River flowed backward and the Liberty Bell rang in Philadelphia. The last minor quake in the state, though not part of the Kentucky River fault system, occurred at Sharpsburg in 1980. It is significant that the Interstate-75 bridge at Clay's Ferry is built over this fault. "Every time I drive across that bridge," Dever said, somewhat humorously, "I think about that fault." E.B. Estes, a state resident engineer, recalled that in the early 1960s he saw the fault at the base of one of the 50-foot deep piers of the new southbound bridge before it was filled with concrete. Quicksand seepage complicated the bridgebuilder's task. Benign for thousands of years, will this fault ever reassert itself?[15]

By the end of the great Pleistocene era's ice sheets, the Kentucky was already meandering in its course, entrenched into a valley close to where it lies today. However, *piracies*, the capturing of part of a stream, and abandonment of channels, would go on for some time. Piracies were first discussed by geologists in the late nineteenth century and consisted of stream modifications in which one stream takes over all or part of the course of another. Tributaries of the Licking and Salt Rivers, for example, have taken away some old Kentucky River drainages with the uplifting of central Kentucky. Moreover, to the south, the Tennessee River (apparently there was rivalry even back then) pirated some old Kentucky River tributaries. There is some evidence that the Salt River was originally part of the Kentucky. In the upper part of the river, above Irvine, the course of the river has had little to deflect it from its northwesterly flow since earliest times. However, the story is quite different past Irvine.[16]

Abandoned channels are evident in any meandering river basin. The oxbow lakes and cutoffs of the shallow Mississippi River are numerous in the section south of St. Louis, but that river cuts only through soft material, dirt and sand for the most part. The Kentucky has cut through rock in its meanderings, unlike no other river in the region, and few in the world. Jillson made a special study of these abandoned channels and found several along the lower region of the river. The Pot Ripple channel in Henry County was abandoned after cutting down 200 to 225 feet during the Pliocene epoch. Other abandoned channels, such as the Elkhorn in Franklin, the Hickman in Jessamine, Garrard, and Madison Counties, the Nonesuch in Woodford County, and the Drennon in Henry County, testify to a restless river, ever seeking the least line of resistance. Even today the process is at work, if on a smaller scale. For example, John Donaldson, who lived on the Kentucky in Jessamine County, owned an island in the river that has been a source of contention between two counties and several previous owners. In the early twentieth century, two families, one on the Madison side and the other on the Jessamine shore "lawsuited" over the 20-acre-or-so island because it was prime corn-growing land. After various floods the main channel would shift from one side of the island to the other. Decades later, the Jessamine County side of the channel is filling in with

The Kentucky River Fault at Clay's Ferry. (Willard Rouse Jillson Collection, Berea College)

debris, creating a slough that may eventually become solid land. Donaldson paid taxes on this Jessamine County land in Madison.[17]

All rivers create oxbows, panhandles, and other bends. Over time the outside of a stream, which flows more rapidly than the inside, cuts deeply into the outer bank, causing deformation, slides, and change. Frankfort, for example, is located on an old oxbow bend of the Kentucky, with Fort Hill being cut off from the original river flow. Flood waters can rise so abruptly that they can break through into new channels. Monterey in Owen County is located on the fill of an old meander in the lower part of the river. But if anything separates the Kentucky from most other rivers, it is the entrenched meanders that give it such spectacular cliffs in the Palisades region from Frankfort to Boonesborough. Beginning in the Pliocene, the Kentucky in the Palisades slowly but incessantly cut through limestone to bedrock, encasing the river in high, spectacular cliffs that keep it from spreading.[18]

Biologists who have studied the central Kentucky River region have found unique ecosystems. "There is nothing else like it," biologist William S. Bryant argued. "This is probably the most unique part of Kentucky." Plants vary according to amounts of moisture and sunlight on the cliffs. Yellowwood, sometimes called gopherwood, a relic of past Tertiary period vegetation, 65 million to 2 million years ago, still can be found on the cliffs, isolated, yet occupying a niche it has for so long. Moreover, the river continues as a corridor for the migration of plants and animals. Some have even suggested that the deadly copperhead migrated on flood-born debris into central Kentucky from its native habitat in the highlands.[19]

What does the Kentucky look like today, as it flows from the eastern mountains to the Ohio? What is at the surface as one looks across the Kentucky River landscape?

In the Cumberland Plateau, where the Kentucky's headwaters begin, the Three Forks drain a large area. The largest of the tributaries, the North Fork, flows some 155 miles before meeting the South Fork, itself 77 miles long, and forming the Kentucky at Beattyville in Lee County. The Middle Fork, 93 miles long joins the North Fork a few miles above Beattyville. The fall of the Three Forks is more abrupt than the main Kentucky River, which falls 0.9 feet per mile, while the North averages 1.7, the Middle 2.5, and the South 3.1. The North rises above Whitesburg, in Letcher County, where it is joined by Leatherwood and Carr Creeks, on which the Corps of Engineers has built a dam for flood protection, before passing Hazard. At one point "Sharp Rock," appearing like a shark's dorsal fin, protrudes nearly in the middle of the stream 2 miles above Beattyville. As the North flows through Breathitt County, other creeks, such as Troublesome and Quicksand, join its waters. At Jackson the North Fork at one time made a sweeping oxbow called "The Panbowl," separated by a cliff less than 140 feet wide. At this narrow point, a mill in the nineteenth century utilized the 8- to 9-foot difference in water height by employing a tunnel to create a steady flow of waterpower. Panbowl has now been cut off by Highway 15 construction, creating a lake. Caney, Frozen, and Walker Creeks join the North Fork before the Middle Fork merges with it.[20]

The Middle Fork rises nearly 30 miles above Hyden in Leslie County, with such creeks as Beech, Greasy, and Cutshin, before joining the North Fork. Another Corps of Engineers dam has created the Buckhorn Lake on this tributary. All of the Middle Fork's drainage is contained within the Daniel Boone National Forest. The South Fork rises above Manchester in Clay County. Goose Creek and Red Bird Creeks join, as do several others, below Oneida before passing Booneville in Owsley County, only 10 miles upstream from Beattyville. So far the Three Forks and their tributaries have flowed through mostly noncalcareous Pennsylvanian rock. The heights and depths of the Three Forks varies, generally growing wider as they progress downstream. One major exception is "The Narrows," or "The Narrs," in local pronunciation, on the South Fork. Here the stream constricts so tightly that during the winter and spring tides only the most courageous and skillful oarsmen could guide their log rafts through the roiling water. The Three Forks were never dammed by the state or by the Corps of Engineers, but into the twentieth century fish traps and water mills existed in places. Since the late nineteenth century some oil and gas wells have operated, off and on, in the Three Forks area and in Lee County. Today, the Three Forks run unimpeded to Beattyville, although they are much polluted. An oft-repeated joke around Hazard says something to the effect of, "Flush the toilet, they need the water in Lexington." Unfortunately there is much truth to what has become this folk adage.[21]

In its upper reaches the Kentucky averages 250 feet in width, and in the lower stretches, 400 feet. The attempt to keep a 6-foot minimum channel has long since failed in many places beyond Frankfort. After flowing by Beattyville, officially 254.7 miles from Carrollton, the first dam on the Kentucky is located at Heidelberg, just below the Lee County seat. One of the longest creeks in Kentucky, Sturgeon Creek, enters the river here. Flowing on through Lee County, Yellow Rock Bend announces the formation of a fine quarry stone, which is still mined there on the river by the Kentucky Stone Company. The river continues its winding course past Dam Number 13, flowing past Old Landing and on into Estill County. Entering the Knobs region and passing over Dam Number 12 at Ravenna, the Kentucky moves past Irvine. Station Camp Creek, where Dr. Thomas Walker camped in 1750, enters the Kentucky here. The Warriors' Path crossed the Kentucky at the mouth of Station Camp. The river now must break through the Eden Shale belt. These shaly hills of Upper Ordovician age hold some of the poorest land in the region. All along the river are old and interesting names often of unknown origin, like Shaving Machine Bend in Estill County. Drowning Creek's name, however, is obviously appropriate, as the creek is well known for its treacherous waters.[22]

After flowing through some of the most thinly populated regions of the state, the Kentucky is about to enter the fastest-growing part of the state, the Bluegrass, particularly the Lexington-Fayette County area. This area places great stress on the river. Although sewage treatment is better in this area of the river than in the region above Irvine, incessant growth causes greater and greater demands for more water. The Kentucky-American Water Company and the cities of Winchester,

Lancaster, Versailles, Frankfort, and Richmond draw increasing amounts of water from the Kentucky. Past Dam Number 11, straddling Estill and Madison Counties, rock cliffs begin to appear more commonly on the river. Just before the 96-mile-long Red River enters the Kentucky at Maupin Bend in Madison County, the Kentucky passes Devil's Backbone, a series of outstanding ledges. As the river continues its big bend around Madison County, entering the calcareous Ordovician Lexington Peneplain, it flows past the Ford Steam Generating Plant in Clark County, operated by the Rural Electric Cooperatives. Otter Creek enters the river, used by the first settlers at Boonesbourgh. Dam Number 10 is also the site for a state park, which has recently added a modern swimming pool. The pool was built because the beach was so often closed to swimmers due to high coliform counts resulting from fecal contamination of the Kentucky. Boonesborough will also be the site for a Kentucky River History Museum. At Boonesborough, the river crosses the Kentucky River fault system and first encounters the resistant limestone and dolomite of the Ordovician High Bridge Group. It is here that many people officially designate the beginning of the Kentucky River Palisades, although cliffs of similar beauty, though not as high, exist in the upper river basin.[23]

Now the river is in the Inner Bluegrass, the Lexington Peneplain, passing over major faults and under the massive Interstate 75 bridge at Clay's Ferry, and swinging around Bull Hell Cliff, 169 miles from Carrollton. Ordovician formations along this stretch of the river are defined and named by geologists based on their differing characteristics: Clay's Ferry, Camp Nelson, and Tyrone. Not far downstream is Raven Run Creek and the Raven Run Wildlife Sanctuary near Bill Lail Island, the only "official" island on the Kentucky. At the site of the Valley View Ferry, the oldest operating business in Kentucky, Dam Number 9 again breaks the river's natural flow. Jack's, Tate's, and Silver are lengthy Madison County creeks that drain into the Kentucky. Along the entire length of the Kentucky, sand and gravel bars often partially block the channel, almost always across from where a major creek runs into the river and often in the bend of the river. Paint Lick Bar, for example, covers a bend across the river from the creek of the same name. When the Corps of Engineers had complete control of the Kentucky, an annual trip by a snagboat and dredge kept the river relatively clear of debris and sandbars that can often be redeposited some distance away during a major flood. Now the upper river is left to its own inadequate flushing action because of the fourteen dams impeding its course.[24]

Dam Number 8 is the site of a spectacular rock ledge that constricts the normally average width of the Kentucky in The Palisades. More descriptive names such as Round Bottom Bend and Devil's Elbow recall colorful river lore as the river moves toward Camp Nelson, a once lively distillery town. Important as a Union fortification during the Civil War, the longest covered bridge in North America once stretched across the river here. At Hickman's Creek near Camp Nelson is one of the narrowest parts of the lower Kentucky. Separating Garrard and Jessamine Counties, the river gorge reveals unusual rock formations. Candlestick Rock and Halfway House, or Chimney Rock are formations that stand below the bluffs on famous Polly's Bend. At mile 118 above Carrollton lies the mouth of Dix River, now only a short stream dammed in 1925 by Kentucky Utilities. Once the world's highest railroad bridge over a navigable stream when completed in 1877, High Bridge is within sight of Shaker Landing, where Shakertown at Pleasant Hill operates an excursion boat in season. A short distance away is Dam Number 7, the only dam on the Kentucky with a small hydroelectric plant, operated by Kentucky Utilities. The cliffs along this part of the Palisades are quite spectacular, with limestone broken into seeming building blocks by horizontal bedding planes and vertical joints on fractures. On past the old settlement of Brooklyn and under the new concrete bridge, the river sweeps around another bend where fluorspar and calcite mines were once operated by the Chinn family and others. The old Chinn homestead at Mundy's Landing offers an engaging view of the river. Twin Chimney Rocks jut out from the rock cliffs. Chimney or candlestick rocks, some nearly one hundred feet high, were left in place after surrounding rock weathered and fell onto the river terraces.[25]

Onward the river flows, with serpentine meanders past Captain Preston's Landing, named for a prominent riverboat captain of the early twentieth century, past Oregon and Dam Number 6 in Mercer County, and the stillborn but well-planned town of Warwick across the river. The Kentucky is now into the truest part of the inner Bluegrass, Woodford County. Just before reaching Dam Number 5 is Tyrone, the site of a large Kentucky Utilities steam generating plant, a rock quarry, and two spectacular bridges. The Blackburn Memorial Highway bridge and a nearby Southern Railway bridge are interesting structures, though not quite as impressive as High Bridge. In Anderson County where Turkey Run Creek empties into the Kentucky is Lovers Leap, a rock ledge jutting over the river. Not long after entering Franklin County at about the 70-mile marker, the Kentucky flows under twin Interstate 64 bridges near Big Eddy Bend. Frankfort, 66 miles from the mouth of the Kentucky, is the largest city on the river. There are more boat docks and recreational usage here than at any other place on the river today. Several bridges span the river above Dam Number 4, the point where the Corps of Engineers still maintains navigation to the Ohio River because one barging company continues to operate out of Frankfort. The St. Clair "singing" bridge has been a pleasure for generations of children. A restaurant now conducts business on the site of the old Kentucky River Mill just above the old millrace at Dam Number 4. The old George T. Stagg distillery, now Buffalo Trace Distillery, on the river at Leestown, is the only such business still functioning directly on the river. At the beginning of the twentieth century, dozens of distilleries operated on or near the river. Because of his legendary discriminating palate, one man was able to differentiate between whiskies based on the location of their water supplies on the Kentucky. A few miles upstream from Frankfort is Steamboat Hollow Creek, Bend, and Bar at one of the Kentucky's many sharp bends. Before the Kentucky leaves Franklin County, Elkhorn Creek enters the stream after sliding past the old community of Polsgrove. Although the Palisades end at Frankfort, the river continues to provide many beautiful scenes all the way to the Ohio.[26]

Now separating Henry and Owen Counties, a sharp bend at Monterey in Owen, named for the battle during the Mexican War, is the site for Dam Number 3. Across the river in Henry County, the small village of Gest has lost out to the population exodus that has depopulated many small towns in rural America. The Kentucky makes a spectacular sweeping 6-mile oxbow bend around Clements Bottom, some of the most beautiful farmland in the region. At Lockport, Dam Number 2 was once the site of the popular Thomas's swimming beach until the immediate post–World War II era. The Kentucky flows past Gratz, another small town with another landing, Leitch's, named for another famous Kentucky River pilot. Lead and zinc mines once operated above the river bluffs, where the limestone cliffs no longer dominate. These mines provided employment into the World War II era. The often photographed Marshall's Bottom in Henry County can be viewed from the highway that leads to Perry Park. Originally called Ball's Landing, a resort community now prospers at Perry Park in Owen County. Drennon Springs across the river in Henry County was once a thriving resort in the nineteenth century until a cholera epidemic forced its evacuation. At Dam Number 1, 3 miles upstream from Carrollton, the Kentucky makes its last great bend. First called Port William,

Willard Rouse Jillson at Chimney Rock on the Kentucky River, ca. 1920. (Cusick Negative, Kentucky Historical Society)

Carrollton has long suffered from the floods of the Kentucky and Ohio Rivers, but it has also prospered from the commerce of both.[27]

On our trip down the Kentucky we have traversed a watershed equal to 4.4 million acres in a third of the state's 120 counties. The plethora of unusual names for Kentucky River features includes Noname Creek and Sea Lion Branch, as well as at least two Lovers' Leaps, two Daniel Boone Caves, a Belle Point, a Bellepoint, and no less than five names invoking the Devil, such as Pulpit, Backbone, Meat House, Hollow, and Elbow. On the North Fork is one Hell Creek. Early Kentuckians apparently had no compunctions about the colorfully explicit place names they applied to the geological and natural features of the Kentucky. One wonders why there is no invoking of angels, saints, and other heavenly intercessors, except for St. Helens, a small community on the Middle Fork in Lee County. Names come from varied, often unsuspected origins. For example, Sea Lion Branch got its seemingly incongruous name from the sinking of a boat of the same name at mile 157 on 28 October 1919.[28]

The central Kentucky course of the river flows through a major *karst*, a region of porous limestone containing sinkholes, caverns, and underground streams. Most limestones in the region are soluble. Weakly acidic water dissolves the calcium carbonate from limestone as it soaks through fractures in the rock. Inorganic or organic acid speeds up the process. As the opening enlarges, water flows through, increasing the size. Geologist Jillson estimated that the Inner Bluegrass contained thousands of sinks, where the roof of a small cave had collapsed, and many underground streams. A good example of such terrain is the undulating topography so evident at Calumet Farm in Fayette County. Creeks in the Inner Bluegrass often disappear underground to reappear not far away. Springs flow from caverns, influencing early settlement in central Kentucky. The Royal Spring at Georgetown, for example, continues to provide a steady source of water for 20,000 Scott Countians. However, like water from any aquifer, it is vulnerable to contamination and must be constantly monitored. Because of this underground system of streams and drainage, the Inner Bluegrass has fewer surface streams than other areas with similar rainfall. These conditions contribute to the growing pains of central Kentucky and the attendant pollution of the water table in many areas. It has just been too easy for the unthinking to dump refuse into sinkholes, leaving horrible, perhaps irreparable damage to the water table.[29]

Most Kentucky soils are thin, with rock inches beneath the surface. The numerous rock quarries in the basin testify to this important economic benefit of the geology of the Kentucky River. Since pioneer days limestone has been used for housing and fences. One of the finest is "Kentucky River Marble," a crystalline magnesium limestone, or dolomite, from the Oregon Formation. Real marble is a metamorphic rock. Sedimentary rock from the Oregon Formation has been used for Daniel Boone's Monument and the old State Capitol in Frankfort and for Henry Clay's Monument in Lexington Cemetery. This stone takes on a polish like true marble. Another construction stone is Tyrone limestone, which has crystals of clear calcite called "bird's-eyes," and which weathers over time to a chalky white coloration. The major uses of the massive limestone in the Kentucky River areas today are for highway construction and agricultural lime. These deposits are inexhaustible. In pioneer days there was enough clay in small pockets for making brick used in home construction. Bybee Pottery in Madison County still uses sedimentary blue-gray clay mined from a farm near the Kentucky River.[30]

Although stories about Swift's Lost Silver Mine continue to fire the imagination, there are no precious metals or gems in Kentucky. Iron pyrite, or "fool's gold," can be found, but there is no real gold in the sedimentary rocks of the Commonwealth. Rocks similar to the diamond-bearing igneous rocks of South Africa occur in Elliott County; however, no diamonds have been discovered. Other minerals on or near the Kentucky River have "just about played out," except for the shale oil, which has never been exploited. Iron deposits ran out in the nineteenth century, and other areas like Pittsburgh and Birmingham became the leading iron and steel centers. But the Kentucky River region held other minerals that lasted into the mid-twentieth century. These include calcium phosphate, calcite, fluorite, lead, zinc, and barite. Phosphate mining played out in the early twentieth century. On the south bank of the Kentucky River near the mouth of Shawnee Run in Mercer County, near Mundy's Landing, lie calcite deposits used in putty, paint, and auto tires. The vertical vein of calcite, deposited by hydrothermal fluids moving upward along fractures and faults, varies from 6 to 16 feet in width in the High Bridge group. One form is called "dog tooth spar," with an elongated crystal coming to a point. The Chinn family milled calcite into a fine flour called "Spanish white," transported it by boat to High Bridge, lifted the cargo to the top on a conveyor, and then shipped it on the Southern Railroad outside the state. On the barge it was called a "cargo" and when shifted to the railroad it was called a "shipment." At $20 per ton loaded, a day's shipment was worth $1,000 in the days when a postage stamp cost two cents. "Iceland Spar," the finest calcite mined in Kentucky on the Crutcher farm near Camp Nelson brought a much higher price. A few other companies operated for a short time in this form of surface mining.[31]

North of the Kentucky in the Bluegrass, barite, an unusually heavy white mineral, has been mined in the past. With a heavy specific gravity, four and one-half times that of water, barite occurs in vertical veins in the Lexington Peneplain. Barite has many uses—from an impervious filler used on canvas for sacking country hams locally, to an ingredient in auto tires, enamel for pottery, and ink. A most important modern usage is as an ingredient in drilling mud to keep oil wells from blowing out around the drill hole. In the old days finely ground barite was used as an "adulterant" in flour to increase its weight and the profits of the miller. Outlawed in the first national pure food acts, perhaps this is the origin of half of an old mountain adage: "There will be more preachers and millers in hell than anyone."[32]

Fluorite, or fluorspar, was also mined into the era of World War II on the south side of the Kentucky by such companies as Chinn at the Faircloth vein, which ran from 6 to 30 feet in thickness. It is a beautiful mineral that ranges in color from yellow to white to purple. Important as a flux in the production of iron and steel in the early days, this mineral is also used in the making of hydrofluoric acid. Later manufacturers included it as an ingredient in glass, refrigerants, and plastics. Some of the largest deposits of fluorite occur in western Kentucky, but even that business has also declined since the fifties because of Mexican imports.[33]

Lead and zinc deposits became known in pioneer days along the Kentucky in the Lockport and Gratz areas. Hopes that silver would be found in the lead deposits proved to be for naught. Several veins of varying riches have been mined off and on through the years. During World War II, the lead industry at Gratz was subsidized by the United States government because of the war crisis. When the war ended the subsidy ended and so did the lead mining. There has always been some thought that if zinc is found in small pockets at the surface, then in the Knox formation at a depth of about 800 to 900 feet richer deposits must exist. Companies spent substantial amounts in the sixties drilling and coring, but could not find deposits in great enough amounts to warrant mining.[34]

By far the greatest resource of all has been Kentucky's soil. The vaunted fertility of pioneer days, when legend had it that even a hickory cane would sprout in the rich Kentucky soil, is gone forever. Soil conservation efforts have not always kept this irreplaceable resource from being depleted. Soil types vary from one region to another, with sandy or loamy soils predominating in far eastern Kentucky, where the Kentucky River rises, to the often alluvial and silt loams of the Jackson Purchase in far western Kentucky. Clayey soils of various compositions tend to show up just about anywhere in the state. The heavier clays of eastern Kentucky have always bedeviled farmers. Even in the Bluegrass region, the soil is often thin and subject to erosion. Riverine farm-

Twin Chimney Fluorspar Mine, Mercer County, Kentucky River Gorge, ca. 1920.
(Kentucky Historical Society)

ers, since time immemorial, have depended on annual deposits of silt
to replenish the fertility of their fields. Kentucky River farmers in Estill
and Lee Counties still depend on this age-old process. But like many
agricultural states, Kentuckians need to be better stewards of their soil.[35]

The resources of the Kentucky River, past and present, indicate
that in the future the greatest concern will be about water and the
ecosystem that supports a sizeable habitat in a forty county area. The
people who have inhabited the watershed did not always take good
care of their resources. Slowly the realization is growing that the basin
must be protected from the continued depredations that have so often
placed the Kentucky River on the brink of collapse. The crisis of the
Kentucky River continues as the interaction of people and their demands on the Kentucky conflict with this venerable river's ability to
cleanse itself.

CHAPTER THREE

Riding the Tide
Logging and Rafting on the Kentucky

Due to a lack of capital and entrepreneurial faith, Kentucky's economy recovered very slowly after the Civil War, even appearing to stagnate as its neighbors to the north and south became more vibrant. The few Kentuckians with money searched for ways to catch the economic boom of the late nineteenth century, while its poorest citizens eked out a living on hardscrabble farms that dominated the Commonwealth. Exploiting tremendous stands of first-growth timber offered one way for many Kentuckians to latch on to the American dream of prosperity that electrified the rest of the country in the booming national economy.[1]

Tulip poplar, several varieties of oak, as well as hickory, elm, walnut, and other trees had barely been exploited by the pioneer folk that began pouring through Cumberland Gap and down the Ohio River in the late eighteenth century. Although much virgin timber had been used for housing, furniture, and fuel, Kentucky's hardwood forests were barely tapped at the end of the Civil War. Indeed, the forests of eastern Kentucky were so plentiful that few people were concerned that the old-growth virgin timber might be quickly diminished. In the late nineteenth century, logging and rafting of logs became a part-time vocation for many farmers along the Big Sandy, Licking, and Kentucky Rivers and their tributaries in eastern Kentucky as well as for timbermen on major rivers of the western part of the state, the Cumberland and the Green.[2]

Always searching for ways to make a little cash, mountain men looked around them. They could subsist without being part of the national economy, but in order to join the mainstream they had to produce something. The iron and salt industries of the region were almost dead at the end of the Civil War. Coal was difficult to mine and ship and remained only a pipe dream of budding entrepreneurs like John

C.C. Mayo until after the turn of the twentieth century. They had visions, as did the Army Corps of Engineers, of canalizing the Kentucky and her tributaries so that their black gold could be shipped to the outside world. Building fourteen locks and dams on the Kentucky River did not appreciably help the coal industry; only railroads did that. Moreover, the locks and dams actually served as a hindrance to the timber industry. But in the 1870s, Frankfort had two locally owned sawmills and a planing mill near Lock 4. The Kentucky River region appeared poised on the brink of more development of its timber reserves.[3]

Although local sawmills and sawmill boats operated on a small scale on the Kentucky and up the Three Forks from the Civil War until well into the twentieth century, only the development of large-scale operations with outside financing radically changed the mountains. Buyers began scouring the mountains for the best timber to keep up with the demand for construction, furniture, and industrial wood products in the burgeoning national and international economies. These agents would measure the logs, always from the smaller end, and give the seller a price. One man recalled this as being known as "The Doyle Rule," which always worked to the advantage of the buyer. At least 4 inches was allowed for waste during the sawing process. This also cut into the profit of the seller. The price might be as little as $1 to as much as $3 per hundred board feet.(A board foot is 1 x 12 x 12 inches. To find the number of feet in a log, you measure its diameter at the small end, subtract 4 inches and square the remainder, then multiply the result by the length of the log and divide that by 16.) In the 1890s a well-constructed raft might bring between $150 to $300 dollars to its owner, perhaps the result of a year or more of work. The buyer would sometimes pay one-third down, with the rest coming on delivery. The experience was not always happy. "Lee Hensley was a buyer; he had a hammer and the measuring stick," one man recalled. "He would give you what he wanted to." "That company man was an awful hard measuring man," said another. "He didn't give us no breaks at all, it all went to the company." Often only one buyer would bid for the logs. Sometimes logs could not be delivered to market. Moreover, many times the buyer would pay nothing except upon delivery. It was a buyer's market.[4]

Logs were marked on both ends at some point in the logging and rafting process with a metal striking hammer with raised letters. This "branding" assured some semblance of order on the river as thousands of logs floated free. The brand for the W.J. Roberts Company of Frankfort was a circle "R." The brand for the Mobray and Robinson Company in West Irvine was a circle "H," for the previous owner of the company. Before a sawmill bought the logs, families would sometimes brand their logs; the family of Ike Short used an "S," Ernest Robinson's father incised "BR."[5]

Some trees were so large near the base, 4 feet or more in diameter, that it was nearly impossible to get them to a sawmill or float them down the river. Many trees required a scaffold to be cut down. It was reported that dynamite was sometimes used to break apart the biggest trees. The circumference of one chestnut, or tanbark, oak was measured at 19 feet. Floated logs ranged anywhere from 18 to 40 inches; anything larger, particularly oak, would not float for long. At first, logs were floated down the Kentucky on a winter or spring tide, unimpeded except for natural barriers in the river—islands, rocks, and snags. Not until 1891 did the first of the newly constructed locks and dams above Frankfort, Number 6, necessitate lockages during low water. In 1910 the General Assembly passed a statute outlawing unrafted logs because of the damage they caused to newly built dams on the river above Frankfort. Logs sometimes impaled themselves in the oak plank dam facings, or they fell over the dam, beating against the lower wooden apron. However, if the tide ran high enough, 4 to 6 feet over a dam, logs and rafts could easily clear it without harming the new structures.[6]

Some forests were so tightly grown with trees and underbrush in the predominant narrow mountain valleys as to make exploitation nearly impossible without modern heavy machinery. Although some foresters would cut trees before the corn had been "laid by" in summer, most trees were cut in late fall or early winter after they had lost their leaves. At this time of the year, farm work had slackened enough so that a farmer and his helpers, often his sons and other relatives, labored in the woods, even in the worst winter weather. Loggers worked either for a sawmill or they might sell their logs to a *pinhooker,* an independent buyer who scouted the hills and valleys for good timber, hoping to make a profit on the margin of sale to a sawmill. Most logging men were farmers who worked the forests on a part-time but laborious basis, but there were always notable exceptions.[7]

Homer D. Allen's grandfather, Jim Ball, bought 2 miles of virgin timber along the South Fork near Oneida and worked it for over twenty years in the late nineteenth century. His workforce included several men who lived and boarded with him. Allen remembered, as a child, hearing the sound of the big saws biting into wood: "You could hear them all the time. . . . You talk about skills today, why, they had skills back then," he continued. "You couldn't pull them off the hills. They didn't want to do anything else. My granddaddy paid them cash. He'd go with the first raft to Frankfort, stay in a hotel, and stay until the tides were over. He had a bank account down there. The men rode the train back to Beattyville and then walked back to Oneida." They repeated the process, riding the rafts to the Bellepoint sawmill in Frankfort until the tides ran out and could no longer float rafts out of the South Fork.[8]

But first the trees had to be felled. Two men with well-honed crosscut saws and axes could cut down ten to fifteen trees a day. These tools were expensive and carefully sharpened. When he lost his favorite ax, one man jumped into frigid February waters to save it. Labor could be hired for around a dollar a day plus meals about the time of World War I, even cheaper before 1900. The fallen trees had to be trimmed of branches, cut to usually no more than 12 to 16 feet in length, and much shorter if the log was more than 4 feet in diameter. In the early years of logging, oxen, usually large red shorthorn steers, were trained to haul the logs on the forest floor. At that time, it was thought that horses and mules were too light and could not pull the heavy hardwood logs. With only a rudimentary harness of wood, leather, and ropes, a pair of oxen could haul a large log a great distance, but not always without resistance. In hot weather they would lie down rather than work. An interviewee in the "Living and Working on the Kentucky River Oral History Project" recalled, as a child, being given the job in hot weather of pouring cool water over the animals to encourage them to get up and work again. Eventually, experimentation proved that horses and mules could haul logs, and being much faster, they replaced oxen. The logs would be pulled to a pit, a process called *pitting*, then rolled onto a wagon at a lower level using a *cant hook*. The cant hook, or *peavey*, was a tool used to turn over logs and move them short distances. A wooden lever with a metal point and a hinged hook near the end, the cant hook was indispensable in moving logs along the ground or from pit to wagon. At some point the wood had to be stripped of bark, a process called *stripping* or *barking*. It was far easier to strip seasoned timber, because the bark had already begun to separate from the log.[9]

The mountain loggers were ingenious in adapting to their work environment. Wagons had to be heavily constructed to carry the weight of the big timber. Wooden slides were built to make use of gravity, but more often muddy banks were just as good. In some places, track had to be laid, made either entirely of wood or fitted with a small strip of metal, in order to get the timber out of the mountain fastnesses. In one adaptation mules or horses pulled logs on a cart with cupped, or hub-wheels over a pole road, which resembled a wooden railroad without the crossties. Interviewee Sam Wilson of Lee County built a tram with wooden ties and rails because the logs were so large. "I think I spent a whole afternoon trying to skid one log with oxen," he said in an interview, laughing. The land was so rough and tightly woven with trees and undergrowth that when he asked "Uncle Bill Bush" if he had ever seen a snake, the old timberman replied: "Why no, son, it's so rough they can't get in or out." Small steam engines were often used by the bigger operations for moving logs out of the forest to the collection point at the streamside or directly to a sawmill. The larger the operation, the more capital required for such labor saving and more productive devices.[10]

On some of the tributaries of the Kentucky, particularly on the smaller branches and creeks that flowed into the Three Forks, splash dams provided a head of water in order to have enough flow for logs. Joseph B. Hignite owned such a site on the Hignite branch of Bullskin Creek, a tributary of the South Fork. During most of the year, the stream had little if any depth. When rain did come, the stream would run out, quickly returning to its normal shallowness. In the dry summer and fall months there would be no flow at all. This damming increased the flow of a rather shallow but steep mountain stream. Splash dams could be triggered, releasing relatively large quantities of water. A splash dam consisted of a series of log cribs, with an opening of at least 14 feet. Horizontal planks were held in place by vertical log "fingers" until a "trigger" was removed, collapsing the dam so that water could rush through the gap. Although primitive by modern standards, the splash dam enabled loggers to get their product down into the larger streams when no other way to market existed. The dam, held together by ropes, could be retrieved after the flow of water had diminished and reset to build up another head of water behind the dam. This process might be repeated several times during the winter and spring rafting season. Free floating logs such as these were either captured on a larger deeper stream for making into rafts, or allowed to float on to a large sawmill, where they were snared by a log boom in the river. Often a water mill, grinding wheat and corn into flour and meal, was part of the splash dam operation and provided another source of livelihood for mountain entrepreneurs like Hignite.[11]

Making the raft, usually pronounced "raave" locally, took time. Some were made better than others, some being little more than random logs cobbled together in a most haphazard manner. But most raftsmen took pride in completing a nearly aesthetic device. "They were hard to tear up," Ed Combs recalled. "Logs that was rafted good would take a lot of punishment." All the logs would be 16 feet or so in length at the bow and taper to 12 or so at the stern of the raft. The average raft might be between 60 to 70 feet in length. Because of the possibility of locking, combined rafts could be no longer than 140 feet in length, the shortest lock being 145 feet long. If rafts were longer, they had to be broken up for lockages. Narrow rafts were necessary for the tight tributaries of the Three Forks. If a raft was too long and spun in a swift current, completely grounding on each bank, the raft would break up. If the raft turned around without striking the bank on either side, it could be righted, repositioned, by skilled raftsmen. Once on the wider main channel of the Kentucky, two or more rafts could be tied side by side and end to end for more efficient travel. In the last days of rafting on the Kentucky, a series of rafts hundreds of feet long were strung together and guided by a small gas-powered boat, backing its way to Frankfort. Backing the boat apparently gave better control of the rafts as they followed the main channel of the Kentucky, only guided—not pulled—by the tiny boat. On wider rivers, such as the Cumberland after it crosses into Tennessee below Celina, three 16-foot-wide rafts were tied together into what was known as a "Cumberland River Drift." No such expediency existed on the Kentucky because of the narrow river with its sinuous curves and numerous impediments that existed all the way to its mouth at Carrollton.[12]

Actual construction of the raft might take weeks, or only days if enough laborers were available. If the logs had already been stripped of limbs and bark, the process progressed much quicker. Too, if they had been carefully piled at the bank of the stream, the job was far easier. But if too close to the bank and not secured, many a log floated away on an unexpected tide, and much hard work was lost as well. For a raft that floated well and stayed together in the strong current of the tide, workmanship and skill in construction was important. Numerous interviewees in the "Living and Working on the Kentucky River Oral History Project" of the late 1980s and early 1990s had some knowledge of rafting on the river, having seen the rafts on the river into the 1920s as children. But few had ridden on a raft, and most of those only briefly in the waning days of the trade. Unfortunately, few people were interviewed who ran the river in the heyday of rafting from the late nineteenth century until World War I. For his book, *The Kentucky*, Thomas D. Clark interviewed a few of these people, including renowned raftsmen "Blowey Jim" Bishop, Bill Peters, and Bill "Turkleneck"

Log raft on the Middle Fork of the Kentucky River near Hyden, Leslie County, ca. 1900. (J. Winston Coleman Collection, Transylvania University)

Eversole. However, Clark did not record or make transcripts of the interviews and much has been lost. The "real" experiences of logging and rafting on the Kentucky developed below have been culled from numerous interviews conducted by the author and by Todd Moberly.[13]

"I remember seeing men with frozen britches legs," Edward Campbell recalled as raftsmen labored in terrible weather on the Middle Fork of the Kentucky. His only brief raft ride as a child is memorable solely because a drunken man fell off the side. Everyone on the raft laughed as the man scrambled out of the cold water, invigorated by his unplanned plunge. Another man recalled that as a small child he badly wanted to ride with his father on a raft on the South Fork. "No, you see there is the 'Narrows' down there and they wouldn't let me. I wanted to. My daddy did it many times." How plentiful were the rafts? According to one interviewee, "Now, when I was a boy growing up, they ran timber out of these rivers. And most of it was run out of these Three Forks. I've seen the rafts over here on the Middle Fork and for maybe a couple of days you could almost jump from one to the other." How vivid are the memories of the rafting days for interviewees? "The most excited time I have seen was at Lock 8. I seen a man get his hand cut off with a cable," while moving rafts through the lock. Most informants recalled seeing the logs on the water's edge or the making of the rafts themselves. The rafts provided a natural playground for adven-

turesome children, but as a youngster Emil Napier of Beattyville recalled an unhappy time on a raft: "I rode it one time, that was enough.
I like to froze to death."[14]

The process of making a raft was crucial for a successful run on
the Kentucky. Before the raft could be assembled, materials had to be
gathered. If the raft was to be held together only by *chain dogs*, two
chisel-pointed wedges attached by a short length of chain, the work
could proceed immediately. But these devices were expensive, usually
owned by the sawmill, and had to be carried back home after the raft
was delivered to market. Sometimes chain dogs were used only to tie
rafts together after they had entered the wider flow of the Kentucky
River proper. The old-fashioned craftsman eschewed such devices, preferring to pin together the raft with wooden pins and *tie poles*, or whal-
ing. "The worst trouble with using chain dogs was that they were heavy
and expensive," a son of a raftsman recalled. "It was more simple and
less expensive to use hickory pins." Tie poles made of hickory saplings,
4 to 6 inches in diameter split in half lengthwise, were not only quite
strong but flexible. Two or more lengths might be used on the longer
rafts. The logs were rolled to the water with cant hooks. To float well
in the water it was best to intersperse "floaters" like yellow poplar or
linn, a type of basswood, with the heavier "sinkers," such as oak, walnut,
beech, and hickory. The first log rafted, sometimes the first two, would
ideally have been a large poplar, with the men standing in the water if it
was not too deep or too cold, otherwise a johnboat would be used.[15]

The log and tie poles would be held in place with ropes. Holes,
1¼ inch or 1½ inch in diameter, would then be bored with an *auger*, a
type of drill with a long metal handle, through the tie poles and into
the log. Hand-hewn pins of oak, hickory, or dogwood the same diameter as the drilled hole, about 10 to 12 inches in length with a rounded
head 2 or more inches in diameter, were part of the process. Some men
spent most of their spare time using an ax, a draw knife, and a *shaving
horse*, (a wooden device for holding the pin material) making pins by
the hundreds either for their own use or for sale to other raftsmen.
Workmen shaved the pins to a point on one end for easier insertion
into the logs. The hole drilled in the log would usually be the same size
as the pin. Raftsmen drilled a slightly larger hole in the tie poles so that
there would be some give in the raft as it floated on the current. The
pinning operation took the efforts of several men, with two or more
holding the log in place, several inches away from its neighbor, and
two or more men aligning and driving the pins into place with either a
wooden mallet called a *maul* or a steel *pole ax*. After a log had been

successfully pinned in place, another was floated into position for a repetition of the process until a raft of perhaps sixty to eighty logs had been rafted. The number depended on the size of the logs. Sinker logs greater than 2 feet in diameter were normally too heavy to be successfully rafted, as they would either pull down the raft into water or require too many floaters for a financially successful raft. Ideally, about 20 percent of the logs were floaters. In 1917 at the time of the publication of her book, *The Kentucky River Navigation*, Mary Verhoeff estimated that one-third of the average raft was white oak, then chestnut oak, beech, and chestnut, with much second-growth walnut and yellow poplar. The average raft at that time was 60 feet long by 10 to 15 feet wide and contained 8,000 board feet or more of timber.[16]

During and after the rafting process, the raft was securely tied to large trees on the bank. If tied too near shore, the raft might become prematurely grounded. A close watch on the rising and falling of the stream was important. When the raft was completed, if he had not done so already, the buying agent from the sawmill might then measure the logs, branding them with the company logo. Now the owner had to wait for the proper tide. After the raft had been finished, a rudimentary wooden or tarpaulin shack might be constructed near the middle along with a fire pit of mud and stones to keep from burning through to the logs below. However, most rafting trips on the Kentucky were of short duration, and most raftsmen preferred to stop at night and take advantage of room and board provided along the river. An interviewee at Oneida on the South Fork remembered well the peak days of rafting on that tributary of the Kentucky: "I've seen the South Fork of the Kentucky River, for a half-a-mile or more, maybe three-quarters of a mile in front of this place here [Oneida], they'd get a lot of rafts rafted and they'd get them to the other side of the river and tie them up. Rafts would be all tied up along there. They left a channel in the river. They worked all the time," waiting for the right tide.[17]

The longer the logs weathered, often alternating between dry land and shallow water for several years, the greater the possibility of the heavier logs sinking deeper into the water. One interviewee recalled riding a "sinking raft" that rode very low in the water. This type of raft could only make a short trip to market and was extremely uncomfortable to ride in cold weather. Raftsmen with wet feet became men with short tempers who did not look kindly on another raft in their way as they painfully guided their own downriver. Sometimes the river channels were filled with rafts during the best times to run on the tide. It was important to get a raft downstream at the optimum time. The decision was usually left up to the steersman, the man who commanded the raft. He watched the flow of the stream, and when it had risen a minimum of 4 feet he would call for his crew to join him at streamside. However, too much of a flood might be dangerous, even disastrously foolhardy, for successful rafting. But all was relative to the time of year, the weather conditions, the desire of the owner to get the raft to the sawmill market as soon as possible, and, most importantly, the steersman's judgment. A real mountain entrepreneur might have several rafts to get downriver, necessitating several rafting ventures. If you left too early, the tide might be too high and swift, with the water flowing from the middle of the channel toward the bank, particularly on the outside of a curve. Only the most experienced raftsmen could control their crafts on the narrow Three Forks during these conditions. The best rafting was on a falling tide, when the slower current tended toward the middle of the river.[18]

The raftsmen guided their unwieldy craft with long oars, anywhere from 22 to 36 feet in length, one at the bow and one at the stern. These were constructed from a single piece of light wood like poplar with a flat-hewn blade a foot or more wide that was dipped 6 to 8 feet into the water by the raftsmen. The oar was attached to a *headblock*, a brace at the back and front of the raft. Headblocks were made like the tie poles, but diagonally reinforcing the raft at both ends. A *tickle pin*, secured the oar to the headblock, being inserted into an elongated hole so that the oar could be raised and lowered easily. When all was in place, the steersman would take his station with another crewman on the stern oar and three men would control the bow oar. The three crewman on the bow, having the more difficult pull against the current, took their orders from the steersman, who, with his helper, had less pressure on the stern oar. The steersman decided all maneuvers in the river, when and where to tie up for the night, and whether to proceed or not, depending on the rise and fall of the river and the location of obstructions in their path.[19]

The "Narrows" on the South Fork and rocks and islands on the Three Forks bedeviled the raft crew on occasion. As one man described it:

> Sometimes the men wouldn't go through the Narrows. They was afraid. They would come and want to know if any of the grown boys would go. We would gladly get to go. We would get about two dollars for it. We would go on to Turkey Gap. We would make about a 20-mile run but it was fast water. And we would go and come back home by dark with two

dollars in our pockets. . . . On that side of the river way up to Patty's Rock and from there from where you left Patty's Rock that raft used to pick up and fly almost. It couldn't hardly bump the cliffs over there. The river was hitting it so hard it was knocking it back. And that was what the men were afraid of. They was afraid to go through there. . . . I think the engineers surveyed it once and said it was a 29-foot fall there in a mile. And a raft was outrunning a horse almost by the time you got to the bottom of it. . . . Patty's Rock—that's when we begin to get nervous.[20]

Only the utmost skill of the steersman and his crew, coupled with luck, brought them safely to the sawmill and the successful conclusion of their voyage. The steersman carried neither navigation chart nor notes, but depended entirely on his hard-won knowledge of the river. He memorized the location of rocks, sandbars, and other hazards from previous experiences riding the tide. He also had to know the peculiarities of the currents in certain parts of the river and how to swing around a bend without grounding. All of this took years of experience, first as a crewman. A steersman had to earn his position, but he was not alone. Perhaps sitting around the fire at night, a steersman learned the hazards of river life from old-timers who had made many trips before. They passed on other river lore as well. The less steering the better, and inexperienced crewman could be dangerous when they overworked the oars. Another steersman recalled some men at the bow "was working me to death" on the stern and "they was working themselves to death. And not any need 'cause we had good water. I'd tell them to stop. I just quit and then they let up. They was aggravating me to death. They pull first to one bank and then the other." This steersman was happy that this time he had only a short rafting trip from St. Helens to Heidelberg.[21]

The orders given by the steersman differed from one crew to another. It might be as simple as the commands to "pull her to the left," or "pull her to the right." If the bow got too near the bank, the steersman could straighten out the raft by *crosslifting*, or "steering the raft in the same direction as the front in order to correct the angle at which the raft would go around a bend." Other crews might use somewhat different signals. Interviewee J. Gordon Combs of Breathitt County recalled the excitement and danger of his first rafting trip:

My dad, I'd been after him all the time to let me go with him down the river all the time. I was really too small. [But] he agreed and said that "Now if you'll listen to what I tell you, I'll let you go." So, he got up a group of men and he went up Caney [Creek] and got on the raft. It was still on this big rock. We got my uncle. We got on the raft and my uncle said, "Now walk over, everybody." They's six of us including my uncle, he's the steersman. He said "Walk over on the side next to the water, I think she'll float." And we did and kindly jumped up and down. You could feel it and hear it scraping off the rock. Finally, it just dropped into the water and took off down the river. They's three of us at the bow and three on the stern. We made it real nice until we got to a bridge, my Uncle French, he yelled out, "Pull her to the right!" Or, "Pull her to the left!" And most of the time, when he was on a curve he'd say, "Pull her up!" That meant pull her toward the inside of the curve. We were headed between bridge piers, you know? And, the boys on the front, he said, "Pull her to the left!" Well, they went left, but it sent it the wrong way and hit the bridge pier. It made it through, just dragged through, and it turned crossways. And three of us ran off. We ran off onto the bank. We thought my uncle and the other three would get off, but they really couldn't. The raft turned loose and we ran down the riverbank for a long ways, and it was hitting first one side of the river and then the other. And my uncle said, "You better come on in. We're gonna lose it!" I remember this was in February, real cold. But we all, we three swam in and got on the raft and went on down Troublesome Creek. We touched a rock called Bald Hornet a little and never did get the raft straightened out right. We went on down just a little farther and one end bowed the bank and then the other one swung around. After we got off and got it tied it just sunk and went right down. The oar pin had broken, that was the reason that we lost it. So we finally put a new oar pin in and started on our journey.[22]

If danger existed on Troublesome Creek, there was also humor, understated mountain humor, for Combs and his family.

We had another cousin of mine on there, George Washington Allen, and he was real bull-headed. He didn't want to do anything that anybody else told him. And we was on with my dad that next morning, and we got down to the mouth of

Troublesome. My dad said, "Raise your oars!" George said, "Why, Uncle Nathan?" He wouldn't raise his oar. About that time the oar just swung around and hit that whirlhole, the whirlpool, I guess you call it. And it took George way out into the river and sat him down. And he was gone for, it seemed like two minutes. But finally he popped back up, and we finally got him back on the raft.

"And he was a lot better from then on," Combs said with a hint of dry mountain humor, "we never had any more trouble out of him. We went on down and we got to Jackson. And George was just about froze to death."[23]

If the raft trip was going to be less than a day, the men brought food prepared beforehand, most likely fried fatback, beans, and cornbread or biscuits. If they had a fire on board, they could make "river coffee" or perhaps warm themselves with a swig from a jug of moonshine. For longer trips they might prepare food on the raft during the day, perhaps even allowing a crewman to get off and do a little hunting ashore if they had a long trip around an oxbow, such as the Panbowl on the North Fork in Breathitt County. Lee Countian Nevyle Shackelford's grandfather told him, "They'd get so hungry for something green [because] they'd just have sidemeat and maybe cornbread they'd bake up. He said they'd pull up to the bank and tie up the raft and go up and gather wild onions" on the nearly week-long trip to Frankfort. A young raftsman took his father's advice and tied his meal, contained in a shoe box, to the oar, keeping it dry all day long. If the trip took more than a day, raftsmen tied up before sunset, the Kentucky being too narrow and winding for night travel, usually at a point along the river where they were assured of getting a meal and a place to stay for the night. Food and boarding normally cost about $1 to $2 per man, paid for by the raft owner. The men themselves made up to $2 a day plus expenses, with the steersman making at least twice that much. An interviewee recalled making $5 per trip for the 14-mile trip down Goose Creek to Oneida and then on to Beattyville and the Kentucky River proper. Thereafter, not as large a crew was needed, and two or more rafts could be joined together. To supplement their income from the raft, more than one rafting crew would bring along some moonshine for sale "down below," as they referred to the Bluegrass area of the state. Whereas a bushel of corn might bring one dollar at best, a gallon of whiskey fetched fifteen times that much or more in a ready market in Frankfort and other places. The trip from Beattyville to Frankfort took a minimum of five days to make the nearly 190 mile run.[24]

When the crew tied up at night, being sure that the raft was tightly secured to trees on the bank, the men were famished. Homeowners along the Three Forks and the Kentucky supplied their needs. Experienced steersmen knew where the best lodgings and meals could be found and vied to get there before their competitors. An interviewee recalled her mother taking in rivermen near St. Helens on the South Fork. One night they fed a total of sixty-four men, feeding them ten at a time. The meal invariably consisted of soup beans, potatoes cooked in butter, breaded tomatoes, canned corn, and sometimes kraut, all washed down by gallons of coffee. Lacking enough room for the men to bed down, even on the floor, some would retire to the yard or their rafts for rest. Breakfast consisted of biscuits and strong coffee made in two 2-gallon pots. This hard-working woman rolled side bacon in corn-meal, and then fried it. "Boy, did they lap that up," her daughter recalled. This hearty breakfast also included fried corn, fried apples, and eggs. She and her mother fried 12 dozen eggs one morning for hungry rafting crews. This stalwart mountain lady never permitted card play-ing in her house, and those rafters arriving always knew the rules. But one night some men were allowed to play cards in the barn loft after she loaned them a lantern normally used to light the way to church on Sunday night. She recalled that most of the men were well-be-haved, although an expensive pair of silk stockings disappeared one time. Often a raftsman would volunteer to help with the dishes, and this lady always chose one "who looked good and clean" to help with this chore. Young raftsman Gordon Combs recalled his exhaustion at the end of a day of rafting, the biggest day of his life. "I'll never forget they had a big heating stove. I'd been used to just open grates, you know, you never get warm there. The heat all went up the chimneys. But I got real warm there at the heating stove and I just dropped off to sleep. They woke me up, you know, and my cousin and I went to the movie [in Jackson] and that's the first movie that I'd ever been to." Even in his later years this adventure, his only rafting trip, was memorable. "It was a real nice trip; I enjoyed it, and of course I'll never forget it." Another interviewee recalled, "Well, it was a thrill, but I had blistered feet when I got home. The worst experience was having to walk about 30 miles home. That took some of the joy out of it."[25]

Rafts were notorious for tearing up trotlines laid by fishermen in the river channel. The father of interviewee Harrison Broce at Oregon in Mercer County got his revenge on a rafter who continually broke his trotlines. "I remember one time old Eversole fooled around for half-a-day or better; thought he was on a snag, but dad had a big wire cable tied from a tree around his raft, had him tied tight." The old raftsman could not have thought the incident humorous, because he lost valuable time. Perhaps the next time he passed Oregon at Lock 6 Eversole tried not to entangle Broce's trotline again. Other interviewees recalled Eversole, who, as the last of the great raftsmen, worked into the 1920s towing long rafts to Frankfort sawmills with a small gas-powered boat. "We used to go out in a rowboat and walk on them big logs," recalled Bill Fint of the Woodford County section of the Kentucky. Eversoles's rafts were so long that they required many lockages on their way downriver.[26]

Rafting was dangerous and each year the tide claimed its victims. "Old Huldy" Rock and the Narrows on the South Fork as well as Sharp Rock, or Shark Rock, on the North Fork caused problems for rafters during the tides. Nevyle Shackelford's father lost a raft there and fell into the river as well. A man died of exhaustion from the work of keeping a raft riding on the tide. One wonders how much the freezing temperatures and exposure to the elements added to the ill health of raftsmen in their later years. Once, late in the rafting season the North Fork rose suddenly in Breathitt County, a man recalled. The raft on which he was riding broke in two after hitting a large rock. Three more rafts piled into the wreckage. "A fellow got drowned up ahead of us, a Deaton boy. That was in 1924. That was in May. That was the last time I went down." The drowning of a sixty-five-year-old rafter, who could not swim, punctuated the memory of Ike Short, who also recalled that on his father's last venture the raft broke up and the elder Short had to swim out. Another raftsman courted death when, after a raft began breaking up, he fell between the logs into the cold river. "My father could see my uncle's hand sticking up where he had fallen through between the logs. My father ran quickly, got my uncle by the hand, and pulled him up from between the logs in the river. My uncle always gave my father credit for saving his life." A woman recalled a seriocomic story about a time when her father fell into the icy river while rafting. He entered his home saying, "I'm covered with ice," and promptly threw a banjo that her dumbfounded brothers had been playing into the fireplace so he could thaw out more quickly.[27]

Logging and rafting also brought out the worst in people, reinforcing the mountain stereotype for violent behavior. In *The Kentucky*, Thomas D. Clark interviewed people who recalled miscreants throwing rocks at the rafters. Sometimes the rafters answered with a hail of lead which usually squelched the rock throwing. "Old Jim Cushenberry, if you stirred him up," recalled "Boss" Sewall of Frankfort, "was a aw-ful bad fellow. He carried a sawed-off shotgun. He was a terrible old fellow." Sewall also witnessed a gunfight over runaway railroad ties that had floated up on an island on the upper Kentucky River. Deter-mined men shot back and forth across the river until one side withdrew and the winners rounded up their spoils for the twenty-five cents per tie finder's fee. Moreover, there were inherent conflicts over rights to prime logging territory in the eastern highland, many ending in law-suits and some in bloodshed.[28]

Many people, some not connected with the industry, others na-tives of the mountains, observed the parade of rafts down the Ken-tucky. An outsider described his observations on a camping trip in 1907:

> As we lay in our blankets ashore, I saw log rafts passing . . . , each manned by three or more muscular fellows, who usu-ally had a small dog-tent amidships, with small cooking-fire burning near-at-hand. Each had his "watches" at long, strong sweeps [oars] and often carried a "44" strapped to his hip. At Irvine, where the river emerged from the mountains, there whined a sawmill. Miles further down at Ford and at High Bridge and other places, there whined other mills. But lum-bering is now a thing of the past; the primeval forest is gone; the western border of the plateau has become a second-growth reserve, named "Cumberland National Forest."

A native recalled the thrill of the rafting days, "Law, yes, I've seen log rafts on the river [South Fork]. I'd say I have. I've seen them dump them off at the mouth of Cow Creek right down here and wade in that icy water in the spring and raft them, and wait for a spring tide to take them out. If the tide was late, the river would be covered."[29]

A Kentucky statute law stipulated that the finder of a lost log be reimbursed with a minimum of twenty-five cents for each log found in the river and returned to its owner. Some sawmills paid fifty cents or more if the log was delivered directly to the mill; many boys and men along the river made money fishing out runaway logs. It was hard work and put money into the pockets of people that otherwise could make little from the river's bounty. Using a footboat, John W. Irvin of the Doylesville area in Madison County could always find a few stray logs, making some spending money as a youth. "That's the way we made pocket money," said Preston Johnson of the Valley View area of Madi-son County.[30]

Some river people resorted to foul means in order to make money out of the logging runs. Rather than making twenty-five cents for returning a log to a mill or its rightful owner, a thief could make a lot more by *dehorning* a log. The state passed a law making this act a felony. "If its a 12-foot-long log," Vernon Alcorn explained, "they'd saw a foot off each end and make a ten out of 'im. Well, if they can't find no marks on 'im, why, you can't identify 'im. Yeah, they call that dehorning." An Irvine man, imprisoned for dehorning logs, read up on law before returning home, becoming a more respectable citizen than when he left for the Frankfort penitentiary. Once the weather became so cold that a family tied up a raft at Jackson, planning to return in warmer weather and catch a tide to Beattyville. When "Uncle Nathan went to look for his raft it was gone." Kentucky River log bandits had wiped out weeks of labor and stolen the equivalent of hundreds of dollars.[31]

The men worked hard, and those who reached such worldly ports as Frankfort played hard in "Crawfish Bottom," locally known as the Craw. A good number carried guns and were not afraid to make their will known to the inhabitants of the capital city. If they didn't have a jug of moonshine with them, they could readily buy "red liquor," as they called bonded bourbon whiskey, and beer, a beverage they often could not find at home. As Clark so well described this tableau over a half century ago:

> Down in the Craw logmen could forget their trials and tribulations and give themselves over to at least one night of complete debauchery. Away from the mountains and their families they could enjoy complete freedom. A good place to start was either Salander's saloon or Jim Jenning's "Last Chance." Maybe a copper-lined moonshine lover could stand enough "factory-made" whisky to patronize both places. From Salander and Jenning's the logger wandered deeper into the Craw section, which clung to the famous river cliff like a half-drowned animal. Here, behind the staid and dignified Greek Revival capitol building, was all the wickedness of the Biblical twin cities in concentrated form.

But all of that is long forgotten now and the Craw has since been made into a respectable office and hotel complex as well as public housing area.[32]

Many people thought of the rafting life as romantic, now and then, much like the earlier days of flatboat and steamboat commerce on the nation's rivers, the days of Mike Fink and the legendary half-alligator, half-horse rivermen. There is even a "Raft-Man's Song," attributed to an unknown Woodford County troubadour. The music notes say "Many years ago, men rafting down lumber from the mountains would sing this song while floating down the middle Kentucky River." One cannot be sure what is meant by "middle." Is this the middle part of the Kentucky River proper or the Middle Fork? Anyway, the words are interesting, evoking typical nineteenth century melodrama in which an omniscient voice calls to the young raftsman, "Wake up, wake up, You drowsy sleeper, Wake up, wake up, It's almost day, How can you lay and sleep and slumber, When your true love's a-goin' a-way." This is the only song found specifically about Kentucky River rafting. However, raftsmen undoubtedly brought with them downriver a wealth of mountain ballads such as "Barbara Allen," "I Gave My Love a Cherry," "Pretty Polly," and many others. But if there was some element of romance about the raftsman life, apparently so footloose and carefree, it also had a dangerous side, a means to an end, making a living for mountain families that had few sources of income.[33]

Kentucky author John Fox Jr. took note of the rafting life in his melodramatic masterpiece, *The Little Shepherd of Kingdom Come*, first published in 1903. Although situated in the days just before the Civil War, the rafting experience of young Chad Buford is convincingly true to life. What more compelling story could there be than a boy seeking adventure, a first step toward manhood by joining his adopted family menfolk and the local schoolmaster as they ride the tide from Kingdom Come Creek to Frankfort. But first the circuit-riding preacher must ask for divine intervention when there is not enough water in the creek. He pleads "'We do not presume to dictate, but, if it pleases, Thee, send us, not a gentle sizzle-sozzle, but a sod-soaker, O Lord, a gully-washer, Give us a tide, O Lord!'" The dramatization of this trip is replete with mishaps that many raftsmen endured. Chad himself is injured slightly and his dog Jack breaks a leg when their whirling raft "bows," striking first one bank and then the other. "The raft humped in the middle like a bucking horse—the logs ground savagely together," is a fine description of the violent tide that many raftsmen faced. But Fox resorts to a bit of hyperbole when he announces the raft was "On the way to God's Country at last," that is, central Kentucky and Frankfort. When they near Frankfort, Chad sees for the first time such wonders as a railroad as well as the state capitol building and lightning rods sprouting from rooftops. Chad's misadventures continue deeper into the novel when he gets lost in Frankfort, having missed his train ride

A young tie hacker in the eastern Kentucky mountains. (The Filson Club)

toward home. If a bit "over the top" for the tastes of the modern reader, *The Little Shepherd of Kingdom Come* is evocative of the old rafting days.[34]

Mountain loggers found other uses for their timber. Not only logs, but railroad ties, barrel staves, and shingles were floated to market on the Kentucky River tides. "They had two tides," Homer Allen of Oneida recalled. "One was a raft tide and one was a tie tide." The first was higher and the latter was not as swift. Of course, with the advent of the railroad, products could be more easily and efficiently shipped to market. With expanding railroad markets, there was a ready market for ties. Moreover, ties lasted only an average of seven years. Railroad ties were hand-formed with a broadax well into the twentieth century in the mountain counties and either free-floated or rafted like logs. Called *tie hacking* by many, the process tested the skill of the axeman. For some men the work was only part-time, but for others they were listed as "tie hack" in census records. Oak was the favored tie hacking material because of the way the wood would split. Splitting and hewing required great skill as well as planning to get the maximum number of ties from a single log. The ties were usually either 6 x 8 or 7 x 9 inches and a standard 8½ feet in length. Steel and wooden wedges were used to split the largest logs into several pieces. With a broadax

Well-made rafts of railroad ties waiting for a tide on the Middle Fork at Buckhorn, Perry County. (Kentucky Historical Society)

beveled only on one side of the cutting edge in order to get a smooth side, this skilled craftsman generally used a crooked hickory handle so as not to bruise his knuckles. A Grayson Countian once hewed forty-two ties in one day. In 1910 a finished tie brought ten cents to the skilled tie hacker, but by this time sawmills began specializing in railroad ties and soon replaced the individual. Ties were free-floated at first and rafted later on. When rafted normally, chain dogs were used to hold the double-tie rafts, 17 feet wide and a 100 feet or more long. A tie tide need not be as large as a regular rafting flood, because the railroad ties were more uniform and floated more freely and higher in the river.[35]

Mountain logmen and their families also produced white oak barrel staves and shingles. Tanbark was later shipped out by the carload on the railroad. Barrel staves were in such great demand at the turn of the twentieth century, they too were floated on the tide to collection points on the lower Kentucky River. "I've seen the river just about solid with staves," reported Ed Combs about his 1920s home at Athol on the Middle Fork. Herbert Marcum's father ran a stave mill with other men along Red Bird Creek in Clay County. After the large corporate sawmills took over the market and cut out the small producers, an estimated 2 million white oak staves were left to rot.[36]

Raising "sinkers" that have lain on the bottom of the Kentucky, in some cases for decades, was one last way to make money from the old logging days. If a log is covered by mud, oxygen will be denied and the wood will be well-preserved. As a matter of fact, this method has been used in Japan for years in preserving logs shipped from American forests. Decades from now the logs can be recovered in as good a condition as the day they were submersed into mud. Over the years Kentucky rivermen developed a method of bringing valuable walnut and other logs to the surface. They have pulled hundreds, perhaps thousands, of logs from their watery resting place. It helps tremendously if there is a record of a lost raft or folklore about a particular part of the river where logs are suspected to be buried. The work is labor intensive and demands much river knowledge. Depending on the depth of the water, a length of pipe with a spike on the end is used to probe the depths. When a log is found, a core is removed by using another pipe. If the log is valuable, a *spud*, a device for grabbing the log, is lowered and driven into place. Then the log is raised by a cable on a winch. All this takes a great amount of skill, with the reward being a log that might be worth hundreds of dollars. One man recalled he would sometimes dive below the surface to check out the logs. Particularly in the upper part of the river, interviewees often told of treasures such as logs, coal, and iron still buried in their locale. Much might be assigned to folklore, but there must still be buried in the Kentucky and its tributaries hardwood logs worth untold millions in today's prices. Many of these logs are first-growth hardwoods that will never be seen again. One man recalled some logs so large, 4 feet or more in diameter, they could not be raised; he went to the grave with knowledge of the location of his father's last raft, which sank with eighty-one fine logs. In recent years there is no record of entrepreneurs raising logs from the river, and it is doubtful that anyone will ever again try to raise "sinkers." Like many other river trades, this one too is lost forever. Many men have gone to their graves knowing the location of invaluable logs long buried in the mud of the Kentucky River.[37]

The rebuilding of the original five locks and dams and the construction of nine more upriver did little to improve the economy of Kentucky. Once the railroad reached nearby Beattyville, even the necessity of water transportation for coal production had been eliminated. Yet, because of the inertia of government policy and pork barrel legislation, the final locks and dams were completed, the last at Heidelberg, just below Beattyville, in 1917. Moreover, construction of the dams hindered the timber trade, and after 1910 the Corps would no longer tolerate free-floating logs in the Kentucky because of the damage to dams. In 1904, Number 10 was almost torn out by a logjam. With the pushing of railroads and better highways into the mountains, even old veterans like "Turk" Eversole finally gave up in the late 1920s, and rafting existed no more on the Kentucky. Eversole lived out his days embellishing his rough-hewn image in the minds of many Frankfort residents with his unique behavior. When a boy strayed onto his shantyboat, the old man invited him to stay and eat. After looking at Eversole's repast, a boiled hog's head with the eyes staring at him, the young man replied, "Mister Eversole, I'm not very hungry and they're expecting me at home. I expect I better get home."[38]

Corps records give some idea of the size of rafting on the Kentucky. In 1887, for example, the record of lockages for the five existing dams at that time indicated that many rafts, a thousand or more, were going all the way to the Ohio and to the sawmills in Indiana and at Louisville. This was the same year that the Beattyville Beartrap proved to be a disaster for both timber and coal transportation. In 1888 the Corps observers reported only one good rafting tide for the entire year. By the mid-1890s, rafts became the major downriver traffic. The 1905 report recognized the dams as "detrimental" to rafting and that the construction of the locks and dams had had "so far, no effect on freight rates." About the time of World War I, the value of rafting railroad ties skyrocketed, but tapered off before long in that boom-and-bust cycle to which mountain folk have become so accustomed. This era marked the last gasp for rafting. Ice gorges in 1905 and 1918 destroyed many rafts and logs, causing a loss of millions of dollars. "Cutting the trees off the bank" as the ice finally broke loose, eyewitnesses recalled the awful rending sound. In the late twenties and thirties, rafting slowed to a trickle. The annual reports of the chief engineer noted some rafting on the river as late as 1940, and that was probably only a single raft.[39]

Communities along the Three Forks and the Kentucky were a crucial part of the timber trade. Small sawmills could be operated in the mountain valleys for a short time with a limited investment. Even some floating sawmills filled an industrial void for a long time, but as railroads pushed ever deeper into the mountains, large sawmills followed. The mills started in the lower part of the Kentucky Basin, with Frankfort being a center for the industry in the late nineteenth century. As construction of the dams moved upriver, so did the large sawmills, eventually reaching as far as Jackson. Sawmills became an important part of the Kentucky River timber trade, providing jobs for hundreds before the Great Depression. Small towns grew up around the sawmills. The Southern Lumber Company at Valley View had a three-story steam-powered sawmill complete with electricity that "lights up the office and mill by night" as well as a telephone system.[40]

In the earliest days of logging, logs free-floated down the Three Forks and the Kentucky to large sawmills, beginning in Frankfort. Telephone communication into the mountains coordinated the loosing of logs on the tide, preferably arriving during the daylight hours. Lumber dealers like Tom Congleton sold much of his lumber to New England and Canada. Large mills were built at Beattyville, Heidelberg, Irvine, Valley View, Camp Nelson, and Ford in the late nineteenth century on or near sources of railroad transportation. In 1899 the first complaints surfaced about the log boom used by the big sawmills at Ford. The booms of the Barker Cedar Company and the Southern Lumber Company were cited by the Corps of Engineers as "obstructions to the navigation of the river during high water up to Ford." Barker's location at Valley View just above the newly constructed Lock and Dam 9 also contributed to the problem.[41]

The log boom (see illustration) consisted of a *boom shear*, made of logs wired together, floated out into the river when a sawmill received word that its logs were on the tide. A steel cable unwound from a windlass allowed for precise positioning. Rudders floated at the back of the boom to give it stability in the swift current. Logs would be pulled into shore by men in boats, then worked onto the bank for storage and eventual transmission to the sawmill on higher ground. At low tide the boom was pulled into the bank for storage and maintenance. The boom took a beating from the current and bombardment by logs riding on the tide. With multiple sawmills operating on the river and numerous booms in the water during a tide, it was a constant struggle for mills to garner in their logs and allow others to go on their way. Vernon Alcorn worked for the Irvine sawmill for several years: "My job was to take care of them rafts when they come in." The log rafts had to be securely tied to shore, not in the "swipe of a river," but away from the main current and protected from drift that could pile up suddenly on a rising river and break the raft apart. "You got to get them out of that drift," Alcorn recalled. "Right smart job about it and right smart job to know where to put them. Another thing, if the raft is about sunk, you better get him in and take him to the mill and get rid of him; hold with the ones that's floating up good. There's a whole lot of figuring out to it."[42]

In 1894 an executive of the Asher Lumber Company of Ford de-

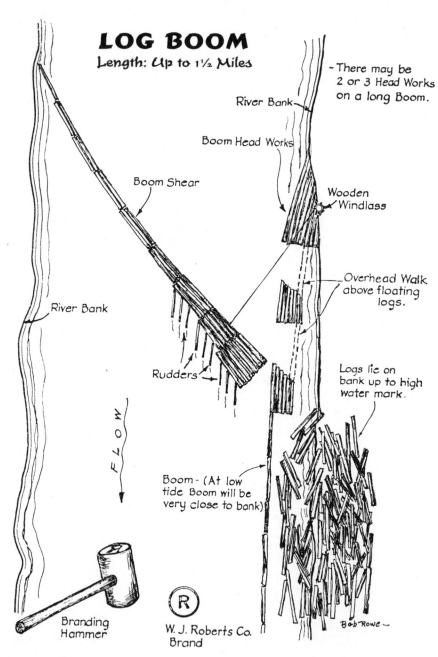

LOG BOOM
Length: Up to 1½ Miles

- There may be 2 or 3 Head Works on a long Boom.

River Bank

Boom Head Works

Boom Shear

Wooden Windlass

Overhead Walk above floating logs.

River Bank

Rudders

Logs lie on bank up to high water mark.

F L O W

Boom - (At low tide Boom will be very close to bank)

Branding Hammer

W. J. Roberts Co. Brand

Ⓡ

Bob Rowe

Drawing of a log boom. (Bob Rowe, Frankfort)

fended his company's use of a log boom there and at Frankfort as the only way to get large quantities of timber to his mills. He also noted that his men maintained a 100-foot gap so as not to interfere with other river traffic. Moreover he scorned the continuing building of dams up the river as not good for his industry. The Burt and Babb Company of Saginaw, Michigan, took over the Asher Lumber Company of Ford in 1896 and petitioned the state and the Corps of Engineers to keep use of the log boom. In that period most of Burt and Babb's better lumber went to Great Britain. The log booms continued to be a point of contention for those using the river until they were outlawed in 1910 along with the running of loose logs. After that there was no alternative but to raft logs, a trend that had been growing since the 1890s because of the advance of the locks and dams upriver.[43]

The heyday of free-running logs ended in the winter of 1905 when an ice gorge extended from just below Beattyville to Irvine, a distance of 30 miles. Many producers and sawmills had much at stake. Extremely cold weather at or below zero extended for days in mid-February. Logs ground together in the 20- to 30-foot-high ice packs, wiping out the work of many mountain timbermen. Sawmill operators in some places used dynamite to try to break up the gorge, but with no effect. The attempts of the Kentucky River Poplar Company at Irvine to stretch cables and chains across the river to catch their logs failed after the gorge finally broke up. As the ice moved downriver, it soon reached Ford, where an estimated five hundred rafts were caught, unable to move. To compound these problems, when the temperature rose, a flood of water washed out Lock and Dam 10 at Boonesborough just below Ford. With the pool lost, it became impossible to lock through the remaining rafts when the tide receded. The "ice tide" of the terrible winter of 1918 again devastated the rafting season. "A rain loosened it up, broke all that up," Bill Broadus recalled, "came a big tide in the river, cut trees off the bank." "You could hear it for miles," another interviewee recounted.[44]

A "timber boom" fueled the Kentucky economy from 1870 to 1920. In the peak year of 1909, over a billion board feet of lumber was sold, but by 1927 the amount had fallen to less than one-third of that figure. With large sawmills at Irvine and near Jackson, and timber holdings in Perry, Knott, and Breathitt Counties, the huge Mobray and Robinson Company depleted 15,000 acres of timber. In the mid-twenties with its forests gone, the company donated thousands of acres of land to the University of Kentucky and what became the Robinson Agricultural Substation and Robinson Forest. Another company, the

Last rafts to come down the Kentucky River at Frankfort. (National Archives)

Kentucky Lumber and Veneer Company, also had extensive mountain holdings, with a major mill below Jackson on the North Fork.[45]

West Irvine, opposite Irvine, the county seat of Estill County, prospered as a Mobray and Robinson sawmill town from 1906 until closure, resulting from the Great Depression. Previous companies, like the Kentucky River Poplar Company, at the same site suffered with the ebbing and flowing of the national economy. Oral histories illustrate the dynamics of that community and the lifestyle of that place and time.[46]

"It was considered a good job," recalled an interviewee who grew up there. Although wages were only thirty cents an hour for a ten-hour day, with a salary of $18 per week, management also included a house. "Really, our little West Irvine community was ahead of our time because we had electricity," another interviewee recalled. "We had a five-room consolidated school which had a furnace in it." Like all children her memories and those of others may be a bit rose-colored, but they recall a childhood full of wonder and promise before the coming of the Depression and World War II. "I always wanted to ride that chute [the conveyor that brought the logs from the river to the mill], but none of the bosses would agree to it." All the children were most impressed by the burning of excess waste, mostly sawdust and trimmings. "They had a great big iron thing, we used to call the 'hell hole.' The conveyor would take all the old slabs and sawdust out and dump it over and there was a fire that burned continuously. As long as the mill was running it never went out. There was always a pile of embers there ready for another piece to fall in." "I love the smell of sawdust," a woman claimed, having grown up with it ever present. Once four repairmen fell into the dreaded place, one man losing his life. All the children who lived there recalled the little sawmill towboat, the *Fred M.*, which scurried about moving logs toward the conveyor to the mill.[47]

Childhood days at West Irvine on the Kentucky were happy ones indeed, especially for the boys. "I enjoyed playing on the rafts," one interviewee recalled. "We'd run off every day." With plenty of unsold lumber and scrap around there was always something to build. One family used free lumber to build a shantyboat and tied up near the mill site. "The river was a way of life," the young shantyboatman recalled; "it was a source of food. There is something about it that if you stay there long enough it'll get to you. I still love it today. I had a very happy childhood." Although discouraged by their parents and the sawmill officials, girls and boys would play around the lumber piles, looking for violets and other treasures.[48]

But if childhood memories are still bright, for those who worked there, their toil was hard and often dangerous. One young man, whose father operated the nearby toll bridge, worked at the mill during the summers to make money for college. "Now I can tell you, that sawmill work will separate the men from the boys," he concluded after working the summer of 1928 stacking lumber. "I was glad to see September come." Another young man, who grew up at the mill, worked there after the milling ceased in the thirties. "Oh, law, it was hard work, too, because I did a little bit of it after the mill shut down. When I was in high school, I was old enough to go out there. They'd get a order for a load of lumber and they would let us pick up an extra dollar or two. We'd go out there and load up one of those big boxcars."[49]

The higher the skill the better the housing for employees and their families at Mobray and Robinson. The housing area was neat, tree trunks were partially whitewashed, and there was apparent harmony. But there was a price to pay. The family of one worker recalled their father's long hours, which included lacing together leather belts. "If a belt broke, he would lace it back together with the mill running. He'd throw it back on the pulley while it was going. He'd have some burnt places on his arms and way across his stomach" from belts flying off the wheel. One of his jobs included cleaning out the steam boilers. "It's a wonder he hadn't died in those boilers when he went in there sometimes," his son admonished. "He'd go in there on Sunday evening after the mill had been shut down on Friday evening. It really didn't have time to cool down hardly, and they'd wash it out and then go in there. I went in there once. You couldn't hardly breathe it was so hot."[50]

The days of the big sawmills were numbered, undermined by competition and the brunt of Great Depression economic losses. By the time the Corps of Engineers recorded the last raft on the river in 1940, the old days of timbering on the Kentucky were long since dead. The big sawmills like Mobray and Robinson folded their tents and moved out of state while continuing to exploit Kentucky's forests. Trucks, owing to improving highways, and railroads carried out the timber, most of it by World War II second- and third-growth. Unfortunately, Kentucky did not develop secondary wood industries like North Carolina and Indiana. No large furniture factories dotted the landscape as they do in those states, providing jobs and supporting communities. As concluded by Harrison and Klotter in *A New History of Kentucky*, "In a story that would be told and retold in the Commonwealth's economic history, many of the benefits of Kentucky's sizable timber industry would go outside the state." Another opportunity had been missed to help bring Kentucky out of its economic doldrums. And all that is left of the rafting days are faded photographs and memories.[51]

CHAPTER FOUR

Harnessing the River

Ferries, Bridges, and Dams

It sounds trite, a well-worn cliche today, but we human beings really do try to dominate nature. From their first sighting of the Kentucky, Euroamericans envisioned ways in which the river could enrich their lives. Early on these dreams included harnessing the river for its economic benefit. With its seasonal floods followed by long stretches of drought, when not enough water flowed for continual navigation, entrepreneurs plotted means of regularizing the river's depth by canalizing the Kentucky River into individual pools. And there were other concerns as well. Wherever people settled, there was a need to cross the river for the full flow of commerce across the river valley. Ferries sprang up along the river and then bridges, at first made entirely of wood, and later of iron, steel, or concrete, spanned the river's width. The human history of the river has always been inextricably tied to manmade features.

Soon after the beginning of white settlement, early inhabitants developed ferries at places that demanded more regular travel than what was possible at low water riffles that predominated for most of the year. Trade, animals, and people had to be moved if the commerce of Kentucky was to grow with the expanding population. With the chartering of Richard Callaway's ferry at Boonesborough in 1779 through the present-day operation of the Valley View Ferry connecting Madison with Jessamine and Fayette Counties, these conveyances played an important part in Kentucky's history. The history of the Kentucky River ferry included both the famous and infamous among the Commonwealth's early citizens. On 13 October 1800, for example, Andrew Holmes and his wife Tabitha deeded to John Brown their Frankfort ferry, which had originally belonged to James Wilkinson.[1]

Dozens of Kentucky River ferries operated in the nineteenth century in the simplest manner. From a rope or metal cable suspended across the river, a sliding hitch attached to a boat was all that was needed for this so-called "current ferry" to operate in all but the highest floods. Most often manned by only one person, "walking from one end of the ferry to the other," all the operator had to do was counter the effect of the current of the river. Nineteenth century ferries usually consisted of only a flat-bottomed boat, made of wood and only sometimes reinforced with metal straps and ribs. Ferries were notoriously fragile crafts and not always well-maintained. Ramps facilitated the boarding of wagons and buggies. In the nineteenth century typical fares were five cents for a person, twenty-five cents for a horse and buggy, and five additional cents for an extra horse. Many ferries exempted preachers and funeral processions. Sometimes widows were also given a free ride. Tariffs grew as did the size of the ferries to accommodate larger twentieth century trucks and automobiles. When only one or two passengers appeared at the ferry dock, they were very often taken across the Kentucky in a "footboat," a common term for a flat-bottomed, wooden johnboat. Eventually the Corps of Engineers required that the lowest part of a ferry cable "be not less than 80 feet above pool level," in order for river traffic to have clearance.[2]

Many ferries existed in the nineteenth century on the Three Forks, but the most famous locations were on the Kentucky River proper. There still are a few place names on the Kentucky based on old ferry locations. At major towns like Beattyville and a place called Old Landing in Lee County, for example, ferries provided important services. Clay's Ferry, originally named Cleveland's Ferry, operated until a bridge spanned the Kentucky at that point on what became a major north-south artery, U.S. 25. On the Madison County side, "Bull Hell Cliff" necessitated that busses back up to get around the hairpin curve on the precipitous hill. The Jackson Ferry, connecting Doylesville in Madison County with Clark County, operated for many years. At one time that ferry gave a direct access for shoppers who wanted to continue on to Lexington. Interviewees recalled the ferry as being a center of life for that small community. As a young man, one informant used the ferry in the late 1920s to take chickens, eggs, and other local produce from his father's store to Winchester every Friday. "I took it in a horse and a spring wagon," he recollected. "I'd get $75 to $100 a load." A Greyhound bus once used the ferry at Doylesville, but not before all the passengers got off. Joined on the Madison side of the river, the passengers reboarded and the bus went on its way.[3]

The life of the ferry in Kentucky has been limited because of improvements in rail and highway transportation. Many bridge sites on the Kentucky originated as ferry locations. A ferry operated continuously at Boonesborough for 150 years, at one time owned by Maurice D. Flynn's grandfather. A state highway bridge replaced it in 1930 and was itself replaced by a $6.6 million concrete and steel structure in 1994. In times of high water, ferries could be very dangerous conveyances; even under normal conditions disaster could strike. On 10 September 1925, the Clifton Ferry in Woodford County capsized, drowning six sheep and a cow, after a truck rolled backward. Happily, the *Courier-Journal* could report the next day that "several men, eighteen sheep, and a bull managed to swim to shore."[4]

The ferries mentioned above are all gone now from the Kentucky. Only the Valley View Ferry, at the mouth of Tate's Creek, is left, a testimony to the need for such transportation services even as we enter the twenty-first century. The oldest continuously operating business in Kentucky, the Valley View Ferry has a long history of owners beginning with John Craig in 1785, when he was granted a franchise by the Virginia legislature. In 1812 Craig sold the ferry and surrounding acreage to David Baker, who applied to the Fayette County Court for permission to operate. The ferry changed hands several more times in the nineteenth century. The Land family held part or total interest in the ferry from 1870 until 1950 when Claude C. Howard purchased it. In 1991 Howard sold the ferry to Jessamine, Madison, and Fayette Counties. Former Madison County Judge Executive William Robbins arranged for the sale and the subsequent board made up of representatives of each county. Unlike the old days, the ferry now operates only during the daylight hours. High tides also bring the service to a halt. Extensive and costly renovations in the range of $200,000 during 1998 included new steel towers to hold the cable across the river. The little towboat, *John Craig*, was also renovated. Sometimes traffic totals 250 vehicles a day for the two-car ferry in what has now become a free service.[5]

The words of Ed Land Jr. speak eloquently and knowingly about the bygone days of the Valley View Ferry and the surrounding community in the early 1920s. In particular, he spoke highly of his father's engineering abilities.

> The first one that I remember was that wooden boat. It was all wood and when you drove in the boat, the aprons, you drove down in the hull part. That boat was pulled across by oars. Those oars was out of saplings, something like 15 to 20

feet, with a paddle nailed on the end of it. And they paddled that boat across. That's a hard way of getting across, that was the way they done it. And it was all the time a leaking. They drove that corking in it and it would leak, and they'd put in a board and it'd leak. It was kinda unsatisfactory. So he (Ed Land Sr.) designed a steel boat. It was made in Madisonville. I came home from school one day, I was about six years old, and it had been delivered and was tied up on the other side. I didn't think much of it because it was just a hull. No deck, no banisters, no way of getting in or out of it, just a box made out of steel. Of course, that was the way he had it designed. Then he got some men around there and they put the deck on it. They put a deck, built the aprons out, put banisters on it for railings. Then it began to look like a ferry. And that was an improvement over the old wooden boat.[6]

Next, Land's father designed a more seaworthy craft. In the following sequence of his interview, his son also displayed a sense of humor.

I was a great big boy then, twenty-one or twenty-two years old. The American Barge Company was to bring it up the Ohio River and kick it off at Carrollton. My father took me to Carrollton in a car, and I got a room at a hotel and waited for them to bring this boat up. And finally the American Barge Company, they were taking steel to Pittsburgh, and they come up in that big barge. I never will forget, I was standing on the bank and I thought this ferry boat was just a footboat beside it. They kicked it off and I tied it at the mouth of the river. The Kentucky River was out of its banks. It was high, past flood stage. Of course, Carrollton was a long ways from Valley View and I was getting homesick. About all I can ever say I done in Carrollton was drink beer. Carrollton was quite a town. I stayed there three or four days until the river got down just a little.[7]

When the boat arrived to tow the ferry up river to Valley View, young Land's mettle would be tested.

Ed Black and Tevis Perkins came down the river in this little gasoline boat to tow the ferry upriver. And, of course, they got there that night and, of course, they was like most river people; they liked to have a beer and to have a drink. And they was in seventh heaven, but I'd saw enough of Carrollton. I was ready to head for Valley View. So I told them the night before. I said, "You all get all the beer and whiskey bought you gonna have, because we're pulling out in the morning." And they told me, "Well, we can't 'cause the old river is up; they're not even locking." I said, "We're going over the locks." And the first two locks we did, we went over the dams. The river was so full. But the third lock, the river began to fall just a little and it left a riffle across there. This little gasoline boat got that barge right up on top of the riffle and it didn't lose no ground, didn't gain none. It just set there. I put Tevis Perkins ashore on a footboat with a cable. He rode up the river and tied to a big tree and me and Black pulled on the rope. We pulled over the riffle on the dam. When we got to the next dam [Number 4 at Frankfort] we had to wait another day till it got down enough so that we could go through.[8]

This vessel, delivered in the late thirties, is the ferry still used today. Land continued his recollections:

This boat's got a 19-ton capacity. That's what it was built for. When it came up, the railings and banisters that's around it had to be put on it, and the aprons that you see down there had to put on it. They put a wire, about the size of a number nine, and it went across and it had slack in it. And you picked that wire up and started walking and the boat started pushing out. That was the way they ferried with that wire. We kept oars on board in case of an emergency. He added an extra wire. If you catch the river just at a certain current, the current will take that boat across the river without a motor running, or an oar or anything.[9]

Land also recalled the dangers of the river at Valley View Ferry with Lock and Dam 9 only a few hundred yards downriver.

I remember one time they was a family by the name of Burgess. Tobacco all came that way on wagons, and he had two wagons and teams and they started across the river on the ferry. The cable broke and that set the boat adrift. Of course, they grabbed these oars, and tried to push the boat out of the channel. And they were getting there but the boat was moving faster down the river than they was going out of the current. And he had a boy, great big boy, that was running down the bank on the other side talking to his daddy. [He] said, "Get in that footboat and come on off." My daddy told them, "If you get down to the falls [the dam] and see we can't get it out of the channel, we'll get in that footboat and go to the bank. We'll let her go." He told Burgess, "You'd better unharness your horses so they'll have a chance to swim out. They haven't got much of a chance, but we'll give them all the chance we can." And that boy would holler, "Come on off of there, Pappy." And he'd holler back, "Just as soon as I can get these horses unharnessed." The boat was going on down the river all the time. It was getting pretty close to that dam. And the boy'd holler, "Pappy, come on off there! You can get another old pair of horses, but I can't get another Pappy!" [Land laughed heartily at this juncture in his story].[10]

Being a consummate story teller, Land allowed the story to build, unhurriedly, to a crescendo of excitement. "As luck would have it, Tom Sullivan was lockmaster then at Lock 9. He saw the ferry coming and saw it was in trouble. He walked up the left side of that cribbing [the lock wall]. He was standing on that and my daddy throwed him a rope, and he tied it to one of those buoys. The men that was on the boat got to pulling, and they pulled that boat just enough to straighten it up and when it hit on the corner it hit middleways. It could swing and went over the dam, but it swung and come into the lock pit."

They worked their way back upriver by pulling ropes in the slackwater near the bank. Land ended his story with finality, "So that's one of the things that happened with the Valley View Ferry."[11]

Later, when the ferry added motorized propulsion with a small paddle wheel boat, Land recalled a time when the Kentucky froze from bank to bank.

The ferryman, when the ice tides come, you had to run that boat about every hour or two to keep that channel open where the boat ran. You kept the ice broken. It'd be so thick you could get out and walk as it went across. The boat had a Fairbanks Morse motor, one of those kinds that looked like every lick was the last one, but it came back for more like one of these two-cycle John Deere tractors. But they were very satisfactory. My daddy designed those belts, those three belts and three wheels. By switching from one belt to another, the motor would propel the little paddle wheel boat either forward or backward.[12]

Claude Howard recalled his early days of ownership:

It makes a good living if you operated it yourself and take care of the business right. State Highway 169 goes to Nicholasville, Lexington. Since Lexington's getting very largely populated and Nicholasville is also, I would say they'd be more people using the ferry than there ever has been. Each town is coming down Tate's Creek from Lexington, from Nicholasville, and from Richmond. So quite a few uses it now that works at Nicholasville and Lexington. The boat's in pretty good shape now and all ready to go since we've overhauled it.[13]

Other observers of ferries could remember cattle often jumping off the ferry, most of them making it to shore safely, although not always to the same side of the Kentucky. The Valley View Ferry and the one on the Cumberland in Monroe County are the only ferries still operating on Kentucky's internal waterways. Valley View is a peaceful scene on a spring day with the nearby bridge piers that remain from the Richmond, Nicholasville, Irvine, and Beattyville Railroad, which locals called the "Riney B." After the L&N Railroad purchased the line earlier in the century, it pulled out in the 1930s, and the bridge was salvaged by army engineers during World War II. The site is so idyllic it was used for a scene of *The Flim Flam Man*, starring George C. Scott and Sue Lyon.[14]

Most ferries ended their days as rotting hulks when better highways, particularly after World War II, opened more regions to the wonders of modern transportation. Bridges on the Kentucky played an important role in a more modern transportation network. There are approximately twenty-two highway bridges, including the double Interstate 71, Interstate 64, and Bluegrass Parkway structures, a Brooklyn Bridge, and at least half-a-dozen railroad bridges. By far the most massive is the newly rebuilt single Interstate 75 bridge connecting Madison and Fayette Counties and the famous High Bridge, still a monster that spans the Kentucky for the Southern Railroad. Frankfort, the largest city on the Kentucky, has the most bridges.[15]

The earliest bridges on the Kentucky made use of the region's abundant timber. The quintessential American bridge, covered with a wooden superstructure for reinforcement and a shingled roof to protect the wood floor against the weather, reached its zenith in the mid-nineteenth century. Usually designed with rigid trusses bolted into place, internal arches were often added to longer bridges for extra strength. In 1990 only thirteen of an estimated four hundred original covered bridges remained standing in the state of Kentucky. None existed on the Kentucky River, but this had not always been so. The longest covered bridge in the state's history, designed by German immigrant Louis Wernwag, who had earlier built the St. Clair Street covered bridge in Frankfort, spanned the Kentucky River at Camp Nelson at the mouth of Hickman Creek. Completed in 1838, the massive double lane 241-foot-long structure spanned an important crossing place connecting Danville and Lexington. A single arch gave the bridge exceptional strength for its time. Although often credited as the longest cantilever wooden bridge in America, the State Highway Commission condemned it as a hazard in 1926. A petition of 500 citizens and creation of a group called "Citizens of the Blue Grass" failed to save the old bridge. Engineers estimated it would cost $30,000 to repair the old wooden Hickman Bridge, as it was locally called, and $100,000 to build a modern one. For two years ferries operated around the clock at Camp Nelson until the new bridge could be dedicated to the transportation needs of a new era. The old wooden bridge stood until 1933, when it collapsed into the river. In its turn the new Camp Nelson bridge suffered the same fate as it predecessor, being condemned after severe flood damage in early 1997. The Loyd Murphy Memorial Bridge, completed in the early 1990s, now rises far above it.[16]

On the Dix River the Kings Mill Bridge, like the Hickman Bridge, spanning a river without a central pier to hinder navigation, served its community from the mid-1870s until covered by the waters of the new Herrington Lake in 1925. It too was replaced by at the time what was a modern bridge, the Kennedy Bridge—796 feet long and 254 feet above the lake. The Kennedy Bridge still stands but tests the courage of the modern driver with its narrow two-lane roadway high above the deep waters of the lake.[17]

Rivalries often surfaced when construction money became available. For example, proponents of a bridge at Tyrone won out over those who proposed a similar structure at Clifton, and Anderson and Woodford Counties were connected. Moreover, some bridges did not always get built on schedule. Highway Commissioner J. Lyter Donaldson pushed through approval of a new bridge at his native

Carrollton in the early 1940s. The old Carrollton bridge over the Kentucky cost the astounding sum of $100,000 when completed just after the turn of the twentieth century. World War II halted construction of its much-needed replacement near the mouth of the Kentucky "in a move to save critical materials and manpower." Local citizens bemoaned the fact they would have to continue to use the old narrow bridge there. It would not be until 1952 that Carroll Countians and Donaldson, now a Carrollton banker and lawyer, dedicated their long-sought-after bridge, which cost eleven times more than the old structure. However, at another site, the exigencies of the war pushed through completion of the new Clay's Ferry Bridge in 1945. Because of the Army Ordnance facilities in Fayette and Madison, construction there received priority steel shipments during the last months of World War II. Called the "Sky-High Bridge" by the *Courier-Journal*, the structure was dedicated as a memorial to World War II service personnel. Updated in the late 1990s, to twin three-lane structures, these massive bridges carry thousands of vehicles every day, the inhabitants of which probably neither notice, nor care about the river below.[18]

In the mid-nineteenth century almost all roads, or turnpikes as they were called were toll roads, privately owned and most often poorly maintained. Slowly this changed to the state-owned system that we know today. But there were also toll bridges; the last operated on the Kentucky in Irvine into the 1930s. Judge O.W. Witt was president of the company that owned the bridge near the big West Irvine sawmill. The father of interviewee James Hubert Tuttle, who ran the bridge from 1926 to 1939, lived in the little tollhouse and collected the fees charged for using the bridge. After being robbed one night by a masked man, "he got scared and bought a bulldog, a mean rascal." With the dog resting on the porch, there were no more robberies. The canine watchman even scared off miscreants from using the bridge without paying the toll. During the economic crisis of the Depression, the toll dropped from twenty-five cents to twenty for an automobile and to three cents for a pedestrian. Keeping with the old tradition, people going to church and to funerals were not charged to cross the bridge. A new "free" state highway bridge made the old toll bridge redundant and it was torn down for scrap during World War II. With a $125 per month salary and a small house thrown in, the Tuttle family lived comfortably even though they were on call twenty-four hours a day. To young people living at the sawmill, the toll bridge was also a source of entertainment, as when a few young men tested their coming of age by diving from the bridge.[19]

Frankfort is the "Capital on the Kentucky" as well as the largest city on that stream. There are more bridges in and around Frankfort than any other city on the Kentucky. After two covered bridges at the south end of St. Clair Street collapsed, a later wooden structure successfully connected south and north Frankfort at a cost of $65,700. Lasting from 1847 to the mid-1890s, the bridge was immortalized in several paintings by Paul Sawyier. On 24 March 1894, the famous St. Clair Street "singing" bridge opened for traffic at the same site. The open grate floor "creates a variety of musical pitches as vehicles cross," and has been a delight to children of all ages for generations. Because of the growing importance of the L&N Railroad in central Kentucky, just prior to the Civil War a Fink truss bridge spanned the Kentucky at the mouth of Benson Creek. The railroad added a pedestrian walkway in 1868, giving Bellepoint a much-needed connection to the city during floods. In 1894 the bridge was raised 8 feet, complying with an order from the Secretary of War, so that steamboats could navigate even in times of high water. A replacement recently opened at this same location.[20]

Frankfort needed more bridges, and New Deal money came to the rescue. After several studies and political squabbles during the 1930s between Governors Ruby Laffoon and Happy Chandler, the new War Memorial Bridge opened, connecting Capital Avenue with the main city. Dedicated on 14 June 1938, the bridge cost $329,331.10. Growth necessitated the construction of five more bridges in Frankfort and Franklin County since the early 1960s. Two opened on Interstate 64 in 1962, and others on State Highway 676 and at Miro and Clinton carried U.S. 127 into Frankfort on a new bypass.[21]

High Bridge still stands at mile 118 on the Kentucky, over a century and a quarter after initial construction and within sight of the mouth of Dix River, Shaker Landing, and Lock 7. In the beautiful Palisades region, the steel bridge mocks the river below with its massive bulk. Although the Jessamine County community that once shared its name is now long gone, High Bridge continues to be an important north-south Norfolk Southern Railway link still held by the municipally owned Cincinnati Southern Railway. The bridge today is a favorite of passengers on the *Dixie Belle* excursion boat that plies the waters of the Kentucky during Shakertown's summer tourist season at Pleasant Hill. Passing under the bridge cruise-goers are dwarfed by the rusting steel. At other times, central Kentuckians become painfully aware of the bridge after an unwary teenager tumbles to his or her death. But there is more to the story that must be added because of the fascinating history of this, by far the largest steel structure on the Kentucky River.[22]

A bridge over the Kentucky River gorge between Jessamine and Mercer Counties was first conceived with the chartering of the Lexington and Danville Railroad Company by the Kentucky General Assembly on 5 March 1850. Kentucky was starved for a better transportation network, and a railroad connecting these two towns offered a solution to that impasse. At the eventual High Bridge site, however, the canyon is a formidable 1,300 feet wide and 280 feet deep. In 1851, when John Augustus Roebling took on the task of designing a bridge for this site, he was treading on untried engineering ground. He envisioned a suspension bridge over the Kentucky's chasm; at the same time, he was constructing a 900-foot-long suspension railroad bridge near Niagara Falls. Suspension bridge design had been around for a long time, but now engineers like Roebling and others attempted to span huge distances with bridgework suspended from iron cables. One such bridge at Wheeling, West Virginia, collapsed in mid-1854. Roebling pushed on with his work at Niagara, completing a bridge with a railway deck above a carriageway. The question remained: Could a suspension bridge carry not only the weight of locomotive and its cars but also withstand the vibration set up by the moving traffic? Nevertheless, Roebling's company, on the cutting edge of mid-nineteenth century technology, constructed twin stone towers and anchorages at High Bridge, Kentucky, at a cost of nearly $100,000. But the project ended after the terrible panic of 1857 and bankruptcy of the Lexington and Danville. During this same era, Roebling designed the suspension bridge at Covington on the Ohio River. Although the Civil War intervened, this bridge was completed in 1867, making it at that time the longest suspension bridge in the world at 1,057 feet. In many ways the Covington Bridge is the prototype of Roebling's Brooklyn Bridge. With steel cables replacing wrought iron ones in 1896 and with later refinements, the Covington Bridge still stands as a monument to visionary nineteenth century bridge technology.[23]

Meanwhile, Roebling's towers, opposite the Kentucky River's palisades in Mercer and Jessamine Counties, stood like silent sentinels to the folly of trying to bridge the great river gorge. It took both visionaries and political clout to complete the project in the rough-and-tumble days of post–Civil War Kentucky politics and economics. With the L&N Railroad having a stranglehold on the state after the Civil War, some Kentuckians in the Kentucky General Assembly and the city of Cincinnati looked for a new route south.[24]

In the 1871 gubernatorial race, Democrat Preston H. Leslie defeated Republican John Marshall Harlan. Leslie immediately faced the challenge of the Cincinnati Southern Railroad bill, enabling legislation that would open a path through northern Kentucky southward. It divided his party and led to new state political coalitions. Vigorously opposed by the L&N, "the question was one of power, money, and dominance," historian James C. Klotter has said, "and the bitter battle lines divided parties and factions." Lobbyists flocked to Frankfort like migrating birds. The Southern Railroad wisely countered old Confederate veteran and influential L&N lobbyist Gen. Basil Duke with their own old Confederate veteran, Gen. John C. Breckinridge. Politicking, and undoubtedly the passage of money around Frankfort, was thick and heavy. The issue became the most contested of the early 1870s, pitting Kentucky's Old South image against the new plunging boosterism of the Gilded Age, a view that many Kentuckians associated with the dreaded Yankees who had won the Civil War. Would Kentucky join the new booming railroad age or not? After initial failure of the bill in 1870 and 1871, the lower house of the General Assembly passed the bill, and Lt. Gov. John G. Carlisle, a resident of Covington across the Ohio River from Cincinnati, broke a tie vote in the Kentucky Senate, passing the enabling legislation. The Cincinnati Southern Railroad had won the right to expand into the Bluegrass State and on to Chattanooga. Central Kentucky would be the preferred route for the new railroad, and the chasm at High Bridge stood at the nexus of that line.[25]

In 1874 the Cincinnati Southern purchased the remaining properties of the defunct Lexington and Danville line for $300,000. Chief engineer William Adams Gunn rode on horseback along the proposed route, possibly intending to make good use of the old Roebling towers. Actually, the towers did not go with the purchase of the railroad right-of-way. An old lien on the towers was purchased by Harrodsburg lawyer Ben Lee Hardin, who hoped to make a neat profit from the sale of the towers to the Cincinnati Southern. The railway company, which apparently never intended to use the towers, told Hardin to remove his towers from their property. Eventually the parties reached a settlement in this dispute.[26]

The question now was what type of bridge to construct, for the new railroad could not connect Cincinnati with Chattanooga without it. Into the picture came another legendary bridge engineer, Charles Shaler Smith of the Baltimore Bridge Company. Should it be built on four bridge piers, spanning the river with a sectional truss bridge? The latter type of bridge was now at its apex of design, and iron was still the preferred and cheapest material available. Smith decided to use a long-known though little-used type of structure, the cantilever, a bridge whose span is formed by two cantilevers projecting toward each other, eventually joining at the central point. More simply stated, the "cantilever principle is simply the balancing of a portion of the structure on one side of a support by the portion on the opposite side of the same support. Similarly the halves of the middle span were built out from the piers, meeting with exactness in mid-air." Easier said than done. The question was: Could Smith build a superstructure light enough to bridge the canyon successfully while able to carry the increasingly heavier railroad stock? Stress and wind factors were uppermost in Smith's mind, and he took up the challenge with a passion.[27]

First, the municipally owned Cincinnati Southern had to sell bonds, in the initial sum of $150,000, for preliminary studies. Meanwhile Smith was at work. His cantilever bridge would be built outward from each cliff with a temporary pier on dry land, supporting the structures as they extended outward over 250 feet above the river. Two permanent stone foundations to bedrock stood on the bank on the Jessamine side of the river and just on the edge of the Kentucky on the Mercer shore. Extending upward from these reached the iron piers, 177 feet high, 375 feet apart, each composed of four legs, with the pedestal resting on double friction rollers. At the top of each pier a 12-inch pin connected into the lower truss. Being in the middle of the Kentucky, the meeting point would not be supported by falsework or scaffolding. The entire work, known as a *Whipple* or double intersection truss, was riveted together except at the cantilever connection points. The middle of the bridge, from one pier to the other, became an extended girder under Smith's direction, in effect, three 375-foot spans joined together. Smith's bridge was not entirely his own. L.F.G. Bouscaren, chief engineer of the Cincinnati Southern, demanded that the "chords" be cut on the lower trusses, and that sliding tenons in iron sleeves be installed. Reasoning that the bridge would need to expand and contract with temperature changes, Bouscaren believed that these stresses could cause structural damage of unknown proportions. From that juncture the "superstructure then consisted of center span trusses, 525 feet long, cantilevered 75 feet at each end beyond their supporting towers to receive the ends of the shore spans, the trusses of which were thus reduced to 300 feet."[28]

Amazingly, after preliminary work, the Baltimore Bridge Company began construction on 16 October 1876 and finished on 20 February 1877 at a total cost of $404,856.58. High Bridge, being on the

The original High Bridge, ca. 1905. (Hibben Collection, Kentucky Historical Society)

very edge of the technology, became one of the most-studied structures of the late nineteenth century. Built outward from the cliffs and from each iron pier the bridge met flawlessly in mid-air. Bridge engineers made pilgrimages to the site to wonder at Smith's masterpiece, with Bouscaren's improvements. According to bridge specialist Eddie B. Smith, "At the time of its construction it was the highest railway bridge in the world, the highest bridge on the American continent, and the first real cantilever railroad bridge in the United States."[29]

Various tests were carried out on the bridge before placing it into service. The most advanced test concluded with four heavy locomotives meeting at the center span, their engines puffing away. Cincinnati Southern officials celebrated with champagne on 20 April 1877. Gov. James B. McCreary, a Confederate army veteran, made an impromptu speech that apparently had the intention of burying the old hatchet of the Civil War. After the speech came the final test. With the surrounding hillsides lined with hundreds of spectators, an engine, drawing twenty-four loaded cars, entered the bridge at 20 miles an hour, and then slammed on all of its brakes. The bridge did not even wobble, and

An outing on High Bridge, awing sightseers for generations, ca. 1911. (Arthur Y. Ford Albums, Photographic Archives, University of Lousiville)

The massive new High Bridge. (Caulfield and Shook Collection, Photographic Archives, University of Louisville)

engineer Charles Shaler Smith could not have been prouder. Two years later Republican president Rutherford B. Hayes formally dedicated High Bridge or, as it was known in a Smithsonian Institution exhibit, "The Dixville Bridge."[30]

High Bridge became an immediate hit with the public. Excursions by rail came from far and wide. A station and the small town of High Bridge developed on the Jessamine County side. Even the normally dour Shakers of Pleasant Hill fed and housed tourists at their nearby village. Boat excursions also increased on the river below as passengers wanted to get a look at this new marvel of transportation. Artist Paul Sawyier would soon work his way up the river as he developed his impressionist talent. He painted the bridge as an ephemeral sight, appearing in the distant fog, unsubstantial. The bridge was amazingly light by modern standards, built just heavy enough to carry traffic. Edge Moor Iron Company of Wilmington, Delaware, supplied the iron for the Whipple trusses and the towers, altogether weighing nearly 4.5 million pounds. "A bad rivet," engineer Eddie B. Smith has said, "it would have unraveled, as most failures did at that time. There was no backup, no redundancy."[31]

But it did not fail. However, like all manmade structures it became obsolete, in this case much sooner than anyone in 1877 would have guessed. High Bridge became more and more dangerous as locomotives and traffic increased in weight. In 1910 Cincinnati Southern decided to replace the bridge, but how to do so became the question of the day. Again, an outstanding engineer, Gustav Lindenthal, took on the task. One suggestion was to build an entirely new steel bridge nearby, with a supporting arch from one rim of the canyon to the other.[32]

Lindenthal decided instead to build a massive steel double-track superstructure encasing the old structure. Cincinnati Southern locomotives would slow but never stop running during the construction process. Three new steel trusses, 353 feet long, were designed so that two E60 locomotives could pass successfully, with the greatest "dead load" capacity of any bridge in the world except for the Forth Bridge in Scotland. In the end workmen laid only one track during the 1911 reconstruction process. Fearing the damaging effect of floodwaters, Lindenthal had the old stone foundation piers capped with concrete. After construction of the new steel bridge, the old, inner, iron structure was torn down for scrap metal at a more leisurely pace.[33]

The *Lexington Herald* reported the new bridge open for traffic in September 1911. This time there would be no large crowd, no visit from the president of the United States, no other major festivities to praise the new structure. Railroad officials shook hands, toasted the new bridge, and got on with the business of making money. The wonder and the awe of the old High Bridge had been lost. The American Bridge Company had built the new High Bridge 31 feet higher than the old one at a cost of $1.25 million.[34]

Engineer Smith perhaps best summarized the differences between the old and the present bridges:

> In Sawyier's pictures the old bridge has this ghostlike appearance. The current structure doesn't have this. It's dark, massive. It looms over you and consequently it makes the space look smaller. You don't see this wide canyon you see in Paul Sawyier's prints or in the photographs of the original bridge. The sense of wonder is not there anymore. Being overbuilt in the first place, there is not a lot of maintenance to do. It is no longer painted because of the expense. It made money and it still makes money. It is now part of the Norfolk and Southern, which leases the property from Cincinnati.

However, the old railway station is gone and the town of High Bridge has long since faded into distant memories.[35]

It remained only for man to tear down the last romantic signature of the bridge, the stone towers with their graceful arches. With double tracking now a necessity on the line, workers dismantled the towers in 1929. "That was something to see," longtime Burgin resident William Ison declared in an interview. "That was the prettiest stone and arches you ever saw." A final indignity is that no one seems to know what happened to the beautiful stone from those towers.[36]

In the mid-twenties another permanent structure would be built not far away from High Bridge, two miles up the Dix River. Originally spelled "Dick's," after a Cherokee Indian chief known as Captain Dick, the 45-mile-long tributary of the Kentucky once had scenery as spectacular, if not more so, than its parent. Most of that was covered by Dix Dam. Kentucky Hydro-Electric Company, in effect a subsidiary of Kentucky Utilities, had great plans that included not only harnessing the Dix River for waterpower, but other sites on or near the Kentucky River as well. At Jackson on the North Fork and at Beattyville, where a proposed dam that would back up water 35 to 40 miles, the company planned for the future. Smaller turbine units at Dams 8–14 on the Kentucky did not exhaust their scheming. All this coincided with the attempt by Samuel Insull to build a major project near Cumberland Falls. The country was ablaze with such efforts in the boom days of the 1920s. Even the town of Winchester asked for permission from the Federal Power Commission to install turbines at Dam Number 10. In the end Kentucky Utilities only built one small hydro turbine plant at Dam Number 7, 1½ miles below High Bridge.[37]

At its headquarters in Louisville, Martin J. Insull, the brother of Samuel Insull and vice president of Middle West Utilities, a part of the multilayered Insull public utilities holding companies, presided over the Kentucky Hydro-Electric Company. L.B. Herrington, vice president of Kentucky Hydro-Electric and also Kentucky Utilities, did most of the planning for the project. Harry Reid, a Kentucky Hydro-Electric vice president and president of Kentucky Utilities Company, filled out the top leadership of Kentucky Hydro. It was a very cozy arrangement, and with such interlocking leadership, Kentucky Hydro-Electric would sell power to Kentucky Utilities and Louisville, and all would make a healthy profit.[38]

Kentucky Utilities, incorporated in 1912, officially began operations at Cheapside and Main in Lexington. The brainchild of New Yorker Harry Reid, who started his dream of a statewide electric company with a small plant in Versailles, KU rapidly expanded toward southeastern coal mining country. Companies in Virginia and other places were purchased. Small power plants, serving only one town, were inefficient and not always trustworthy, as when the smokestack at the Richmond station folded over one day in a high wind. Being unable to maintain a draft, the stack could no longer keep the boilers going for the little power plant, but the local manager quickly thought of a solution. He solved the problem by blasting away at the stack with his shotgun until he had shot enough holes in it for it to draw properly, "and Richmond's lights were still burning." Kentucky needed more power and Kentucky Utilities believed it needed it in a big way.[39]

L.E. Myers Company, a Chicago firm, won the construction contract for Dix Dam. Beginning in the fall of 1923, approximately two thousand men worked around-the-clock shifts until completion of the dam in mid-1925. Impoundment of the lake began in early 1925 with the spring rains. At a cost of $7 million, the dam would be the largest rock-filled dam in the world and the highest dam east of the Rocky Mountains at that time. Lake Herrington backed up 35 miles into Mercer, Boyle, and Garrard Counties. The turbines in the powerhouse could turn out 24,000 to 30,000 kilowatts, depending on the water level in the lake. Placed in a gorge with 350-foot walls, reaching from the Mercer County side of the old Dix River gorge to the Garrard side, the dimensions of the dam were indeed monstrous, nearly 1,100 feet long at the top and 287 feet high. The base at the riverbed was 750 feet wide. After being faced with a hand-built masonry wall, the lake side of the dam was covered with a layer of concrete. A 24-foot "horseshoe tunnel" led to the steel penstocks that entered the turbines on the back

The construction process at Dix Dam. (National Archives)

side of the dam. Electric transmission lines led off toward the Louisville market. Moreover, Kennedy Bridge and the Chenault Bridge had
to be built to replace covered bridges submerged in Herrington Lake.[40]

Like High Bridge, Dix Dam became a big hit with sightseers and
tourists. The *Lexington Herald* predicted the latter would become "one
of the important showplaces of Kentucky." Part of the rationale for the
Dix Dam and Herrington Lake was flood control, and the Army Corps
of Engineers took notice of that purpose. Kentucky Utilities may have
owned the dam and surrounding acreage but not the lake itself. Financing growth of KU continued to be a problem, particularly after
the Great Crash of 1929 and the unraveling of Insull's utilities empire.
L.B. Herrington worried about this incessantly, from the market crash
and subsequent reorganization of KU until his resignation in 1933. It
was still "a hell of a company," his son Alex P. Herrington concluded.
The anti-Insull *Courier-Journal* was already deploring the loss of scenery caused by such projects as the Dix Dam and voiced strong opposition to Insull's designs for a dam on the Cumberland River.[41]

In the middle of the construction period, one of the worst racial
incidents in Kentucky history occurred. About eight hundred African
Americans worked at the site and lived nearby with their families. They
did the hardest work, laboring in the pits at the bottom of the dam.
"Away from work, both white and black men spent their time gambling, drinking, and fighting, though usually on a segregated basis,"

according to historian George C. Wright. On 9 November 1924, a white man was killed by two blacks, "who were convinced that he had cheated them at cards." A large white mob soon attacked the section where the black people lived, driving them toward Burgin and the railroad depot there. Herded into the little town, many of them wounded, the blacks waited until railroad cars could take them to safety. James Bond, investigating for the Commission of Interracial Cooperation, reported that others were found wandering in the countryside. Marauding whites had stripped the camp of possessions that belonged to black families. The *Lexington Leader* editorialized that "it was purely a massacre of that element of hard working Negroes by that class of whites who carry a grudge and foment trouble when coming in contact with Negroes."[42]

The L.E. Myers Company reacted quickly and received aid from the Kentucky National Guard. Thus protected, almost all the black workers returned. After detaining some whites for their destruction of the African American camp, Mercer County officials released them. Two black men, however, were not treated as lightly, receiving stiff prison sentences for murder. Historian Wright concluded:

> By the mid-1920s, white leaders all over the state agreed that steps had to be taken to eliminate mob rule. The beating of black farmers in isolated areas could be ignored and covered up, but an incident as blatant as the forced removal of 800 black men could no longer be tolerated. Most important, however, the labor of the men at Dix Dam had been necessary for the successful completion of the project. Obviously, some of the whites resented blacks working on the project and wanted them fired, but their disdain for Afro-Americans was not enough to have them removed. The company needed the workers and had, therefore, assisted the state in providing police protection to ensure that the blacks could perform without overt threats of violence.[43]

There were other problems as well at the Dix Dam site. Although a story about a workman falling and being covered forever with concrete is untrue, there is a larger concern. Engineers will attest to the fact that all dams leak, and Dix Dam was leaking before it was completed. "It's leaked since the day it was backed up," long-time KU employee Clyde Hayslett revealed in an interview. "It's never quit leaking. The biggest problem is in the expansion joints." On one occasion a bulkhead "blowed out," he recalled, washing 36-inch valves over 100 yards down the Dix River. After core-drilling for access to the holes in the dam, workers like Hayslett grouted them with a slurry of concrete, the larger holes also filled with sacks of cinders. Once a diver lost a lead shoe in a large hole, the suction being so great. Another claimed, according to Hayslett, "Man, you could have driven my pickup truck in it. That hole was getting ready to drain the river." Another diver, not having the best of attendants on the surface, got his airhose tangled: "It got kindly hair raising there for a little bit. And this guy. I never heard a man cuss so in my life. He was down there hung up. He was a nice fellow, but, you know, he just got excited in there." Down at 125 feet in the cold dark waters of Herrington Lake such behavior is perfectly understandable. As late as 1991, divers installed a 150-foot by 40-foot rubber belt 7/l6 inch thick to seal an expansion joint. Filled with concrete, the "rubber blanket," KU predicted, "will give the dam extra support and allow for some movement." The weakness of the dam is "saturation" with water, according to one longtime observer. Some residents of the "Capital on the Kentucky" fear a catastrophic collapse of Dix Dam during a record-setting rainfall and subsequent devastation of their city.[44]

"The best laid schemes o' mice and men do oft go astray," so the immortal Robert Burns wrote in 1785. He could have been writing about the construction of the fourteen locks and dams on the Kentucky River. Great political pressure from Kentucky politicians, businessmen, and others coincided with similar forces from other states in the latter nineteenth century, forcing the Congress of the United States and the Army Corps of Engineers into developing policies and plans for the nation's waterways. Few would argue that the major rivers like the Ohio and Mississippi needed canalizing, but did comparatively small streams like the Kentucky require the same attention? Probably not, but we now have the insight, the 20/20 vision not possible well over one hundred years ago.[45]

"Tight ass and popcorn," is the way James C. Thomas, a longtime Corps of Engineers employee, described one point on the upper Kentucky River. "Rocky point and a very narrow river," he continued, "that's what everybody on the river called it, called it 'tight ass and popcorn.'" Born on the Kentucky, he loved it much more than the mighty Ohio, on which he worked most of his career. "Too many locks and you can't lock but one barge at a time," Thomas concluded. The Kentucky is so narrow and crooked, he described navigating the treacherous currents as "flanking" rather than steering. "You run down on a point and kill 'er out, without stopping her. Then you let your head stick in the current, see, and you're over on the point. It hits the side of your tow and takes you right on around. You wouldn't have a chance trying to steer it, because you would have your boat over on the bank or whatever is over there. You'd be lucky if you didn't knock a hole in it. Sink her. You have to respect the current and the ice, 'cause you can't do much with it." Another old riverman, who operated towboats on the Kentucky in the last days of traffic above Frankfort, described his record by proudly declaring, "Well, I never sunk no barge. Yeah, there's bad curves on that river. Anybody that can pilot on that river can pilot anywhere. You had to be on your p's and q's to run the Kentucky River, 'cause it was a bad river to pilot on." A lockkeeper also summed up the problem: "The Kentucky never was no towboat river anyway," sometimes taking three hours to lock through a towboat and two barges in the narrow and short locks.[46]

Why didn't better judgment prevail, stopping the march upriver of locks and dams all the way to Heidelberg? The answer lies within the inertia of large institutions like the Corps of Engineers and the political system of America. First, perhaps better judgment might have prevailed if the original five dams had not been constructed in the first place in the early 1840s. Devastated by the stresses of the Civil War and lack of maintenance in the immediate post-war period, they were enticing hulks, waiting for just the right combination of boosterism and political logrolling in Gilded Age America. Even as long ago as 1930, nearly $22 million had been expended for construction and reconstruction of the Kentucky River system.[47]

Railroads were already pushing into the mountains of eastern Kentucky, offering a more assured system of transportation, when Kentucky politicians won approval of the Beattyville Beartrap Dam in the mid-1880s. On that project, even the Corps of Engineers initially balked, particularly complaining about the site fixed by Congress. That ill-fated construction should have proven more to all concerned than it apparently did. Soon dams were being built up the river, incrementally raising pools toward Beattyville. Because of the small locks on the original sites at Numbers 1-5, each was 38 x 145 feet, and the decision not to tear them out and enlarge them, Locks 6–14 were only increased slightly in capacity, being 52 x 146 to 148 feet. Other states competed for construction funds for rivers similar to the Kentucky, putting terrible pressure on the Corps. The Corps did not choose wisely, preferring instead to succumb to the political climate of the day and spread the government largess around. Therefore, the Kentucky River locks and dams were built as cheaply as possible, dooming them to years of costly maintenance that continues to this day. Timber crib construction continued upriver to Number 8. Finally, at Number 9 at Valley View, the Corps stipulated concrete cell construction. However, even here the auxiliary dams, built because of washouts around the new dams at Valley View and Boonesborough, were constructed on timber crib foundations. That type of logic, or political expediency if you will, doomed the Kentucky River Navigation to the small scale operations that would prove uneconomical once railroads expanded their services.[48]

Yes, Mary Verhoeff, you were right when you wrote *The Kentucky River Navigation* in 1917. As her biographer concluded, "Citizen Mary Verhoeff, of independent means, was under no such necessity [as was the Corps of Engineers to defend their construction of the Kentucky River dam system]. For her to predict in 1917, only a few months before the project would begin to prove itself in use, that 'the improvement represents a waste of money, labor, and engineering skill' and 'it is doubtful that the river commerce will be appreciably augmented by shipments from the coal field when the slack-water system is finished and navigation is opened to Beattyville' was to put herself at least as precariously on a limb as the Corps had done, and with far less compelling reason." What she said would have made modern consumer advocate Ralph Nader proud.[49]

In three categories—geographical fit, quantitative fit, and secular fit—amateur economist-futurist Verhoeff was correct, according to David Ross, editor of *American Canals*, the quarterly bulletin of the American Canal Society. Geographical fit excluded the Kentucky River's canalization, because in order to use the river, coal first had to be trucked to Beattyville, an unnecessary mode of transportation with the growth of the railroad and construction of better highways. It was easier to transfer from one railroad to another. In the category of quantitative fit, the locks were too narrow for the increase in size of barges that would be developed in an "economy of scale" necessary for efficient twentieth century water-borne transportation. Secular fit was also not met, because even though water transportation is supposedly cheap and slow, towboats could not make enough trips on the narrow and often turbulent Kentucky River in their attempt to outrace more effectual railroad and truck transportation. Moreover, the 6-foot channel of the Kentucky did not permit heavy barges and it was often impossible to maintain even that depth on the upper Kentucky. Ross concluded that although Verhoeff "took on that most virile of institutions, the U.S. Army Corps of Engineers, in its own field of expertise, she had the courage to say flatly that it was wrong, and she had the brains to be right."[50]

However, some officers in the Corps had second thoughts about the Kentucky project from time to time, and they were not afraid to voice their caveats. In the 1881 annual *Report of the Chief of Engineers*, James W. Cuyler covered himself well, after discovering that the old dams to be reconstructed were in worse shape than he had expected. But he accepted the rationale that "business now carried almost exclusively by railroad; most of it, it is believed from its character, would seek water transportation if same were available." In other words, coal being heavy freight and not perishable, could be more cheaply shipped on the Kentucky River than by rail. Of course, he was in error. In the same 1890 annual *Report of the Chief of Engineers* that declared the Beattyville Beartrap Dam to be in the wrong place, the Corps reported a "notable decrease in total tonnage," because grain shipments for several distilleries around Tyrone were now being taken there by rail and highway. Moreover, "all freight shipped to Beattyville and parts in the mountains formerly shipped via Ford is taken to Beattyville via the Kentucky Union Railroad."[51]

As expenses mounted for construction, even maintenance costs skyrocketed with the normal wear and tear on the structures. Moreover, there were always accidents, as when the *Falls City* tore out a lockgate. In the 1899 annual report, an army official demanded that "The steamer *Falls City* should be held responsible for cost of repairing all damage done by collision with the gates," the reason being, "the pilot having rung the wrong bell." The usual procedure was for the boat captain to signal two short blasts from his whistle when requesting locking. Apparently the captain of the *Falls City* gave the wrong signal at some point.[52]

The 1904 report of the Corps reverted to wishful thinking when the chief engineer declared he expected no increased usage of the system "until the improvement is carried to the head of the river, where it is hoped that much coal land may be developed and the product shipped by water." Corps officials recognized the catch-22 situation they found themselves in: If they built locks and dams that were supposed to help the steamboat traffic, then the dominant user of the river from the 1870s to the 1920s—logging and rafting—would be harmed by damming the Kentucky. Moreover, free-running logs tore up the dams during high water and hindered steamboat traffic. There was no easy answer, particularly from the viewpoint of an analytical engineering mind. So, year after year, the annual reports laconically concluded: "It is believed that the improvement has had no material effect on the nature of the commerce" on the Kentucky. The next year, as one might expect, the Rivers and Harbors Act of 1911 authorized completion of the Kentucky system. By the time Congress and presidents like William Howard Taft began to question the wholesale pork barrel legislation that had contributed to the Kentucky River imbroglio, it was too late—the system had been built, leaving a legacy of continued waste, misspending, and controversy.[53]

There is an old joke among pleasure boat owners, "If you want to throw money down a hole, buy a boat." The Kentucky River navigational system would also apply to this same adage. In the end, the inertia of Corps planning and budgeting, with occasional waffling by an army engineer or two, coupled with the insistence of Kentucky politicians to keep the project alive until its completion in 1917.

Fourteen obsolete dams now exist on the Kentucky. Regardless of their uselessness as navigational aids, pools of water created by the dams from Irvine downriver provide drinking supplies for hundreds of thousands of central Kentuckians in one of the fastest-growing areas in America. Although the river can be spanned by such features as the ultra-modern Interstate 75 bridge at Clay's Ferry, the river still must be faced on its own terms someday, both ecologically and environmentally.

The visions of harnessing the Kentucky have often fallen by the wayside. For over two centuries, the dreams have often been at odds with the environment and with changing economic realities. If ferries and bridges made it possible to cross the river in places, making little disruption in the natural river, the building of fourteen locks and dams irrevocably changed the river for generations to come. Thus, nineteenth and twentieth century Kentuckians not only tried to harness the river but to conquer it. Even today many people view the river as something to dominate, not to live with in peace. Others ignore it except in times of drought or flood. With modern transportation and technology, it is all too easy to think that a river, especially one as small as the Kentucky, can have no influence on our lives. However, the Kentucky often appears to have a mind of its own. As one lifelong Doylesville resident declared, "This river really gets wild."[54]

CHAPTER FIVE

The River Always Wins

Flooding, Drowning, and Drought
on the Kentucky

Most of the time the Kentucky River is beneficent, providing plentiful water for the business of life. However, the river can quickly become a most dangerous place. Flooding, drowning, and drought are three of the perils that residents face if they live there for any length of time. The human quest to control nature often clashes with the whims of a river.

"The River Always Wins," the title of a *Henderson Gleaner* editorial about the great Mississippi flood of 1993, can be applied to all rivers. Can you control a river as large as the Mississippi or as small as the Kentucky? If so, what means do you use: dams, levees and flood-walls, or a combination of these? Are all floods inherently bad? The floods of the Kentucky River have often been beneficial. One mountain farmer recalled flood-borne soil alleviating the need for spreading fertilizer in the old days. "I've seen the settlings 18 inches deep," Sam Wilson of Lee County recalled, noting that it grew good corn even though floods usually destroyed one crop in three. Moreover, the tides benefitted the mountain men when they wanted to float their logs and rafts to market. But there has always been another side to the river. "That river is going to do what it wants to do," a longtime Kentucky River watcher exclaimed in an interview.[1]

Flooding not only causes physical damage and loss of life, it can also destroy entire communities, disrupting a way of life that can never recover. The great Mississippi flood of 1927 displaced and killed thousands. It expelled African Americans from the Mississippi Valley in droves when traditional relations between blacks and a dominant white aristocracy broke down. Similarly, floods on the Kentucky River over the years have severely altered the culture, convincing many that nature rampant had to be attacked by the resources of the federal government.[2]

Early floods on the Kentucky have been documented, though not well. Frank Wurtz, a Swiss immigrant, collected data on earlier tides and observed floods from his post as lockkeeper at Frankfort. He talked with old rivermen and erected a cedar post at the lock after the high tide in 1867, thereby having a benchmark for floods in 1817, 1832, 1847, 1854, 1867, and 1880. During the 1883 flood, one "fully 5 feet higher than the tide of 1847," his post washed away. He later discovered that someone had found his historic benchmark and had used it for firewood.[3]

Two major floods struck the Kentucky River Valley in 1919. On 1 January the Kentucky rose 10 feet in ten hours at Frankfort, destroying sawmill facilities and flooding many towns along the river, Ford in particular being inundated. The Kentucky is like that—one place along its path will be hit very hard while another will suffer lighter damage, depending upon rainfall on the micro-watersheds of each creek and branch. In November 1919 the tide rose 3 feet in one hour at Frankfort. The next year, water backed up through sewers in the "Craw" in that same city. The early January flood of 1924 struck the entire Ohio Valley, including the Kentucky, and bad floods hit again in late December 1926. In 1927 terrible flooding hit the upper part of the Kentucky, forcing hundreds from their homes. A witness recalled, "the lightning was so intense, the whole country could be seen." Neon, Whitesburg, and Hazard suffered severe damage. But there was nothing to compare with the floods of the 1930s, which added further sorrow to the worst economic depression in history.[4]

With the bad flood of 1936 in recent memory, the Ohio River Valley had never witnessed such a flood as that of 1937. The entire valley would be affected, but the region downriver of Cincinnati would be particularly devastated. The rainfall for January of that year set records when an average of nearly 16 inches fell across the state. Frankfort had twenty-one days of measurable precipitation. Taylorsville had over 7 inches of rain on January 24. All streams in the state flooded. As the Ohio rose to flood stage, tides in tributaries like the Kentucky backed up even further, being unable to drain into the larger river. Officials in Maysville declared martial law. With a crest of 47.2 feet, half of Frankfort flooded. High waters completely isolated the Old State House. The *State Journal* reported in bold headlines: "Unprecedented Flood in Height and Suddenness Sweeps Frankfort." The flood of 1937 on the Ohio surpassed the previous record rise in 1883 in Louisville. Paducah suffered the greatest damage of all, with 95 percent of the city inundated. Moreover, the cold weather of January tormented the stranded and rescuers alike. In all, a 12,000-square-mile area of the Ohio Valley lay under siege from the terrible flood.[5]

Flooding in Frankfort created a crisis at the Kentucky State Reformatory. With water rising to 6 feet within the walls, racial tension erupted into riots as prisoners moved to the second floor. Twenty-four prisoners made a break for the gates, but only one man escaped after guards fired warning shots. Without drinking water or electrical power, Warden James Hammond described conditions in one word, "horrible." He saw to the evacuation of the twenty-nine hundred prisoners to the "Feeble-Minded Institute" on the hill above the prison. There prisoners were temporarily housed in units cobbled together by carpenters brought in especially for the purpose. National guardsmen helped quell the fears of Frankfort citizens of continued uprisings. One guardsman, called up for duty from Richmond, remembered the stockage of barbed wire and tents. The bad weather added to the discomfort of prisoners and guards alike. "That wasn't a whole lot of fun for them," said Kenton Moberly. "It was cold." The most dangerous felons were taken to Lawrenceburg and Lexington jails for safekeeping until more permanent plans could be made. Gov. Happy Chandler pushed for completion of the new prison in LaGrange, and the old Kentucky State Reformatory was soon abandoned, never reopening after the 1937 flood.[6]

Frankfort's woe's were not over. Kentucky Utilities opened the Dix Dam spillways, adding to the wall of water that attacked the city. With power off, water stood 3 or more feet deep over most of the city. Houses on Mero and St. Clair Streets had water up to the second stories. After a gas main on St. Clair exploded, interrupting the gas supply, women cooked on outdoor grills. Fifteen hundred people in Bellepoint were cut off from the rest of the city at the peak of the flood, with four-fifths of the entire city of Frankfort underwater. The water plant closed when the tide flowed over it. "It's never been this high before," many people said in 1937, and they were right. "The '37 flood wasn't in our house, it was over the house," Bill Douthitt recalled about his boyhood home. "That was on Wilkinson Boulevard. That daggone thing was over the house. I'm telling you, I never will forget it. There was about that much [indicating about a foot] of the top of the house sticking up. The rest of it was over the house. It's a wonder it hadn't floated away." People came to the aid of Frankfort and other flooded sites across the valley. Some paid a high price. Andrew J. Palmer's brother left College Hill in Madison County to help out in the Commonwealth's capital, caught pneumonia, and died.[7]

Other communities along the Kentucky were hit hard. At Oregon in Mercer County, the ferry connecting to the Woodford shore washed away in the tide, never to be replaced. "The river is now a barrier rather than a highway," declared Amalie Preston, the daughter of an old Kentucky River family with roots in steamboat days, in a 1989 interview. At Monterey, the flood covered the entire town. But all was not lost. One family landed a six-room house in the river bottom and "sold it to a fellow" after the floodwaters receded. In West Irvine a man recalled the water just never seemed to go down. Water got into the second floor of their home and when cleanup time came "the floors looked like waves on water. I never heard my mother gripe and complain. My dad said 'We won't be here next year,' but he was still there when he died." At Lockport, the second dam on the Kentucky above Carrollton, Charles Dees recalled as a boy his distress at the rising waters. "We moved out of our house one night, went across the street and got in the church and thought, 'Well, we'll be safe here.' It didn't help." The only family possessions that did not get wet were his boxing gloves and a shotgun. These were saved when a church pew miraculously "floated up and kind of tilted back and stayed dry." Many other families were not as fortunate.[8]

The 1937 flood, "bottom sweepers" the old timers called tides like this one, wiped out several large stores along the Kentucky that had been used for generations of customers. The little gasoline boat, *Hanover*, operated on the lower Kentucky until the flood. "She never made another trip after the flood," recalled longtime Kentucky towboatman John Donaldson. The Thomas store in Lockport was inundated. Near Marshall's Bottom in Henry County, one farmer stood to lose several pigs, which were in an excited state. "He said they pulled in," reminisced an interviewee, "said they [the pigs] came right to the boat, just came hustling down there to that boat. They knew they was in trouble. He pulled into the mainland and turned them loose." The little town of Port Royal in Henry County was spared from the 1937 and other floods. Being one mile from the river, a woman recalled that residents liked to joke "We would be in bad shape if the river ever got up here."[9]

No county was hit harder by the 1937 flood than Madison. All the towns along the river flooded, including Doylesville, College Hill, Valley View, Clay's Ferry, and Boonesborough, suffering heavy damage, even loss of life. "You learn to live with it," one man recalled. "With a flood you know you're going to have a mess with it. So you roll up the carpets, put the furniture on a sawhorse. You move up to the second floor. You adjust." And yet a few miles away, Richmond also housed refugees from as far away as Louisville, including "the little Richmond refugee boy," the nickname for Joseph Walker Henken. After being driven out of several shelters in Louisville by constantly rising flood waters, the Henkens came to Richmond along with dozens of other victims. Born into a Catholic family, the baby and his parents were taken by the local Presbyterian minister to the Catholic church in Richmond for the baby's baptism. The grateful family named the boy, Joseph Walker, after the Protestant cleric. Several churches and homes served the refugees from Louisville. "I made a million cookies," one woman said. Some Madison Countians took their boats to Louisville to help with flood relief. Heavy rains in Richmond also forced closure of the local water plant.[10]

There is always the immense task of cleaning up after a flood. George Chinn humorously told about his boyhood home at Mundy's Landing on the Kentucky in Woodford County: "We used to say we spent six months on the river, six months under." Resilience is a necessity when faced with river mud in your home. One lifelong resident of the valley explained well the cleanup procedure:

> You've got your walls to wash down. If you've got pumps under pressure its good to hose it down. If you can hose it down, that's the best way in the world to get rid of the bulk of it. But when it rises, you've always got mud and dust. It gets into places where you can't even see it, but it's there. You can cover it up with paint, but when your paint starts peeling, there it is again. I've experienced it all. There's one thing worse than a flood, that's fire. Whenever the flood gets over your furniture, you may as well throw it away. The flooring always warps, but it goes down over the years.

However, sometimes the flood is generous. After capturing a whiskey barrel, one could pour boiling water into it or steam it, a process called dogging, to get a small amount of liquor from the charred oak staves. There was always drift carrying chickens. A young boy in Frankfort caught a dozen pumpkins floating on the tide. A woman recalled even seeing a cow floating on a drift of flotsam.[11]

The floods never seem to stop, being almost annual events bringing destruction. Floods sometimes occur in the same area two or more times in a year. After not being struck as hard as the Kentucky below Irvine, the upper basin took a hard hit from a flood in early February 1939. In Hazard the North Fork rose 30 feet seemingly overnight and crested at 36.5 feet. That same flood was slightly higher than the 1937 flood in Irvine. One lockkeeper recalled the high tide of 1939 because he and his family had to use a rowboat to go to their outhouse. Three years later Beattyville and Oneida recorded tides nearly as high as those of 1939. That tide surged on toward Frankfort, but only reached a foot over flood stage when rain lessened on some of the nearby creeks. In the last days of World War II, a "bottom sweeper," second only to that of 1937, struck the entire Ohio Valley, backing up the Kentucky all the way to Frankfort.[12]

The nation demanded more flood control from the federal government, and the Corps of Engineers began to answer the call in the 1930s. The terrible floods of the thirties forced Congress into action. At first most of the effort would be for channel improvement to improve runoff. Later there would be more elaborate plans, including building dams on smaller streams to hold back floodwaters. Levees, broad-based earthen structures, can be used to protect valuable farmland, and floodwalls, narrower based walls usually built of concrete, can be constructed to protect homes. In the thirties, Congress began to push the Corps of Engineers into this area of service to Americans living on or near streams. Leaders like Willard Rouse Jillson, state geologist from 1919 to 1932, while he opposed Insull's Cumberland River dam project, continually voiced his approval of dams for flood protection on the Kentucky and other streams in the state.[13]

As early as 1925, Kentucky Hydro-Electric pushed for a superdam one mile above Booneville on the South Fork of the Kentucky. Many people protested at a public meeting, including H.H. Hensley, who declared "nothing but the hills would stick out of the water" if the power company was allowed to build a 162-foot-tall dam backing water up the South Fork for over 28 miles. In 1939 Franklin D. Roosevelt signed legislation to study the rivers of the Ohio River Valley, including the Kentucky. Some planners advocated a high dam on the Kentucky, blocking navigation above Camp Nelson "to prevent a recurrence of the 1937 flood." The Corps made studies of flood control dams on Jessamine Creek, Booneville, and Buckhorn and for years listed these in annual reports as viable projects. In 1954, the suggestion of damming Jessamine Creek, a large tributary that flows into the Kentucky a few miles above the Dix River and High Bridge, for flood control, drew strong opposition from the *Courier-Journal*, the Kentucky Historical Society, and the Kentucky River Development Association. Their combined voices cited the lost beauty of the gorge of the Kentucky River Palisades as well as the necessity of keeping the river open for future transportation of coal on the river.[14]

In early 1957, Joe Creason, a longtime columnist for the *Courier-Journal*, announced a planned cutoff of the 4-mile-long Panbowl at Jackson on the North Fork, which he described as having "more curves than a chorus line." Costing an estimated $250,000, the fill at the cutoff location would be at a point where the river entering and leaving the Panbowl was only 140 feet apart. Moreover, the earthworks would be the roadbed for an improved Highway 15. But nothing substantial had been done to alleviate floods on the Kentucky when the 1957 flood hit. This tide struck particularly hard in the Three Forks area and on the upper Kentucky. At Oneida on the South Fork the flood inundated the small town, including the Baptist school there. On the Middle Fork, Wendover, the home of the Frontier Nursing Service, experienced the same troubles. Nurse Jane Furnas recalled that on 29 January "About 3:00 A.M. we had a terrible thunderstorm and the heavens fairly opened up. When I got up at 6:30 we could see nothing but water." Seeking help, she and a few others trekked toward the nearest town. "We went on into Hyden Town," she explained, "and were appalled by the sights which greeted us en route; cars had been swept into fields and were caught in trees; the highway was washed out in places and there was mud everywhere; houses were gone and other houses sitting in places where there had been none; stunned people with their muddy, wet furniture and clothing were all along the highway." There had been two deaths of small children as well. The combined tides of the Three Forks rushed on toward Beattyville, which suffered the worst flooding in its history, waters so high local sightseers traveled through the county courthouse in rowboats. Because of the extensive damage in the Kentucky basin, President Dwight D. Eisenhower declared the region a major disaster area and federal aid began to trickle in.[15]

During the 1950s and 1960s, the Corps of Engineers planned several flood control dams for the Kentucky: Buckhorn on the Middle Fork, Booneville on the South Fork, Red River, Carr Fork near Hazard, and Jessamine Creek. Using the Flood Control Act of 1938, the Corps also studied constructing a major dam on the Kentucky River 136 miles above Carrollton in Jessamine County. A dam 170 feet high and 900 feet long would extend a reservoir 126 miles up the Kentucky to Beattyville. Although it is still discussed from time to time, this dam never received either public or Corps approval. Buckhorn is another matter. Completed in 1960 at a cost of over $11 million, the 162-foot-high and 1,020-foot-long earth and rock-filled dam backed up Buckhorn Lake for 34 miles, thereby taking some of the strain off the Middle Fork watershed and the Kentucky farther downstream. Red River created a major controversy and was not funded. Seventh District congressman Carl Perkins from Hyden pushed hard for the Carr Fork project. Completed in 1975, it took pressure off the North Fork. By 1984 the Corps listed all other proposed projects on the Kentucky as inactive, including Red River, Eagle Creek, and Booneville.[16]

But if there was some respite from Kentucky River flooding with completion of dams on the tributaries, the river had a way of reasserting itself. The completion of the Buckhorn and Carr Fork reservoirs lulled people in the Kentucky basin into a false sense of security. Residents in the valley faced the age-old problems and heartaches of flooding, displacement, and even death. Frankfort had begun to make plans for further floodwall construction after the dedication for a section in the North. In 1978 the reality of what a combination of heavy rainfall, bad luck, and poor planning can do struck the valley. Twelve inches of rain in the first ten days of December fell in the middle region of the basin. Flooding in the Red River valley set records at Clay City in Powell County. The Three Forks region and the Kentucky down to Irvine did not suffer as much as the lower river.[17]

Some people are always on the front lines during flood times. Lockkeeping, a hazardous job even in the best weather, became especially dangerous during floods. At Number 11 on the big bend of the river that swings around Madison County, John Lambert often found himself completely encircled by the raging floodwaters. He once saved his automobile and truck from being swept away by chaining them to a large tree. Corps of Engineers regulations required "stripping" the lock of all equipment before it was covered by water. This procedure often delayed the lockmen's retreat, requiring that they be brought out by boat to dry ground. During one such flood at Lock 4, John M. Sparks found himself and another lockkeeper surrounded by rising water, unable to escape. With other supplies exhausted, "We lived on cornflakes and a bottle of Old Granddad Whiskey for three days and three nights." When a boat came in with a pot of soup and hot chocolate, "we really appreciated it," he said with a laugh. A lockkeeper's daughter recalled the isolation during flood time when she lost contact with her friends for several days.[18]

Madison County communities on the river were devastated by the 1978 flood, continuing the depopulation of the valley. "Everybody moved out of Doylesville," an area resident recalled. "It was quite a shock for me to see how the town changed." The flood ruined the Doylesville Baptist Church with water 3 to 4 feet deep in places, and families had to be rescued by boat. Water so heavily flooded the

Boonesborough Rock Quarry that one section could not be recovered for future operations. Nearby Ford on the Clark County side flooded, and the coal-fired generating plant of the rural cooperative had to close as coal piles washed away.[19]

When the waters swept by Jane Early Snyder's Fayette County farm at Clay's Ferry, it was the highest tide she had ever seen. Sidney and Mary Kelley's house and store under the Interstate 75 bridges on U.S. 25 at Clay's Ferry came under siege by water. The tide surged on, gaining height and increasing in volume with each creek that poured into it. Valley View suffered irreversible damage, driving people to high ground. Many would never return to the little village. The flood of 1978 struck all the little towns along its path with great devastation, but it struck the state capital with special fury. The citizens of Frankfort, the largest city on the river, had never seen such water.[20]

At precisely the wrong moment for Frankfort, KU officials opened the gates at Dix Dam on Herrington Lake, creating a controversy that continues to the present day. Kentucky Utilities employee Clyde Hayslett stayed in the Dix Dam generator room until water began coming in the windows. "It really ruined Frankfort. It was no fault of KU. They had a lot of static. I had to talk with lawyers a time or two on this thing, but it was just an act of God, that's all there was to it." Longtime Kentucky River watcher Benny Powell of Danville observed it all. "They had to open" the gates, otherwise the dam might have failed. Others were not so sure The Almighty and safety had anything to do with it, blaming KU for opening Dix Dam. One Frankfort man, who purposely built his house above the 1937 flood level, never expected anything like the 1978 inundation. Another man on Paul Sawyier Street got 37 inches of water in his house, a home that had never suffered flood damage before. Kentucky Utilities "waited until the river was ready to crest," he charged, "and they dumped water right on top of the crest and here it comes. We lost the lawsuit because it got involved in politics. That thing [Dix Dam], is going to fail and when it does it will wipe out Frankfort. I don't think they know what to do with it."[21]

On 10 December the tide crested at 48.5 feet in Frankfort, about 1 foot higher than the flood of 1937. Twelve hundred people had to be evacuated, with many citizens trapped in their houses. The North Frankfort floodwall protected the downtown business district, but water backed up Capitol Avenue toward the state office buildings and the governor's mansion. The sand and gravel yard, the only commercial enterprise still using the lower part of the river, "had a beautiful lake in the sandyard" and had difficulty in finding a place of safety for its towboat. Sweeping on toward Carrollton the tide backed up Elkhorn Creek, covering the Elkhorn Creek bridge at Strohmeier's camp. A house from High Bridge came to rest in a slough just off the river there. David L. Strohmeier recalled a unique flood phenomenon—field mice everywhere, even crowding each other off the fence posts.[22]

The flood of 1978 rushed on toward Oregon. "You couldn't get out of its way," George Moore recalled, "it just kept coming. We just got out while we could. That thing can get you and get you in a hurry. It leaves an awful mess in your house." Harrison Broce caught a church pew in the floodwaters. "There ain't no telling where it come from, maybe out of the mountains somewhere. It got seven feet higher than in '36 or '37 where daddy cut a notch with a pocketknife on a tree." The tide was dangerous, but Broce decided to take a closer look at the river. "I started up that river and the current was so swift them big sycamores was just a whipping and I didn't have no life jacket on, by myself. I thought 'Harrison, what a fool you are,' and I turned that boat around and come back to Oregon." Old houses were swamped for the last time, prompting owners who had endured numerous floods before to give it up. Bud Dedman, owner of Beaumont Inn in Harrodsburg, finally gave up on the old family cabin. If the 1937 flood ravaged Oregon, the one forty-one years later nearly wiped it out, according to Amalie Preston. Amazingly, at one home a table that floated off the porch at one stage of the flood returned to nearly the same place when the tide receded.[23]

Farther downriver the little communities of Monterey and Gratz suffered heavy damage. Gene Tindall's store in Monterey had 3 feet of water in it, "It was a mess." Flood insurance, though expensive, saved the day. Ruby Stewart in Gratz saved some furniture and the country ham she had cooked for supper but little else. "It was the awfullest sight ever I saw," she recalled later. "Gratz is surrounded when the water comes up." She moved to another house, hoping to allude the next big tide. Other people moved from Gratz because of the flood damage and the lack of work locally.[24]

By the time the tide ran out at Carrollton into the Ohio River, citizens were pushing for renewed efforts to control the floodwaters of the Kentucky. Raising of dams on the Kentucky, construction of new ones, and the building of floodwalls did not exhaust the list of proposals. Frankfort pushed for construction of a floodwall on Second Street, one now completed, and the removal of citizens from flood-prone St. Johns Court. Weather forecasting has also been fortified for similar events. But, so far, no new dams have been constructed and the future does not look bright for such ventures. And there is always the conundrum of what will happen at Dix Dam. More recent floods have not reached anywhere near the height of the great flood of 1978, but that does not mean that it could not happen again. Was the 1978 flood the "100 year flood," that the Corps of Engineers expects only once a century? As a matter of fact, some climate theories predict more violent storms in the future. One way of avoiding damage to homes and other property is simply to move away, and the Kentucky River Valley has been seriously depopulated since the flood of 1937. But other people love the river lifestyle, even with the continued threat of flooding. Do the reservoirs at Buckhorn and Carr Fork work? Do they deter flooding on the lower Kentucky? Possibly, but not with the volume of rain that struck the valley in December 1978. It could be even worse next time.[25]

The relatively slow rise that contributes to a major flood on the Kentucky is indeed damaging, but a flash flood on a tributary can be even more terrifying. Often there is hardly any warning and no place of safety. On 4 December 1991, former governor and federal judge, Bert Combs, died in a flash flood near Stanton in Powell County. In late July 1992, a flash flood struck the Bear Creek area in Clay County. At about midnight the water quickly rose to a height of 20 feet as it roared down the creek. In fifteen minutes it was all over, but not before four people died, among the victims, a young mother and her two daughters, five and six years old. Ambulance crews rescued a small boy who escaped only by clinging to the branches of a tree.[26]

The most terrifying flash flood in Kentucky history also hit during July, the evening of Independence Day 1939. Violent storms struck two Kentucky counties that night—Breathitt and Rowan. There was no accurate way of determining the amount of rainfall, but estimates range up to 9 inches in a few hours. Stanley Taulbee, who lived on Negro Branch, which flowed into Frozen Creek, a tributary of the North Fork in Breathitt County, recalled a stormy night after the Fourth of July holiday trip to Natural Bridge. His father, a guard at a nearby WPA facility, returned frequently to his home to warn his family of the impending disaster. "We come back late in the afternoon and it started lightning that night and it was just like daylight. Along towards morning, the creeks began to come up. It had rained for about four hours. You couldn't even see how to walk. My dad said that he'd never seen nothing like it in his life. I mean, he said it was just solid coming down, like a fall, you know, and the waters pouring over it. Yeah, it was a terrible time." The water from the surrounding hillsides funneled into

Negro Branch, a mile above Frozen Creek. Other branches and creeks, normally quite dry in mid-summer joined the deluge of water rushing toward the North Fork. "They's an old fella by the name of George Lane Banks lived back up on the other creek," Taulbee recalled. "He lived by himself and he was drownded and he washed down about 3 mile. He was found in a pasture the next day. On down the road another couple drownded, and their niece, I always called her Tootsie, she was just a little, small child. They was a lot of people drownded."[27]

The *Courier-Journal* headline of 6 July 1939, "132 FEARED DROWNED IN ROWAN, BREATHITT AS 20-FOOT WALL OF WATER WRECKS HOMES," could not have more succinctly described the horror of that night. At first officials predicted the death toll in Breathitt to reach well over one hundred and that in Rowan to be nearly as great. Public health officials moved in quickly to work against the outbreak of disease, even sending six embalmers from Louisville at the request of a Breathitt County funeral director. Gertrude Deaton lost six members of her family. Washed miles downstream she struck a tangle of driftwood that threatened to hold her underwater. Freeing herself, she drifted to another snag and climbed into a tree. "It took several men to remove Mrs. Deaton from her perch," the *Courier* reported. Another survivor told the harrowing story of losing his baby to the floodwaters. "I started to run across the drift toward shore," he recounted the next day. "I stumbled a few times, and the third time I stepped off into the water and the baby fell from my arms. I couldn't find him."[28]

Over fifty years later eyewitnesses vividly recalled the terror of that night, when the death toll officially reached fifty-two in Breathitt and twenty-five in Rowan. The entire region in between was devastated. William H. Garrett saw it all as he tried to return from Rowan to Breathitt then found a drowning victim in his own family. The Kentucky Mountain Bible Institute, operated by the Kentucky Mountain Holiness Association and founded by the legendary Lela B. McConnell at VanCleve on the banks of Frozen Creek, suffered horribly. In the evening before the cloudburst, many of the faculty, students, and families living there celebrated the holiday with an ice cream social. Lorene Rose noticed the darkening sky when she retired later that night, but "didn't think too much about it." About 3:00 in the morning the thunderstorm struck. "The building started to move. We went down the back stairway, but the water had cut us off. So we went up to the attic and got us some old clothes, anything we could find, to put around us. The building started going apart. Some of us got hold of anything we could get hold of to hang on." She grabbed at the rafters of the building, but soon floated in the raging stream, her leg gashed from a piece of careening farm machinery. Floating downstream near Mount Carmel High School, "I'd holler help, help. Someone later said it sounded like a baby crying. I prayed that the Lord would help me get out." Taking off a heavy, water-soaked robe, "I climbed up through these bushes, through these woods, and I saw a snake laying there. And I thought 'I hope that snake don't bite me,' but I got around it and sat down where the grass was." With nothing left of her seersucker nightgown except some fringe around her neck, she struggled up the bank more than 2 miles from where she had been washed from the building. A few days later she came down with a massive case of poison ivy, contacted in her struggle up the riverbank. Two girls were not as fortunate as Lorene Rose; they drowned in the flash flood that disintegrated their home. Young Elsie Booth tried to swim out and drowned. When the water ran out into the North Fork, it had such volume it ran upstream and down until the violence of the tide calmed.[29]

Other victims were snatched from sure death by friends, but the flash flood nearly wiped out the Myers family. According to eyewitnesses and his wife, Horace Myers tried to take two sons to safety, promising to return for his wife and baby. "Stay here," he said, "I'll take the boys to safe, high ground and come back for you and the baby." He and Titus, age 6, and Philip, age 5, disappeared. Then the raging waters swept away Nettie Myers and her infant. "Mrs. Myers went up the river," Dorothy Spencer recalled. "She was rescued by a man in a boat." Days later Nettie Myers could identify her husband only by recognizing a shoe on the body. Her baby's body was never found. For days she would sit, weeping, repeating over and over, "My arms are so empty." "It wasn't anytime until her hair was just as white as it could be," observed Lorene Rose.[30]

The troubles for victims and survivors were not over. The Red Cross brought in caskets and did what it could to help the victims and their families. The state epidemiologist oversaw an immunization program for the flood area. Men in the surrounding community also built pine boxes. For health reasons, associated with the hot summer weather, there was a need to do so quickly. When victims could not be found in the immediate aftermath of the Frozen Creek flash flood, most were found by smell. One victim's body was so decomposed "they couldn't bring it near the chapel," so a quick service was held under a tree. One small boy, whose "body started turning," did not even receive proper burial clothing. These departures from custom were necessary in order to bury the dead as soon as possible. How soon did life return to anything approaching normal at Kentucky Mountain Bible Institute? Actually, rather quickly. State government as well as religious and secular agencies sent in aid. Buildings were constructed on higher ground at KMBI with donations of land and materials. Was this an "act of God", one of those catastrophes for which there is no other apparent explanation? "Some felt it was a judgment," Dorothy Spencer remembered, but most were just "stunned." "Everybody went to work," and money came from as far away as foreign missionaries in Africa to rebuild a bigger and safer KMBI. Even Nettie Myers recovered, spending many more years teaching at the school. Her husband's picture hangs in the Myers Memorial Chapel.[31]

Asked for a report on the Frozen Creek Flood as well as the Kentucky River in general, the U.S. Army Corps of Engineers concluded, "Protection of the Frozen Creek Basin or, similarly, other small tributary watersheds against flash floods such as that occurring on July 4–5, 1939, is neither practicable nor feasible." The Corps' judgment was that, in effect, the flooding had been an act of God that no one could have foreseen or prepared for.[32]

But if there is horror with a flash flood such as that on Frozen Creek, there is also respite, even comic relief, with less dangerous flooding. People have an incurable need for humor that is evident even in time of flooding. The famous "Daugherty Flood" on Tate's Creek at Valley View in Madison County on 2 August 1932 washed away Bob Daugherty's farm. More than one resident of the area described him as "a grouchy old man." When a preacher in Valley View said, "It was a glorious rain, wasn't it?" "Uncle Bob" [Daugherty] allegedly replied, "Glorious hell, it's washed away everything I had." Eva Perkins Sams lost sixteen little chickens herself, but saved the mother hen, she remembered. "Everybody would laugh when they would hear about the Daugherty Flood." One resident's father caught a rocking chair he knew belonged to Daugherty, "and, of course, he put it up on the porch, which was right out on the road" so that all could see.[33]

The Daugherty Flood joined local folklore, even inspiring a song written by Houston Goins, sung to the tune of country music immortal Ernest Stoneman's *The Titanic*.

THE DAUGHERTY FLOOD

Tate's Creek was mighty full
When it got to Jesse Kelley's bull.
It was sad when the Daugherty Flood came down.

It was rafters and boards
And old T-Model boards
It was sad when the Daugherty Flood came down.

Tate's Creek was a booster
When it got to John Hunt's rooster.
It was sad when the Daugherty Flood came down.
Tea cups, forks and knives.
Little chickens lost their lives.
It was sad when the Daugherty Flood came down.

When the barn began to squeak,
Uncle Bob Daugherty began to peep.
It was sad when the Daugherty Flood came down.
When the barn went out of sight,
His poor old face turned white.
It was sad when the Daugherty Flood came down.

Apparently the loss of a few chickens coupled with other sundry ar-
ticles combined with some dislike for Daugherty to bring mirth to the
residents of the Valley View area during the Great Depression. Even as
we face a new century, people who remember the old days at Valley
View smile when they recall "The Daugherty Flood."[34]

The Kentucky River is dangerous even during normal weather, and
all along the river there are stories of drownings. The locks and dams
create special hazards to boaters. On 21 May 1967, six men died when a
cabin cruiser went over Lock 9 at Valley View. Lockmaster Dale Walden
saved three men who tried to swim ashore, but the others were swept
over the dam, which at the time was running at least 6 feet deep over the
precipice. The force of the water pulled the men under. Lockkeepers
recounted numerous similar stories like this in their interviews.[35]

Disregard for the dangers around the locks, many times accom-
panied by abuse of alcohol, too often have led to unnecessary death. At
Boonesborough, Lock 10, a place where boaters often over imbibe,
there has been a considerable number of accidents resulting in deaths.
One Sunday a Corps of Engineers workboat captain watched "two
drunks jump the dam." Nudging the workboat they yelled, "Did you
see us jump the dam?" Fortunately the two men survived long enough
to be arrested by the water patrol. "So many people don't realize what
them dams will do to you. They should have some kind of law so they
know what they're doing, 'cause most of them don't," the captain said.[36]

Sometimes people panic. "A fellow went out and tired to crank his motor one day, put in about 200 yards above the lock. Shoved his boat out and started cranking on his motor; went over and never hit a lick, he drowned. He had oars in the boat and never made an effort. His dad hollered, 'Come on in to the bank, come on in to the bank,' and he still tried to crank the motor," recalled lockmaster Estill Thomas about the incident. At another lock a man jumped from his boat as it went over the dam. The boat survived the fall and even the man's guitar did not leave the boat, but the man died and was not found until the next spring. Another man did the same, jumping into the river just before his boat went over the dam. "The boat came off, down the river, floated, come on down, and they wasn't a gallon of water in it," recollected a lockkeeper who witnessed the tragedy. Sometimes even the most experienced and wary lock personnel get caught by the river's fury. One time a lockmaster and his wife nearly drowned while crossing above Lock 3. "That oar broke and I fell over backwards in the back of the boat, but fortunately I had that extra oar. My wife and me were within 24 yards of drowning. There was no question that if we had gone over the dam we would have drowned." Another time this same lockmaster nearly drowned while fishing near an Ohio River dam. His boat swamped and he got sucked under the dam. A boat came to his rescue. "They began to waving to me to hang on. Of course, they didn't have to worry about that, I was hanging on. They let a line down to me. This boy said, 'Now, you get a good hold of this line,' and I said, 'Now, you don't have to worry about this end; you get aholt of that one.' The only thing I could think of was I had worked on the river all my life and I got drowned fishing. But I didn't drown." Is the river inherently dangerous? Another riverman excitedly replied during an oral history interview, "I been knocked in the river, honey, I come very near getting drowned twice."[37]

For commercial fishermen, who often work the river during high water, hitting submerged trees is a special hazard. Bill Douthitt of Frankfort shuddered, remembering what happened on a cold January day. "The boat threw me out one time coming down the river, the water was up. It didn't frighten me at the time, but it did later on. I had on two pair of pants, long underwear, and a jacket, and a scarf around my neck. I hit something about 50 to 75 feet out in the water. I must've gunned that motor when I hit it, just flipped me out. Boat went on. I come up blowing water and boat was goin' on. I swimmed out, but I don't know how I did. I swear I don't." With rubber bands around his pant legs, Douthitt believed it created enough buoyancy to keep him afloat in the icy water. "When I first went out of the boat, I thought it's just a matter of time. I figured I was gone. But I was gonna make an attempt." When the interviewer asked what Douthitt did when he reached the bank, he replied simply, "I'm smiling when I got to the bank." A woman brought him home. "If she hadn't brought me home, I'd a froze."[38]

Sometimes being saved can be a matter of pure luck. According to Corps of Engineers regulations, the lockkeeper is required to keep a boat above the dam. Once, when a lockkeeper's son had taken the boat below the dam, they saved a man hanging in a tree after he and a friend had gone over the dam. "That river was really roaring," recalled John M. Sparks. "The Colonel didn't like it," the boat being out of place.[39]

Moreover, the violence that often pervades Kentucky life is found along the river. Once a man was found under mysterious circumstances. "He had two concrete blocks tied around his neck. He was an awful big man and they brought him in to the bank. Of course, he was swelled, he looked like a barrel. They'd been looking for him. I guess the reason they didn't find him was he had these blocks tied around his neck. And that was a sad story about that. We don't know whether he committed suicide or somebody, you know, killed him." The river has often been used to dispose of bodies. An Irvine woman was shot to death in the 1930s and her killer was never prosecuted. Because her body was cast into the Kentucky, more than one resident still believes that she died from drowning."[40]

One of the most vivid stories around the Valley View community is the saga of Burgin Howard and Cal Goins. This incident in late December 1926, became forever imprinted in people's memories because of the pathos of good men killed by the raging waters of the Kentucky River. According to Ed Land Jr., son of the owner of the Valley View Ferry at the time, "The river was right at a dangerous stage; it was right at the top of the banks, and that's usually when it's the most current in the river. Burgin Howard came out to the house. He ran the grocery store over there, a very fine store. He'd been to Lexington and he asked Daddy: 'Is the ferry running?'" Having just returned from a funeral in Richmond, Mr. Land assumed that the operator of the ferry had tied up the craft because of the high water. He offered to take Howard across the "backwater" from where he could walk across the L&N Railroad bridge to the Madison side. Land also kept a barn where livestock could be housed when the ferry was closed down. Cal and Herschel Goins appeared, having taken tobacco to Lexington. "I never will forget Cal, he was pretty well liquored up, he got stove caps out and he told me, 'Hey, bud, ain't gonna let my wife cook on no warped, broke-up caps. I bought her a brand new set.' He had on a great big, brown overcoat, army overcoat, one of those big, heavy, thick ones with big pockets. He'd hold his pockets out and I'd put those stove caps in."[41]

The plans of the returning men changed when Houston Cuzick appeared.

> "I got a footboat here," he said, "I'll just go across the river." So they did. They got in his footboat and Daddy went down. He had a spotlight on the ferry, and he threw it up the river and you could see the fodder shocks. That was the kind of drift that run back in those days. It was pretty heavy. And he threw the light up the river. They had to pull up the river a long distance; then they started to cross the current. It was kinda misting rain. "Them banks are too slick for you to be down here," Daddy said, and he sent me home. And they went on down and they started across. Fodder shocks always run sitting up just like it was in the ground. He was hunting so they could get a break and go through there to get on the other side. He was holding it [the light] up there, holding it where they could see that drift running and he heard them holler. First time he just thought it was Christmastime and they's kinda letting off steam. But the second time they hollered, he knew they's in trouble. So he had on an old, yeller slicker raincoat. He threw that off and jumped in the footboat that was tied to the side of the ferry and took off. He throwed that light down the river as he got in the boat. And he would holler and they would holler. It was a funny thing about it, Houston Cuzick couldn't swim much at all much. Herschel Goins couldn't swim at all. When that boat turned over with them, Houston managed to get on top and he reached out and caught Herschel Goins in the back of the neck.[42]

"When Daddy came down, he ran over the top of that boat," Land further explained.

> Houston got in the boat, but Herschel got on the back of the boat and he just clinched, they couldn't pry him loose. He just froze on them. Burgin Howard was a top swimmer, he

was swimming toward the Madison side. He kept hollering and Daddy would answer him. Houston was setting in the back and he'd holler. He could see up ahead in the shadow of this light and see Burgin swimming, and he was telling my Daddy to [pull] to the left or the right. He was right in front of you, and Daddy said he gave one big pull of the oars and he saw him, just in the shadow. He reached to get him and said he felt his collar just slip off the end of his fingers.

Just then they neared the steel piers for the railroad bridge in the intermittent light and darkness. "They's a suction when the water gets current, just like you pulling an oar. You've seen them little, round holes in the water? Well, that's the way it was behind the pier, sucking water. When Burgin Howard got in that suction and Daddy reached for him, it just sucked him right on down."[43]

"They drifted there for a right smart little bit and they never heard no more," Land continued his story. "That's the only time I ever saw my father ever weakening. He gave down when he walked in the house. 'Course him and Burgin was the best of friends and it was a tragedy, but it happened. They found Burgin's body in a drift pile below High Bridge down there along in April or May. Some fishermen found him and his body was might near deteriorated. His clothes he was wearing [were] about gone. The way they identified him, Burgin Howard had gold teeth, or some gold fillings in his teeth. The dentist identified him as being Burgin Howard. And Cal Goins, he never did make a sound; they never did hear of him, and that was the end of it. Of course, I reckon I had enough stove weights to keep him down where he wouldn't raise, you know. So that's one of the tragedies that's happened."[44]

Claude C. Howard, the nephew of Burgin Howard, told substantially the same story as Ed Land, as have others, all second-hand information that has become embedded in their memories with the retelling of the story over and over since 1926. "It alarmed the whole country," Claude said, "he was a well-liked man." Ironically, years earlier, before the construction of Lock and Dam 9, Claude's grandfather slipped through a log raft and drowned in nearly the same place as his uncle, around the bridge piers.[45]

Other tragedies strike around the Kentucky River. Teenagers have a sometimes fatal attraction to High Bridge. "It's kind of thrilling and exciting," one said. "Someone says 'High Bridge' and we just pile in the car and go." In 1988 a high school senior fell through the crossties and hit the rocks below the bridge. Three years before this incident,

Norfolk Southern installed a security fence, but teenagers still persisted in their efforts, almost like a rite of passage, to walk on the monstrous bridge.[46]

The Kentucky River and its bridges also contribute to another all-too-human tragedy—suicide. Bill Fint once observed a man jump from the U.S. 62 highway bridge at Tyrone. "He said after he jumped he changed his mind. And that booger crawled out on the bank and was still living. Blood was coming out of the corner of his mouth when he first came out." However, Fint believed him to be the only survivor of such a plunge. Even lower bridges are enticing to someone wanting to take his or her life. Louis Stivers witnessed a similar incident in Frankfort. "I turned onto the [Memorial] Bridge and I saw this lady on the bridge. It was cold. She took her coat off and laid it up on the rail of the bridge. I thought, that's strange. She leaned over and jumped. I backed off the bridge, and all excited, ran down to Blanton's [Lumberyard]. I ran down to the bank and pushed a boat in. After I got about five feet, another fellow came running down and jumped in the boat and about capsized both of us. We pulled her in, but she was dead. She was so totally relaxed, I couldn't carry her." Later Stivers helped recover the body of a woman who had been swept away in a car. "It was a terrible sight, you know; she was bloated and all." The Interstate 75 bridge at Clay's Ferry has also been used for suicide plunges into the Kentucky. Sometimes people just walk into the river and drown.[47]

The same river valley, with an average rainfall of 42 to 48 inches and annual floods, can sometimes turn very dry. Fall is normally the driest time of the year in Kentucky, and October is the month with the least rainfall. On average there is a major drought every ten years, with occurrences in 1854, 1881, 1894, 1901, 1904, 1930, 1931, 1936, 1954, 1986, 1988, and 1999. The droughts of 1930 and 1931 were prolonged months of water deficit for most of the state. Record high temperatures in the summer of 1930 added to the state's woes. July 1930 was the hottest month on record, with the thermometer hitting 114 degrees in Greensburg, also a state record. Lexington suffered such a shortage of water that the Lexington Water Company laid a pipeline to the Kentucky River. In October 1930 less than 6.5 million gallons a day flowed over Lock and Dam 10 at Boonesborough, the dam that makes the pool from which Richmond now draws water.[48]

Interviewees for the "Living and Working on the Kentucky River Oral History Project," particularly the lockkeepers and their families, vividly recalled the droughts of the 1930s. Some farmers only had crops of corn survive on the river, but in other places, like Muddy Creek in

Madison County "corn would just twist up" from lack of moisture. Sherman Estes said he had a good corn crop, because the "fog off the water, kept the water on the ground." On most farms, away from the creek and riverbanks, the corn crop shriveled up and died.[49]

The lockkeeping Walters family at Boonesborough had to carry water from the river for cooking after their cistern went dry. To wash clothes they carried their Maytag gas-powered washing machine to the riverbank. Finally, water stopped flowing over the dam and a person could wade farther out into the river than anyone remembered. Mary Walters McCauley recalled that even the food tasted of dust. A black family who ordinarily shied away from the river at Clay's Ferry boiled water at the riverside for washing clothes. A father kept his sons hoeing the tobacco crop, admonishing them "If it ever does rain, it will make real tobacco." But "it never did rain," he concluded, after they had hoed the crop five times. Some farmers enlarged ponds with scoops during the dry summers. "I thought we was goin' to starve," one farm woman recalled. Even small children would stay away from the river because it smelled. Desperate for water, one family used dynamite, a bit too much as it turned out, to dig a well on their Kentucky River farm at Valley View. "Rocks fell everywhere," Homer Renfro sheepishly recalled, "It tore twenty-two sheets of tin off the barn."[50]

Droughts in 1954, 1965, and 1988 brought the Kentucky River Valley to the brink of disaster while grabbing headlines in the regional press. The river below Frankfort became a serious health hazard in 1988 because of that city's sewage treatment problems. For several days, the flow of the sewer was the only thing that kept Elkhorn Creek moving, maintained David L. Strohmeier, whose campground and canoe livery business is at the mouth of that creek. Fishermen there complained that they could not keep fish alive in wire cages suspended in the river, because of the low flow of the river and depletion of oxygen in the water.[51]

Like all rivers the Kentucky can be a source of great joy as well as horrifying danger and death. Many boatmen do not have either the experience or the common sense to treat the river with the respect it deserves. The areas around the locks and dams are especially hazardous. During a night locking procedure at Boonesborough, Mary Walters McCauley recalled being awakened by a commotion and flashing lights. "A boy walked off of the lock. The light blinded him." His body was never found. Yet, other times, a fool's luck can save a life. At Number 9 a young man approached with water flowing 4 feet over the dam. When the lockmaster tried to wave him off, the man ran his boat over the dam, being lucky that he had enough speed to "not hit short." Another lockman witnessed another such occasion that ended happily for two drunken sailors at Lock 2. "Two drunks came down through there, they must of jumped 30 feet. They were over at my brother's beach, bailing water. An old fellow went over there. He said, 'Damn boys, what happened?'" After they told the man the story of their narrow escape from death, he replied: "'Go back and do it again, I didn't see it.' They said: 'Hell, we didn't do it on purpose.' It was a good thing they were going fast or it might of drowned them. They leaped it." But on other occasions a drowning victim would be caught in the upper chamber of the lock pit during the night, his body greeting a lockkeeper on his morning watch. John M. Sparks summed up a lot of Kentucky River folks' views of the river: "It was a beautiful river when it wasn't acting up."[52]

Commenting about living all her life on the lower Kentucky at Ball's Landing, now called Perry Park, Aileen Suter perhaps best described the whims of the river: "You have to be kind to it, that's the way it is. That river is going to do what it wants to do. You just have to let it go. The Kentucky River is treacherous. It's got whirlpools and it's got cold places. I'd like to see what's at the bottom of it. It will take anything in its path that it wants to, at any time, because it's swift. You have to be awful careful with it." As we enter a new century, Kentuckians would do well to heed her advice.[53]

CHAPTER SIX

My Mind on the River
The Kentucky River as Subculture

The people who intimately know the Kentucky eloquently told their stories in the "Living and Working on the Kentucky River Oral History Project." Their sense of place is strong, and they have no doubt about who they are or where they come from. People who do not live on the Kentucky find it difficult to understand why anyone would want to live in a capricious place where calamitous floods can be heart-rending.

It is also a place where childhood, though harsh by modern standards, was fulfilling. Many former residents view it now with a great sense of nostalgia. In far simpler times than today there was entertainment of the homemade variety as well as showboats. Even the Great Depression was taken in stride. Fishing on the Kentucky provided food and fun. Kentucky River people also internalized the lessons of the river through good times and bad. The Kentucky River subculture included distinctive expressions in humor, art, music, literature, and poetry as each person has seen it differently.

"It is a great place to live," maintained Amalie Preston, who has suffered all the pain of flooding and all the pleasures of a quiet evening on the river at Oregon. "There is something so soothing and timeless about a river." One woman who has resisted selling her riverfront property to entrepreneurs declared, "If you don't have to sell it off you shouldn't." She knows the dangers of living on the river below Frankfort, but says, "I'm not scared of the river. I don't know why. I guess I've lived here so long." A man who lives in Winchester finds solace while on the Kentucky River. "I've got to have an hour or two of it a day if I can get it. Whether in a boat, or on a boat dock looking at it, it just sort of makes me feel better." "You never get the river out of your system," a man who grew up at Valley View concluded, "it's always there." Another man, with a Ph.D. in biology, derived his love of nature and wildlife management from "raising rocks" along the Kentucky in Anderson County.[1]

John G. Stuart, an eloquent early Kentucky settler, recorded his first venture on the Kentucky in 1806 with all the wide-eyed enthusiasm of youth. Waiting for a tide to sweep his tobacco, flour, and whiskey-laden flatboat to New Orleans from Cleveland's Landing in Fayette County, he recorded everything in his journal. He described one crew that passed as "a specimen of what I may expect to see in my voyage—drinking, swearing, kicking, and farting." Besides losing two prized pocket knives overboard, he also found the constant diet of boiled meat and potatoes not to his liking. When boredom really set in, "we amused ourselves with leaping down our sandbank in the evening." After waiting for nearly two months for a substantial rise in the Kentucky, they "hove off" for New Orleans. The trip to the Crescent City proved eventful, and although young Stuart commented on the "fine girls" he found there, his Kentucky home was always on his mind. The way back was replete with hot weather, buying food from friendly natives, and sore feet; he was elated when he could finally record that "this morning we cross't Dix River."[2]

The childhood experiences of most Kentucky River people have been positive. Later generations who grew up on the Kentucky, even those coming of age in the twentieth century, found it to be just as exciting and fulfilling. "I always had my mind on the river," recalled Claude "Buck" Horn of his hardscrabble childhood on the Kentucky. Horn did all he could to help his family of eleven siblings by hunting and fishing, killing ducks for their meat and feathers, and renting out johnboats to customers who often did not pay. "Dad never had a job during the Depression." While living on a shantyboat, one sister was "injured for life" when she fell off the gangplank. But despite all of this, Horn concluded, "I had a very happy childhood. The river was a way of life. It was a source of food. There is something about it that if you stay there long enough, it'll get to you."[3]

Swimming occupied the leisure time of many boys throughout the length of the Kentucky River Valley. Sometimes their actions appeared foolhardy, even dangerous. At Jackson on the North Fork, William H. Garrett and his friends plunged through the old mill cut where the Panbowl came so close together. "We'd wait, three or four of us boys, until that water got through that hole, then we'd dive through that hole and come out on the other side. One time it tore off my shorts. I came out of the other side like I was shot out of a gun. A big whirlpool took me down and threw me out of the bottom of it." An-

Boys diving from *Falls City II* docked in Louisville, ca. 1905. (Hibben Collection, Kentucky Historical Society)

other interviewee recalled diving off the dam at Monterey and swimming underwater beneath the apron where it was dry. "I dived off that dam and got in under it and sat down. I did that once when my dad was fishing and like to have scared him to death. He didn't know where I went." "I enjoyed playing on the rafts," one man recalled of his youth. "We'd run off every day." Other exciting play included riding the waves of large boats that steamed by their homes or even riding a roof or an old barn that floated down on a summer tide. "Now that was entertainment," Glynn Welsh of Irvine recalled. "The river was ours," claimed Frankfort native Louis A. Stivers. "We would maybe stay in the river three or four hours a day at a time. We'd swim back and forth across the river."[4]

Sometimes the water safety lessons for Kentucky River boys left something to be desired, at least in one case. "The first memory that I have that really stands out is him [Hugh Reece's father] taking me out in a rowboat and pitching me out in the water. I had to swim or drown. I've often wondered, because I never saw my father swimming any, and I don't know if he could swim or not." A picture of naked boys diving off the paddle wheel of the *Falls City II* tied up at a Louisville wharf testifies to the carefree days of the turn of the twentieth century.[5]

If it wasn't swimming, boys enjoyed boating. One youth, finding a derelict boat with the bow missing, used the old craft all one summer by sitting in the stern. This ploy, a classic example of youthful ingenuity as well as a little laziness, kept water from coming in the front of the boat. Another group of boys found a boat that "leaked so badly we had to put inner tubes around it, but we'd row out to the river. We had a window shade that we would pull down, and if the wind was blowing the right way it would carry us like a sail." A local mechanic added to the joys of a local Henry County boy by making a surfboard based on a picture in a magazine in the early 1930s. James B. Roberts rode it behind a powerboat. "People came running down though the cornfields. I don't think they had ever seen anything like that." Alas, Roberts's grandfather sawed it in half because of the apparent danger, and the first surfboard on the Kentucky River joined the woodpile.[6]

If the girls growing up on the river were a bit less adventuresome than the boys, their love of and attachment to the Kentucky was no less strong. "I always did say a kid that didn't have a creek to play in didn't know what fun was," recalled one woman. Aileen Suter of Ball's Landing declared, "I was free as a bird. I've been on every hillside here and climbed every tree in this area." In the 1950s, Amalie Preston's father "would row over into the wake" of coal towboats as they passed Oregon in Mercer County. "My mother screamed 'You're going to drown us all,' but that was fun." Once two young girls were nearly swept over the dam at Boonesborough while taking the mail to the Ford post office along with eggs for the local store. Back safely on shore they all excitedly talked of their narrow escape and shared a laugh when one of the girls blurted out that if they had gone over the dam, the "basket of eggs would have been broken."[7]

A young Valley View girl learned to swim the same way as some of the boys. "Dad would take us out in the river on a boat, and he'd make us turn loose to learn to swim," she said, matter-of-factly. "So we learned to swim." There were other ways for young females to excel on the Kentucky, sometimes exhibiting a bit of daring. Zelma Leitch Filson, the daughter of a riverman, "really threw a tantrum" when her father balked at letting her pilot a racing boat in 1932 in a race from Lockport to Gratz. "'All right, you're so smart,'" he said, "'next year you can just run the racing boat yourself.'" She continued telling her story proudly: "And I did, and I won a race. People were lined up all down the riverbank. Daddy had souped the engine up for me. He knew how to do that. The men who were piloting the other boats were heavier than I, of course. So I beat them both. They gave money, so I won all the money, and I put that in a savings account and used it to go to the World's Fair in Chicago in '33." No contests were held thereafter, because no one was willing to race the unbeatable girl pilot.[8]

There were also tales of ghosts and hidden treasure to fire the imaginations of river youth. One legend about three kegs of gold hidden by a pioneer before being killed by Indians kept people around the Brooklyn Bridge section of Mercer County searching, unsuccessfully, for years. Stories persistently circulated around Drennon Springs in Henry County, 2 miles up Drennon Creek on the Kentucky, about a cache of gold buried at the old site of the Western Military Institute when a cholera epidemic hit in early 1854. James B. Roberts sought his El Dorado, and though he found nothing there, he thoroughly enjoyed the excitement of the search. Susie B. Lair and her cousins in Valley View heard tales from people in the community about a stash of gold hidden under the hearth of her home. Her parents always wondered about the fresh marks around the hearthstones after they had returned from a trip to Richmond and other places. A former Oregon resident also recalled in an interview the family legend about $700 in gold that his grandfather buried without telling anyone about the secret hiding place. Alas, it too was never found.[9]

Oregon seems to be a special place of intrigue on the Kentucky, with childhood stories sure to chill young blood. One tale is of a man who was decapitated when his horse fell. The man rode off, much like the headless horseman of New York's Knickerbocker regions, across the river into Woodford County. The story must have frightened many a local child into pulling up the covers before sleep. As a child, Gilbert O. Britton observed a large cache of tombstones being offloaded from a boat. Eerily, "nobody ever claimed them. They just finally went into the bed of the river with the shifting of sand and mud." Amalie Preston's uncle apparently was once confronted by a ghostly figure in the dark. He promptly emptied his gun into the apparition. The story ended with a special family joke when someone said, "Millard has just killed a sycamore stump." A Preston family tradition has it that someone will see a white dog before a family member dies. Ghosts, or at least stories about them, abound on the Kentucky. At Boonesborough a painter once claimed to have been kicked off a ladder by the ghost of a deceased lockmaster, who had lived in that house for most of his life. The man's widow completed the story by declaring with a laugh, "Whether there is anything to that I don't know."[10]

In the days before radio and televison dulled the minds of young people, opportunities for enjoyment were plentiful on the Kentucky River. In the early twentieth century, several vacation camps dotted a river map. At Boonesborough, Dr. David Williams of Richmond built sixteen cabins as part of a small resort, complete with dance hall. "Everybody in Richmond came down there," recalled a lockmaster's daughter. "On Sundays you couldn't get on that beach" because of the crowds. It was the beach that drew many people to the rather dangerous waters below Lock 10. After the construction of the dam in 1905, the swirling waters created a natural beach that still exists. "It really was a great place to go. Poor Dr. Williams really loved it," but it deteriorated quickly after he died. Eventually the state purchased the Williams property and began development of a state park there.[11]

There were also excursion boats and showboats on the Kentucky to supply the entertainment needs of Kentucky River folk. *Price's Floating Opera*, *The Majestic*, *Captain Hart's Showboat*, and even a vessel with the mysterious name of the *Temple of Health* made voyages up the river, usually going only as far as Irvine before returning downriver before the bad weather of wintertime. Billy Bryant's showboat *Princess* made trips into the 1930s. From as far away as Valley View, residents of Boonesborough could hear the calliope playing the signature song of the boat, *I'm Looking Over a Four-Leaf Clover.* On a stage equipped with oil-burning lights, the shows usually included melodramas, vaudeville, and minstrel acts. Bryant and his family and a crew put on such plays as *Ten Nights in a Bar Room, Leana Rivers, Uncle Tom's Cabin, Mrs. Wiggs of the Cabbage Patch, The Tenderfoot, The Heart of Kentucky,* and *East Lynne.* Margaret True of Camp Nelson could never forget the day one showboat arrived on the river when she was nine years old. While she and her family enjoyed a show one evening, a curtain apparently blew against a kerosene lantern, catching fire and destroying their home.[12]

The *Princess* started its run of one-night stands just up the Kentucky at Worthville and proceeded to such ports of call as Moxley, Ball's Landing, Glen Mary, Gratz, Lockport, Monterey, Polsgrove, Elkhorn, Frankfort, Clifton, Tyrone, Brooklyn Bridge, Camp Nelson, Paint Lick, Valley View, Ford, Boonesborough, Doylesville, Red River, College Hill, Drowning Creek, and West Irvine. On the downriver trip, the shows would be changed, drawing the crowds back again in droves. Children in particular waited with great anticipation for the showboats, relishing the calliope. "They'd start playing that thing as they come up the river and you could hear it forever," recalled Lonnie Ashcraft of Valley View. "Yeah, that would draw them. That showboat was some-

thing. Everybody in the country would come to see it." How important were the showboats as a link with the outside world? Col. George
Chinn recalled that when one such boat announced that World War I
had begun, many men in the audience immediately volunteered for the
war effort. Betty Bryant, the daughter of Capt. Billy, grew up quite
literally on showboats. She recalled Vic Faust, a versatile native Aus-
tralian, who won the hearts of audiences with his "rube" character.
Morever, when Faust reached the Kentucky River he easily supplied
the *Princess* crew with plentiful fish dinners.[13]

Capt. Tom Reynolds's showboat *Majestic* also plied the Kentucky
in the summer months. Zelma L. Filson would attend the shows on the
Majestic at Drennon Springs. Reynolds's daughter not only starred in
the shows but also played the piano between acts. "They'd have a nice
three-act play, and if you had an extra dime, you could stay for the
concert after the play and they would do a lot of dancing. They'd put
on a good show." How "majestic" were these boats? They were usually
only barges, pushed by a small towboat, with a theater stage and seat-
ing for fifty or so patrons. Though pretty tame by modern standards,
they were quite a scene of activity at the semi-isolated communities
along the Kentucky before World War II. With fees of thirty-five cents
for box seats and fifteen to twenty cents for other seats, the showboat
Princess was a sight indeed in the early twentieth century.[14]

J.N. "Boss" Sewall, a well-known Kentucky banjo-picker, began
working on *Captain Hart's Showboat* at the age of nine, "handing out
handbills." Hart would take his boat all the way to Beattyville if there
was enough water in the stream. Combining both live acts and the
latest technological wonder, the moving picture, Hart's boat was a hit
up and down the river. Sewall later had the job of hand-cranking the
movie machine. "I remember one time it was a train picture, and that
train ran in one tunnel, and I just give it a whirl like that and it shot out
of there," Sewall recalled. "They got on me about that," he said with a
wry smile. Sewall learned to play the banjo from "old Bill Hart," who
"was a horse pistol. I seen him hit a fellow one time on the deck of the
boat and he knocked him in the river. Hit him with his fist and knocked
him in the river, and they had to fish him out. Hart was a tough little
fellow," who could walk on his hands between acts, and who was not
above a bit of chicanery. Breaking balloons with a rifle, he kept it a secret
that he used bird shot to improve his accuracy. With admission a quarter,
Sewall found "those old mountain people treated you real nice. . . . That
old river boat was a lot of fun, but was a lot of a hard work." Sewall
rode for the last time on Hart's boat when he was sixteen, taking his

wife on their wedding night to see a show on the boat's last trip up the Kentucky in 1917.[15]

Valley View seemed to be a center of attention not only for show-boats but for other craft as well. Yancy Merrit of Irvine ran a danceboat down to Valley View and as far as Frankfort in the summer. The *City of Irvine* was a welcome sight for entertainment-starved folk on the river. At one time, Merrit's granddaughter recalled, "He had a slot machine on board. If anybody was headed down that they thought was government, well, the slot machine went under something," she laughed. When the boat went to Frankfort, its name was changed to *Capital City*. On more than one occasion the captain of the boat would get drunk in Frankfort, and help would be sent from Irvine to fetch the boat to its home port. "Momma was afraid he would wreck that boat," one Valley View resident recalled. For the Merrit boat and others "people would be standing on the bank when it got there." The *Summer Girl* also ran out of Frankfort in the twenties and thirties. Once on a foggy night the captain fooled the dance crowd into thinking they had gone as far as Lock 6, when in fact he had only moved back and forth across the river within sight of Frankfort.[16]

At Valley View, a Mr. Horton from Richmond would set up a merry-go-round in the summer. One woman recalled, when seeing the clanking contraption for the first time, "I was scared to death and I run to my sister; I said 'I don't know what it is.'" When there was nothing else to do, young people had house parties and box suppers. Eva Perkins Sams recalled on one occasion "one of my fruit baskets brought $15. That was a lot of money in the thirties. We didn't know what going to town [Richmond] was." As a child when there was nothing else to do she and her friends "would put on a show" and charge a penny for admission. "We'd roll up the dining room rug and put meal on the floor so it would be slick, and we would dance," recalled Helen Stevens Witt of Irvine. "We would have a lot of home parties, people would have a bunch at home."[17]

Trade or store boats also gave Kentucky River folk an exposure to the wider world. "Huckster" boats some called them, selling everything from material for summer dresses to candy, the boats plied the river during the summer months before World War II. Local children called one such craft the "candy boat" because the captain knew that free candy would draw a bigger crowd to his floating establishment. "Boy, the banks would be full," recalled James Young. There were other places along the river for entertainment as well. The Ripys of Lawrenceburg built Bat Camp, with two small swimming pools, for their pleasure and that of others on the river. David Strohmeier's family took over Quire's Mayflower Hotel and Fishing Camp at the mouth of Elkhorn Creek in Franklin County. Built in 1921, the hotel operated until World War II. Although the business has dwindled to a campground and canoe livery operation, Strohmeier's Still Waters Campground is one of the few such places that remains open on the Kentucky. Strohmeier exhibited the view of most Kentucky River residents, deploring the trashing of the waters and the growing lack of courtesy of many powerboaters, who "rip and roar up the river" swamping his canoeists. He has also refused to allow any more digging of a large Indian mound by exhibiting a tolerant Kentucky River trait of "live and let live." Asked why he did so, he replied, "Oh, I don't know; I just feel that it's just well to let them lay in peace." Other camps for scouts and the YMCA existed for a time on the Kentucky. Kentucky Military Institute operated a summer camp, Kamp Kaydet, on the Kentucky at Clifton for over two decades. For several years, Sarah Gibson Blanding, dean of women at the University of Kentucky, ran a girls' summer camp called Trail's End Camp.[18]

Swimming at the beach at Boonesborough has been forbidden for years because of occasional high coliform counts and dangerous undertows caused by the churning water flowing over the dam. Its place has been taken now by a junior-size Olympic swimming pool. Beaches that once operated at Lockport and other places along the Kentucky have also been replaced by modern pools and other sources of entertainment. Better highways eventually made it possible for residents of more isolated river communities in such places as Valley View, Gratz, Monterey, and other towns to get to county seat towns.[19]

Many Kentucky River people look upon the Great Depression era as halcyon days. "Back then there wasn't much to do except play on the river," one man recalled. "That was our main source of entertainment." "It was a good life," said a College Hill man from Madison County who would trade an egg for a piece of candy at the local general store. "She'd finally lay, and I'd grab it and run." "We lived on the river, most of us boys," reminisced one Doylesville resident. "If we had to hoe tobacco in the morning, in the evening we'd go to the river. Right at the mouth of Muddy Creek, we had a big cable up in a tree."[20]

Even during the hard times of the Great Depression years Kentucky River people found ways to survive. Keeping to an old river tradition, shantyboat people could live off the land and the river. All along the river, until after World War II, such boats in various states of repair would be found around nearly every community. Perhaps Frankfort is the last place on the river to have shantyboats. What is a shantyboat? Often it was a makeshift, homemade houseboat with little care for aesthetics or paint, but if it floated, it could be a haven for river people. Several people along the river today can trace their heritage to shantyboat ancestors, whom those firmly attached to the shoreline often called "river rats." For example, Avery Imel's father came up the Kentucky on one such vessel and tied up near Ball's Landing. He met a girl on the farm where he worked and "married the farmer's daughter." Raising seven kids they became attached to the land. Shantyboat people were proud and feisty. When a towboat crew turned toward Jim Hundley's shanty, thinking of swamping his craft, "the old man came out with a shotgun and peppered them good."[21]

Farmers usually allowed the shantyboat people to pilfer their corn crops as long as they weren't too greedy. An old saying on the Kentucky was, "The first three rows of corn are for the shantyboat people." Most were law abiding, raising large families and making do with their lot in life. Sometimes they squatted on the riverbank, raising a garden and a few hogs. "They made a pretty fair living," according to an observer in Lockport. A man who grew up on a shantyboat said it was "the most fun part of living I ever had in my life. We never went hungry." Perhaps the best known of all shantyboat people was Turk Eversole, who lived on the Kentucky in Frankfort for many years. Thomas D. Clark interviewed the old man about his Kentucky River experiences in the late 1930s while working on his book, *The Kentucky*. When Clark could not find Eversole, the Frankfort police chief volunteered to act as a go-between. Upon being confronted by the policeman as he was about to enter his johnboat to return to his shanty, the old riverman said: "*Now* what in the hell have I done." Carl Couch, one of the last shantyboat people living at Frankfort in the 1980s, praised his carefree river lifestyle. "It's just like you being raised on the land and calling it your home place," he told a reporter for the *Frankfort State Journal*. "Well, this is my home place."[22]

Community life along the Kentucky remained strong in the Great Depression years. From the Three Forks on down to Carrollton, conditions were much the same. Droughts in 1930 and 1936, the terrible floods of 1937 and the Frozen Creek Flood of 1939 added to the woes of Kentucky River Valley inhabitants. When asked about the size of St. Helens in Lee County, Sam Wilson humorously replied, "Well, it was big enough they had a jailhouse and three saloons." During the Depression "it was rough" around Lee County. Everybody had a garden, chickens, and a cow. Men worked for fifty cents a day hoeing corn, sometimes you could earn a dollar a day for ten hours. Now the moonshiner's place has been taken by marijuana growers. "It's far worse than during prohibition," Wilson maintained, "'cause it don't take no capital."[23]

At other communities in Lee County the hard years were too much. Evelyn completely disappeared from the riverbank, and the settlements at Old Landing, Belle Point, and Heidelberg dwindled to just a few houses each. The out-migration continued from places like Oneida. "You can tell young people around here about [the Depression]," Homer D. Allen of Oneida recounts, "and it's a myth to them; they can't even comprehend it." "We growed what we eat," said another interviewee with finality. "My father was the movenest man you ever heard tell of," said another, never living more than three years in one place as tenant farmers in Clay County. Moreover, in that county during the Depression "a man with new overalls was in pretty good shape."[24]

Further downriver conditions were much the same, yet community spirit and sense of place remained strong. The county seat town of Irvine bided its time, waiting for better days. The floods and droughts of the thirties took their toll on tiny Doylesville, though one woman found it "a wonderful neighborhood to live in." About the continuing floods, "People was used to them kind of things" back then, Walker Covington recalled, but now do not want to put up with such inconvenience when there is higher ground and better economic opportunities elsewhere. "After a while I soon got tired of the river," another Doylesville resident said, and he drifted away.[25]

Perhaps no other community has suffered from the floods, droughts, and demographic shifts like Valley View, at one time projected to grow to a population of two thousand. For a spell around the turn of the century, the *Valley View Argent* touted the "wonderful growth and the many advantages it offers to business enterprises." However, the winds of change bypassed Valley View. The closing of sawmills, banks, and stores along with the last trains on the L&N Railroad, which had originally been the "Riney-B," in 1932 left only the Valley View Ferry as a nostalgic reminder of what the town had been. The old railroad trestle, torn down for scrap metal during World War II, served as a footbridge for many. "If a train happened to come along, we would hang on the water barrels that was on the side," a former resident remembered. Another Valley View man recalled his father raised fourteen children fishing and trapping on the Kentucky. "Yeah," he said, "they was a bunch of us." The 1937 flood appeared to be the death knell for the town. "It's not like it used to be; it used to be pretty and clean," a man recalled. "Right now, it's a ghost town." "I don't like to go 'cause I cry every time I go,"a woman said about revisiting her childhood home there, "thinking about what has been and how it is now."[26]

Downriver in Bluegrass country the same forces stressed and depopulated rural communities during the Great Depression. A comment by Bill Fint of Tyrone would have fit the circumstances of many a river person during those dark days: "During the Depression we didn't have no money, but we had plenty to eat." Frankfort, of course, is the major exception to the poverty of much of the valley. Being the "Capital on the Kentucky," the infusion of state and federal money kept the city functioning, even continuing to grow after the otherwise disastrous floods of 1937 and 1978. The fate of Tyrone, Oregon, Monterey, Lockport, Gratz, and other communites has been otherwise. Some have been swallowed up by the floods never to recover. A city water system and improved roads will help a small town like Monterey (which has been nominated for the National Register of Historic Places) survive into the twenty-first century. But many problems remain, and there is no work on or near the river itself. Except in Frankfort, even the old distilleries have moved out from their places in the Kentucky River floodplain or are safely ensconced on the hill above the river at Tyrone. Only the most hardy, or foolhardy, stay, waiting for the next flood, which may be even worse than that of 1978. The old joke of Gratz native Flora Dawson, "that if you batted your eyes and drove through Gratz, you'd miss it," becomes closer and closer to reality with each passing year. Can these small river towns survive into the twenty-first century as bedroom communities only without the sociality of the old days?[27]

Though many former residents have left the little towns and villages along the Kentucky, they still fondly recall their days on the river and bemoan what the ravages of time and man have done there. Both weather and manmade changes have consorted to place these small towns at a great disadvantage in the modern world. Moreover, transportation improvements and other factors have also led to the continuing decline of Kentucky River communities. Young people leave for jobs. Now the coyote's call reverberates across isolated Kentucky River bottoms, and the marijuana grower has replaced the moonshiner as the region's outlaw. There is little doubt that more small Kentucky River communities will disappear in the twenty-first century as the focus of the Commonwealth moves further and further away from its old roots.

Like river people everywhere fishing has also played an important role in the lives of Kentucky River folk. Though most often thought of today as a wonderful source of pleasure, indeed entertainment, in earlier days fishing was a source of livelihood for some and a necessity for many. Some craftsmen built particular types of flat-bottomed johnboats specifically for fishing on the Kentucky. While Raymond Hicks of Carrollton continued building such boats in the mid-1990s, this craft is dying like many other such endeavors. Tales of big fish abound, just as they do on all streams. For many a person "my mind on the river" included dreams of catching a monster catfish. In hard times, catching fish was often the difference between eating and going hungry. And some folks were not above breaking the law, using dynamite or the insecticide rotenone to stun fish, or illegal nets to catch fish. An Irvine man recalled how he and his young friends mixed lime and aluminum in a jar, making "a little bomb mixed with water and seal it up and it would make a little explosion," addling fish long enough to be scooped up into a boat. A Henry Countian apparently died when the stick of dynamite he threw toward the water hit a tree limb and rebounded into his lap. There are claims of extremely large fish, either catfish or paddlefish, caught all along the Kentucky. Hardly a location along the river does not have a story, usually secondhand, of the 100-pound catfish that did not get away.[28]

Along the Valley View area two men caught a ninety-eight-pound catfish. "That thing looked like a fattening hog laying up there," reported Lonnie Ashcraft about the fish caught in the early twenties. "Man, that was something to see." Into the early 1940s, there were several commercial fishermen around Lockport, including S.F. Spurr, who sold dressed fish for ten cents a pound. During the worst part of the Depression, James Roberts and his family caught so many fish one time that one uncle took his Model-T truck with a load to Carrollton while Roberts loaded his 1926 green Chevrolet with fish and headed to Shelbyville. "We got to Shelbyville, got in downtown Shelbyville, and a policeman come out and said, 'Y'all can't sell fish here.' Said, 'It's against the law.' The chief of police told us to 'Go across the bridge there that crosses Clear Creek, cross that bridge and set there and I'll send the people to you.'" A catfish caught on the North Fork was so large that the man "went back home and got him a plowline," Nevyle Shackelford remembered as a youth. He "got it up so he could get his hand in the gills, and he run his hand down that fish's throat and pulled that plowline up and tied a knot in it and tied it up to a tree."[29]

The fishing methods on the Kentucky differ little from other rivers. For a trotline, "The best bait is 'coon meat, they love that greasy 'coon meat, don't you know," longtime trotline fisherman Avery Imel reported. "I love to 'coon hunt," and therefore he "killed two birds with one stone." Strong cheese worked for another fisherman who often caught 50 pounds at a time basket-fishing. Some seasons were better-suited for trotlines, and other more muddy conditions were perfect for hoopnets. Ruby Stewart often joined her husband, who fished commercially out of Gratz. Soon after their son was born, they took him with them in the boat. Her husband did not like to farm, refusing to learn to use modern machinery when he did. The Stewarts became locally famous for their fish fries, with the fish always soaked in salt water, rolled in cornmeal, and cooked in lard in a large kettle. James Stewart "really knew how to fish. He loved that river just like a little old puppy." Fittingly, he died in his boat one day fishing. Not all women who grew up along the river cared as much about fishing as Ruby Stewart. "I fished one time and didn't catch anything," Maggie Wolfinbarger said, "and never would go back."[30]

Sometimes there was largess on the river. Fish could be scooped up from the Kentucky when a fire struck a distillery at Camp Nelson in the early 1950s. A resident of Oregon noticed the "funny color" of the river's water 35 miles downstream. "Them things was just lying on top of the water. I said they ain't gonna be no work today. I went to dipping fish." "I've heard it said they came to the top of the water grinning," Amalie Preston recalled. "They put them in landlocked pools of clear water to sober them up."[31]

There are still a few commercial fishermen, mostly part-timers, on the Kentucky. Bill Fint of Tyrone caught white bass using baseball spikes to stand on the apron of the dam at Lock 5, until he was given orders to no longer use this dangerous fishing location. "Black people used to come out of Lexington and order a thousand pounds of buffalo fish at a time" in the old days, he said, but more and more restrictions on nets forced him to line fishing. Bill Douthitt of Frankfort lived and worked on the river nearly all his life and sold fish for many years. Along the river near Perry Park, farmer Charlie Gibson mostly fished with hoopnets for white perch, catfish, and buffalo. He prefers to fish alone in the worst weather, because then there are no pleasure boaters around. He said, "They are always in a damn big hurry to get somewhere and then when they get there, they are in a damn big hurry to get back." They stir up the water unnecessarily and pull up his lines or move them. In the late 1980s, two men fished commercially out of Clifton Boat Dock, working trotlines. They sold buffalo, carp, and white perch for $1 a pound and catfish for $1.50 a pound. A 50-pound catfish was their largest catch in the summer of 1988.[32]

Humor is an important part of the "mind" of Kentucky River folk. Upriver in Booneville, Edward Campbell once stood an armed watch while his co-conspirators gigged fish illegally. "I saw they had about a tubful of fish and I emptied that pistol," he said, adding that he had been frightened of being caught. His friends came running asking him what he had seen. "I said 'You fellows got all you need, let's get out of here.'" Another story he related in an interview is one that had been told in other forms. An ex-army man rinsed out a worm can and took a long drink of water at Horse Shoal. "'Why in the army,'" he exclaimed, "'we drunk out of mule's tracks and everything and it never killed us.' He took several more drinks. We went up the river and there was a poor old dead hog a laying there with flies all over it. I said, 'Bruce, can you puke it back up?' He said, 'Hell no, that was the best water I ever drunk.'"[33]

Pranks are a part of Kentucky River humor. George O. Moore caught a sixty-five-pound catfish that "like to drownded me," having to "skin him like a hog." Moore's uncle took the monstrous head of the catfish to Camp Nelson in the trunk of his car. Stopping at a service station, he asked the mechanic to check his spare tire. The man "almost fainted" when confronted by the gaping mouth of the fish. A Corps of Engineers worker recalled going for mail in the upper river valley above Lock 13 in a rowboat. Someone started shooting at him, probably thinking he was a revenue agent looking for a moonshine still. "'Wait a minute, hell,' I said. 'We're not agents, we're just government people going for mail.' . . . They never did shoot no more. That's wild country, by God." A lockkeeper set up a tiny fellow worker by turning on an 80-pound pressure hose and laughing as it raised him into the air. On another occasion, when tools around the lock kept disappearing, he hooked a wrench up to a live wire and plugged it in when he saw the thief pick it up. "One grabbed that and got down on the ground, rolled around. I think it blew a fuse. They got loose, but I don't care what you had in that yard, you could leave it setting there for a month, and they wouldn't bother it," he added, laughing.[34]

Sometimes humor came as the result of a tragedy. The packetboat *Park City* sank with a load of whiskey near Mussel Shoals in Owen County in 1909, fortunately without loss of life. Two residents of that region recalled in an interview that barrels of whiskey from that vessel mysteriously reappeared from time to time, having actually been hidden by locals after the wreck. And then there was an unusual prank using the river's natural surroundings. "One day Dad was watching his cousin plow a field in the valley below," reported a former resident of

Polsgrove in Franklin County. "Aware of the crystal-clear acoustics along the ridge, and knowing that his cousin was nearly deaf, Dad would wait until the mule would reach the middle of a row, then intone 'Whoa' in a slow and deep but not loud voice. The mule would hear my father's command and stop, forcing his befuddled master to get him started again. And so my father found a temporary respite from the boredom of life on the farm."[35]

But Kentucky River humor could also be bitter, even sarcastic, as in a statement by a retired lockkeeper, angered by treatment from the Corps of Engineers over the loss of sight in one eye. "Son, they know how to waste it," he charged. "The best thing you could do to Russia, if you wanted to break 'em, is send that [Corps of Engineers] fleet over there. I bet the Russians wouldn't keep them a year. They'd kill 'em all or have 'em in a salt mine."[36]

There are patterns to humorous stories along the river. Several interviewees told substantially the same story of the man who is about to shove off from the bank to go fishing when he is confronted by a stranger who asks if he can join him. After rowing to his favorite fishing hole, the first man produces a stick of dynamite. He is about to light it when the second man reveals that he is a game warden and must arrest the man for his transgression against state law. Then the first man lights the dynamite and hands it to the game warden and says matter-of-factly, "Are you gonna talk or fish?" Another pattern concerns obviously apocryphal remarks by a greenhorn when he returns home. In one case the story is told of a man who, after returning to Lockport from traveling the river to Frankfort, replied, "It's good to be back in the United States again." Allen Trout in the *Courier-Journal* used the reverse of the story by telling of a mountain youth, who, passing Beattyville on a raft, waved his hat and said, "Goodbye, old U.S.A., goodbye."[37]

Among the many humorous stories about Tom Bondurant, a lifelong resident of Monterey, he is reported to have said the same thing as the boat on which he was working left the Kentucky River, entering the Ohio. "They said old Tom rared back and said 'Goodbye old U.S.A.,'" laughed one of his old friends. Then there is the big man, Paul Bunyan genre. For example, in one case a man came to fight another man, but decided against it after witnessing the giant pick up a pony and set it over a fence. Or there is always the joke ridiculing a certain community's value. When a drunken passenger would not be specific about his destination, saying, "I want a ticket to hell," the riverboat captain replied to a subordinate, "Well, just let him off at Lockport, that's about as close to hell as we can get." In more recent years there have been humorous stories of such things as the algae-eating "river pigs" at Lock 2 at Lockport. Apparently for some time, a sow and her piglets would wade onto the apron of the dam during lower water stages and gorge themselves on the "green slime" growing there. Remarked the owner, "They seem to pretty well know what they're doing." One observer even went so far as to make a home video of these porcine gourmets.[38]

Then there are the many local characters. Tom Bondurant was the quintessential "river rat," a ne'er-do-well but harmless individual who endeared himself to everyone he came in contact with along the river at Monterey. At one time there must have been many like him, scattered up and down the Kentucky River, men who lived off the land for the most part, sometimes living on shantyboats, never requiring much. He was not a vagrant, nor a "street person" in the argot of today, but just someone who did not work much and demanded little from society and his surroundings. Sometimes men like him rode the rails or tramped across the wild backcountry, like the famous "Shiner Slattery," a sometime sheepshearer who endeared himself to the hearts of more than one generation of New Zealanders. But Tom Bondurant was firmly rooted to a place, his place on or near the Kentucky River at Monterey. He wandered not afar, but safely within the confines of a time and place. His life tells us a lot about sense of community, "my mind on the river" in a timeless way.[39]

Those that knew Bondurant and interacted with him have recycled their stories into something almost mythical. "He was a character, Tom was. He was a regular water dog," recalled one man. "He had a pretty good philosophy of life," said another. "I liked the way he thought about things—live and let live." On a more basic level, a storekeeper remembered, "He just scrounged for anything he could get." Often living on the Henry County side of the river, where he owned property, Bondurant would come across to Gene Tindall's store almost every day. "He never bought anything except a can of peaches and a gallon of milk." Carrying his food away in a burlap sack, Bondurant would pole his boat back across the river. Usually "Old Bob," his favorite dog among several, would accompany him wherever he went.[40]

Sometimes Bondurant lived on a cobbled together shanty. Once he caught an old houseboat that had drifted down on a flood. One end of the boat listed heavily, having taken on a substantial amount of water, but Tom made his home there until the boat finally sank two years later. He was a recycler par excellence before it became fully fashionable. "He watched for the drifts and just scavenged the river," Vic Bourne recalled. "I know one time me and my brother-in-law were going down by the mouth of Severn Creek and we looked out in the river and here came a conglomeration of floats and boats and houseboats and runabouts and Tom, who had never been more than a mile away from Monterey in his entire life. I hollered, 'Tom, where'n the hell you going?' He said, 'By God, to the Mississippi if you don't catch me.'" Bourne and others ferried Tom and his bounty, courtesy of a tide, back over the dam toward Monterey. Another popular story is about Tom and his seeming good luck. Bourne recalled seeing Tom in Monterey one hot summer day, complaining about how sore he was. When asked what had happened, Tom replied that "He had got so hot last night he put on his life jacket and he went down to the river and just laid back in the water to cool off, and when he woke up he was going over the dam. He said. 'It like to have beat me to death!' So I said, 'Well hell, Tom, are you going to do that anymore?' He said, 'Yeah, but next time I'm going to tie myself to a willer limb, though!'"[41]

Another endearing story has to do with one of the few times he actually worked for a living, this time for the Corps of Engineers repairing the dam at Monterey. One day Tom got overbalanced and allowed a wheelbarrow loaded with concrete to fall into the river. The foreman demanded, "'Tom, go down there and get that wheelbarrow.' Tom, he was sharper than what he seemed, said, 'I'll get the wheelbarrow, but I don't think I can get the concrete.'" A variation of the story has Tom being called down from a concrete chute just before a storm broke, there being a fear that the chute might plummet into the river. Tom replied, "'By God, it don't belong to me, let it go.'"[42]

After being placed in a nursing home to recover from an illness, Tom referred to the woman who ran the establishment as "nothing but a damn old dictator" for making him bathe. When his friends found out about it they agreed, "Well, that's the end of Tom." One of his best buddies, a young man who had often looked out for the older man's welfare, truly believed this. "The only bath I ever knew Tom to take would be to wade out and just never take his clothes off and splash a little water on and walk back out. This was winter and summer I've seen him do that. And when she cleaned him up and took that layer off, Tom couldn't stand the exposure." There were other characters of the Tom Bondurant type along the river at Monterey, but none will ever match him in the hearts and minds of his old friends.[43]

Each community has its storytellers, and none was better in capturing the essence of locale than Ed Land Jr., who learned yarns from oldtimers in his childhood. Often the stories are about how the city-slickers get taken by country folk. For example, after a local store-keeper had just paid seven cents a pound for a 7-pound rooster, a "very aristocratic looking woman and man, they was dressed up and very high-toned," asked the price of the rooster. "'Well, I'll let him go for just what I give for him. I give seven cents a pound for him.' So he placed him on the scales, and said he weighed exactly 10 pounds, that'll be seventy cents. And I was sitting there. I saw it all happen. I never said anything. After they got gone, I said to him, 'You know that chicken gained 3 pound in about twenty minutes laying there with nothing to eat or drink?' He said, 'Yeah. The man that sold me those scales told me they'd pay for theirselves.'" Another standard story is about a traveling salesman, a favorite brunt of many jokes. "The old man was sitting on his porch down there and this magazine salesman come by and drove up in his yard. And a dog was in the yard barking at him. He hollered at this old man, 'Will your dog bite?' 'My dog don't bite,' the old man said. About this time the salesman got out of his car. The dog like to have eat him up. He got back in the car and hollered, 'You told me your dog wouldn't bite!' The old man said, 'That ain't my dog!'"[44]

But if Kentucky River folk demonstrated much that was admirable, finding humor in everyday affairs, particularly in the days of the Great Depression, they also exhibited some of the same behavior of other Kentuckians, a darker side, when it came to a tradition of violence. "We were part of the bad Littles of Breathitt County," Nevyle Shackelford said, half-jokingly, in an interview that revealed much about the heritage of violence of the Kentucky mountains. "One of my ancestors had thirty bullet holes in him when he died." On the other hand, he revealed he had "borrowed $100 from my uncle, a bootlegger, a moonshiner," to attend his first year at Eastern Kentucky State Teachers College in the 1930s. During Boss Sewall's trips upriver on Hart's showboat, he could not help but notice "some of them men would come with them big 45s buckled on, don't you know."[45]

During interviews for the Kentucky River project it was not unusual for the informant to voluntarily mention violence, quite often of a personal nature, without prompting by the interviewer. A Booneville man said, "Well, gee, that's not the half of it. I've seen 'em shoot 'em down, right in town over there." After witnessing a killing in which one man killed another with a shotgun, he was relieved when he did not have to testify. "I told the others, 'Keep your mouth shut.'" Another man on the South Fork saw a man killed during a church service near his doorstep. It appeared to him that during his lifetime, violence had declined as stealing went up. A Jackson man witnessed a shooting when he was ten years old. After falling, the victim had been given the coup de grace—shot in the back of the head. Several shots hit the iron pipe against which the youth stood. "You couldn't tell whether I was the pipe or not, I was squeezed to it. As soon as the shooting was over with, I got gone. It was a wild place. There was always some shooting going on," including a friend shot on the way to a movie. "There laid my buddy down the street there, [they] shot him in the back of the head." A man who recalled moonshining around Old Landing in Lee County also remembered "they used to be a right smart of violence" along this stretch of the Kentucky.[46]

Violence and killing touched the lower Kentucky River basin as well. In the thirties, an incident of multiple killings occurred near Boonesborough, when moonshining and revenge ended in the deaths of three men. "They had a lot of moonshine whiskey on that river," recalled Maurice D. Flynn, the teller of the story. A stream is always a good place in which to dispose of a body, and in the days before modern scientific forensics, it was often too easy for authorities to declare a washed up body as a drowning victim. Even at bucolic Valley View murder occurred. At Ball's Landing, now called Perry Park, LeRoy New, at the time on the FBI's "Ten Most Wanted" list, inhabited the area for a time with seeming impunity.[47]

Violence struck close to home for several interviewees. At least two informants' families moved downriver to the Bluegrass because of violence. Ike Short's story is one that could be told by others. "My grandfather ran for school trustee, and a bunch of drunks who didn't like him, they just thought they would get rid of him. He had won. I think my grandfather was shot six or seven times. My mother said if they could have got the crowd away, I had an uncle there who was dodging the law. He was a very mean guy and he had killed three or four men. Every time he would raise his gun to shoot, one of these women would step in, he would have stopped it right now. These women were just hollering and screaming." Short's grandfather, transported by riverboat and then by train to Lexington, died of gangrene one week later. His father killed one man in self-defense and narrowly escaped mountain revenge. Short concluded his interview with an ambivalent conclusion: "They ain't as bad as they used to be. They'll kill you now. They'll hold those old grudges."[48]

In *A New History of Kentucky*, James C. Klotter found room for hope about the state of violent behavior in the Commonwealth. For example, from 1933 to 1993 the homicide rate fell from 14.5 per 100,000 inhabitants to 7.0. Moreover, it also appeared that racial violence, at least the threat of lynchings, had declined by mid-century to only a memory of its former virulence. But in the Kentucky River region that had not always been true. At the turn of the twentieth century, blacks inhabited much of the Kentucky River Valley. Like many rural African Americans, their descendants have long since left for the cities and the work they could readily find there. Until very recently in its history, Kentucky society has been segregated by law and by custom. For example, blacks could not use the beach at Lockport. As work diminished on the river, African Americans drifted away from places like Valley View.[49]

However, before World War II, when lynch law and strict segregation governed their lives, relations between blacks and whites along the Kentucky river were often cordial. Within the confines of Kentucky's racial mores, blacks and whites lived in close proximity, coexisting, often working together. It was not unusual for a white family to be tenants of a black owner. The experiences of William E. Hall and his black neighbors at Clay's Ferry in Madison County in early 1923 offer a poignant counterpoint to what typical racial mores were thought to be at that time. "There's nothing like good neighbors and friends," Hall said in a 1989 interview. An elderly black couple often cared for him and his brother when his parents went to town. He knew them as Uncle Bill Toomey and Aunt Pink and loved them like family. Uncle Bill made Hall a little wagon to play with. "I guess I pulled it for miles and miles when I was a little kid. That made me love that old feller." Aunt Pink excelled at making biscuits that she fed to the young white boys along with heavy helpings of blackberry jam.[50]

On a horrific night in March 1923, Hall came to have an even greater understanding of the sense of community that prevailed among his black and white neighbors on this stretch of the Kentucky. A tornado struck Hall's home, killing his father, William, age 38; two sisters, Mary Catherine, age 4, and Rosa Lee, age 13; and a first cousin who was just a baby, the son of Logan Griffith. The memories were vivid many years later.

> Our neighbors here was colored people, but they was some of the finest people you've ever met, old man White and his wife. They was about the first ones to come to us that night. My brother and me wasn't hurt as bad as some of 'em, some of 'em was butchered up bad. One of my sisters older than me, next to me, one of the post on the bed splintered out and

went through her side. They couldn't get her to the hospital, they had to saw each end of that off. She lived until they got her to the hospital but she died. They took my brother and me down to the Whites. We didn't have any clothes on, was just in our night clothes. We was muddy, we was cold; see it was in March, and a cold rain had rained on us. We was a mess. We wasn't hurt as much as the rest of 'em, so they carried us down there. My brother and me didn't like this colored lady. She had an apple tree there right beside the highway, and we'd come by there and we'd fill our pockets full. She didn't like it very much. And we didn't like her for that, but that night she took us in. Oh, we was a mess; we was almost froze to death. She took her good clean blankets and wrapped us up and built a fire and warmed us up. And, you know, we loved her for the rest of our lives. We just thought a lot of her. We stayed right there until they got the rest of 'em out and took them to the hospital. I tell you that was a terrible time. I can hear them screaming and crying. I didn't know whether I was dreaming or if it was really so, but it was really so.

The Richmond paper reported the Hall home had been "carried across the road and smashed to kindling." The four victims were buried on the Hall farm on the hill above Clay's Ferry.[51]

A white neighbor, Joe Simpson, raised $1,100 to rebuild the house and farm buildings, and the family survived. John White, a black man who owned a river bottom, sold Hall his first farmland, twenty-six acres on the Kentucky at Hines Creek about five miles below Clay's Ferry. "If it [the Kentucky] overflowed every other year, it stayed rich and made corn. My wife and I married when I was eighteen and she was sixteen. And we couldn't find a place nowhere. Mr. White rented us a place and had a little bitty old plank house he made hisself. I really enjoyed it. That's where I got my start. I raised ten children." There must be many more unrecorded stories like this, perhaps forgotten among both races alike, illustrating that humanity on a local level can rise above the overbearing racism of an earlier day.[52]

The Kentucky River is also a state of mind. In fiction, music, and art, the river has touched the lives of many people who have lived there and desired to depict it in word, melody, and landscape. Perhaps no one demonstrated "my mind on the river," the Kentucky, as much as artist Paul Sawyier (1865–1917). Though born in Ohio, Sawyier came of age in Frankfort, where his father practiced medicine. Coming from an artistic family, the young Paul studied at the Cincinnati Art Academy and under William Merritt Chase in New York City and Frank Duveneck in Cincinnati. In Frankfort, he worked as a salesman for the Kentucky River Mills, over which his father presided as president, but Sawyier never found a liking for that type of work. Most at home when he roamed the riverside and creeksides around Frankfort, Sawyier developed a lifestyle and painting style that would soon emerge. In particular, until about 1908 he concentrated on painting watercolors, with Frankfort and the river and nearby creeks as subjects.[53]

After a fairly affluent early life, Sawyier fought a never-ending war against falling into poverty. Having to care for his parents because of his father's ill health, he scraped along selling artworks through Frankfort and Lexington establishments, often making only $10 to $15 for several hours of work on a painting. He relied on the use of photographs for models of his work and shared a studio in Frankfort with a photographer. Many of his best early works are of Frankfort scenes, like *Wapping Street Fountain, The Old Capitol, A Rainy Day in Frankfort, Kentucky River Scene,* and *Old Covered Bridge.* An avid hunter and fisherman, he loved to roam the river and creeks when he had the opportunity. There were periods of time when he would be very inactive as an artist and then work furiously for a spell. He could not break free until after his mother died. In 1908 he purchased an old houseboat, and for most of the next five years he painted almost entirely Kentucky River scenes. Slowly working his way up as far as High Bridge, in what one writer has described as "immersed in the dreamlike world" he painted, he produced dozens of scenes. But he also visited other places upriver and for a seventy-five dollar commission painted *Sweet Lick Mountain* at Irvine for a businessman.[54]

My favorite of all is a Sawyier's watercolor on paper scene, *Moonlight Mooring,* one that he painted during this period. It is also one of approximately 175 prints that Paul Sawyier Galleries of Frankfort has produced since the early 1970s. Of that number, at least eighty-five have a theme that relates to Sawyier's love for the Kentucky River, Frankfort, and Benson and Elkhorn Creeks. Most often identified as an impressionist today, Sawyier painted hundreds of scenes, mostly of Kentucky. Willard Rouse Jillson estimated that Sawyier painted two thousand to three thousand canvasses, but William H. Coffey of Sawyier Galleries calculated the number as substantial but far fewer than that. There is an old story that the man who purchased Sawyier's houseboat threw dozens of the artist's paintings into the river. There is little doubt that Sawyier was a prodigious painter, who preferred not to do portraits and seemed drawn to the medium of watercolors more than any other. But if he did not prefer portraiture, his *Rock Breaker*, a realistic depiction of an African American working man, is an example of another style that he could have mastered if given time and inclination. He tended to paint several variations of favorite scenes or structures on the river. For example, the old Frankfort covered bridge appeared in several forms, often in the background of a scene. Coffey estimated that Sawyier painted High Bridge fifteen to twenty-five times with varying quality. *Sky High Bridge* is too indistinct, while *High Bridge 1910* shows a houseboat on the river and makes good use of light. One of his most successful large paintings is *Panther Ravine*, showing Camp Nelson covered bridge with a woman washing in the foreground. This painting has many of the lusty attributes of the French impressionist school. Biographer Arthur F. Jones identified this Kentucky artist as a "minor master" who is a "regional" impressionist, first and foremost. "His creek and river scenes tended to evoke nostalgic dreams of childhood days spent in leisure," Jones averred. Perhaps that is an explanation for the success of the prints today, purchasers looking back at an apparently simpler day and longing for that milieu to which we can never return.[55]

Even when Sawyier moved to Brooklyn, New York, and later to the Catskill Mountains, he still had his "mind on the river" and continued to paint Kentucky scenes, many based on earlier photographs he had made. In a painting like *Kentucky Arsenal*, for example, the Kentucky and the old wooden St. Clair Street covered bridge lie in the hazy background. One writer has described much of Sawyier's work as evoking a sense of "brooding loneliness," which others have ascribed to perhaps his excessive use of alcohol. But if Sawyier did have problems with alcohol, he never exhibited this publicly. Some observers have described him as alternately quite shy with strangers and open with friends. Margaret True of Camp Nelson recalled Sawyier during the time he tied up his shantyboat there. "When I had to go to the grocery, my mother would make me go through the field to keep from disturbing him when he was painting," she remembered. On other occasions, "I just spoke to Paul Sawyier; he was to me just Mr. Sawyier. I saw him at least twice a week."[56]

Sawyier died of a heart attack at age 52 in the Catskills, leaving the possibility that he might have become more famous outside Kentucky. No artist so far has captured the romance of the Kentucky River, particularly at the turn the twentieth century, as well as Sawyier. Many of his indistinct (some modern critics might call them blurry) impressionistic paintings express a wistfulness that is still appealing today. For example, the *Kentucky River with High Bridge in the Background* depicts a warm summer day with the bridge and the old stone towers barely visible in the distance. Like most art forms, Sawyier's impressionism is either liked or disliked by the layperson. Unfortunately, many of his watercolors appear washed out because of the ravages of time. More important for the purposes of this book, his paintings of the Kentucky inspire a continuing love and respect for the river valley.[57]

Impressionism of another sort, in Sawyier's contemporary, Madison Cawein, also illuminated another corner of Kentucky arts. But Cawein, although initially financially successful in the stock market, suffered much the same financial reversal as Sawyier. Moreover, his poetry won some national approval, but eventually fell into artistic limbo to be only recently revived and credited for its farsightedness. Sawyier and Cawein both died young and left the lingering belief among many of their followers that their best, most mature artistic contributions had been lost. However, for this study the early life of Madison Cawein II, the poet's son, gives another strong indication of how the Kentucky River could work its magic on a youth, in this case, a "city slicker" from Louisville.[58]

Nearly three-quarters of a decade later, from far away New Jersey, Cawein recalled the lasting impression of summers spent on the Kentucky at Clifton in Woodford County, where several families had cottages. His experiences sound more like William Faulkner's *The Reivers* and Mark Twain's *Tom Sawyer*. After swimming downriver one day in a swift current, Cawein lost track of time, laid down for a nap, and, footsore from walking barefoot on the gravel road, finally returned to Clifton at about 11:00 P.M. "The old man came out and yelled at me. He was sore but really relieved. He gave me hell, and said they had been dragging the river for me." The younger Cawein, feeling the river's spell, composed a poem, a paean to the river's beauty. "Against Kentucky's ancient hills/The flickering firefly casts her gleam/And on the river's margin spills/One drop from her eternal dream." Years later a friend told him that "I had better not try to make a living by writing in competition with my father, known as the 'Keats of Kentucky,' but had better stick to engineering and physics. It was good advice."[59]

Knowing moonshiners who sold "white mule," along the river, Cawein also got his introduction to life along the Kentucky. "We kids learned a lot of bad habits along the Kentucky River in those days— "smoking and drinking," he recalled. Not liking the taste of wild marijuana, "I preferred tobacco, which the old man raised on his farms near

Versailles. I gathered dry leaves from his barns and rolled my own ciga-
rettes. Old Man Emil gave me a drink of his moonshine when I was
sixteen years old. I nearly choked on it. My best Negro friend was
Sonny Jackson, who would bring me a pint of Old Grandad once in a
while. This I liked. So I learned to drink bourbon at the age of sixteen."
Emil also taught Cawein to drive an automobile at the tender age of
twelve, and the youngster was sent to Versailles to get a block of ice on
a hot summer day. The young Louisville boys even pulled the old snipe
hunt gag on another youth. In 1990, the river still tugged at the heart
of the boy that still existed in the eighty-six-year-old Cawein.[60]

Another native son, Wendell Berry, also felt the pull of the Kentucky as a youngster. After being educated at the University of Kentucky and receiving a Wallace Stegner Fellowship in Creative Writing
at Stanford University, Berry returned to a hillside Henry County farm
on the Kentucky to work the land and write award-winning poetry,
fiction, and essays. He created the Port William community to portray
his view of life there through several generations. He is most concerned
about the loss of community, the dwindling of the small agriculturally
based town.[61]

The Kentucky has always played an important role in the lives of
Henry Countians. "When I was a little boy," Berry explained,

> it was a great geographical experience to come down this
> hill from Port Royal in the river valley. It was always, to me,
> a special, exciting thing to come out off the upland and get
> to where you could see the river. Then come down and see
> the long descent into this valley. I loved it and it was very
> important to me to do that. The river was always very much
> a part of my life. We would hitchhike down there and go
> swimming. There was an old camphouse that belonged to
> my family, and my family would come down. We would have
> a picnic dinner or something. We'd come down as boys, bor-
> row a boat maybe. When my brother and I were bigger, we
> had a boat. We would fish or swim.

Now that Berry lives on the river and farms there, he notices that times
have changed and people think differently about the Kentucky. "To
most people it's just noticeable when it's in a flood and it becomes a
nuisance. You can now cross the Kentucky River Valley on I-71 and
hardly be aware of it. You certainly would have to look for the river in
order to see it. The road has not only eliminated the river as an artery

of transportation and commerce, but now finally, actually dwarfed it and made light of it."[62]

Berry also bemoaned the loss of "country villages" in the Kentucky River Valley as part of the larger trend of the rush to the cities and the continuing refocusing of life away from the family farm. Sense of place is a strong element in Berry's life and in his writing. From the beginning of these Port William novels with *Nathan Coulter,* he has wrestled with the onslaught against the sense of community and of the family farm in particular. *Nathan Coulter* is not autobiographical, but does have some elements of Berry's childhood experiences incorporated into it. "Some of that is made up, some of it's hearsay. Lots of talk that's going on around here at the river. And I think I borrowed some things that I'd heard, imagined some things. You might start out with something you know about, but you never know enough from what you actually know to write a story about somebody."[63]

Berry's environmental concerns are both local and worldwide. He practices what he preaches, using horses instead of modern machinery to farm his hillsides and bottomland on the Kentucky. Although "my cows drink out of the river, without any ill effects that I know about so far, and we still swim in it occasionally," he still worries about the future of the valley and countless others across the globe. According to Berry, the problems of the river are "from cutting the trees, it's from bad farming. Now it's bound to be some extent the strip mining. It's from city-making, it's a lot of paving." Specifically, in *The Long-Legged House, The Rise, January 1975,* a passage from *Openings,* Berry uses the Kentucky as metaphor for what was right with the natural world and what has gone wrong with the modern world. Time is running out on reestablishing the harmony between man and nature that has been lost. In the poem, *January, 1975,* he concludes: "The river has become the gut of greed. Human evil moves in its currents now, each rise a kind of weapon, the old clarity gone."[64]

The Rise is Berry's poetic meditation on the state of his world, in this case the Kentucky, while on a downstream canoe trip during a flood. "It was a cold day in the middle of December," he explains, when this trip took place. This journey becomes a metaphor for the voyager's sensing of something more than the usual canoe trip down the Kentucky. The river can be as merciless as it is beautiful:

> The sense of the power of it came to me one day in my boyhood when I attempted to swim ashore in a swift current, pulling an overturned rowboat. To check the downstream

course of the boat I tried grabbing hold of the partly submerged willows along the shore with my free hand, and was
repeatedly pulled under as the willows bent, and then tore
loose. My arms stretched between the boat and the willow
branch might have been sewing threads for all the holding
they could do against that current. It was the first time I
realized that there could be circumstances in which my life
would count for nothing, absolutely nothing—and I have
never needed to learn that again.

Described as a "latter day romantic" by William S. Ward in *A Literary
History of Kentucky*, Wendell Berry realistically senses what has been
lost in development of the Kentucky River and other state resources.[65]

Even "traditional" country music was influenced by the river when
white and black musicians lived close together working and farming
the valley in the early twentieth century. Particularly in the area along
the river from Madison to Jessamine Counties, "behind the white fiddlers there seems to have been a generation of black fiddlers," according to musician John Harrod. Owen Walker, a black fiddler at Valley
View when Doc Roberts, a famous white fiddler, was a boy, was "a big
man, a rough man, a bad man." Apparently "nobody got away with
anything if they crossed him." The "music scene was fairly integrated,
while the rest of society wasn't," Harrod further explained. African
American Jim Booker of Camp Nelson was the first Kentucky black
musician to record his music, including a melody titled the *Camp Nelson
Blues*. Booker played with white bands and influenced several white
fiddlers in Madison County, including Johnny Masters, with his "whim-
sical style." One sound archivist has estimated that about 70 percent of
Watson's recordings came from "Walker-Booker repertoire." Another
black musician, Jim Smith from the mouth of Jack's Creek in Madison
County, had a band called the Jack's Creek Jazz Band but played old
time "break" music, including one tune that Doc Roberts recorded
called the *Jack's Creek Waltz*.[66]

Those who have lived on the river become attuned, accustomed
to the sounds as well as to the sights that the Kentucky projects. Getting used to water incessantly going over the dam at Boonesborough,
lockmaster's wife Delphia Walters recalled an unusual occurrence during a severe drought in the 1950s: "When the water stopped going
over the dam every one of us got up. Because of the noise of the river,
you go to sleep by it. We all got up to see what was the trouble. I'll tell
you something else about that dam. When that water gets low, with

just a little bit going over, it sounds just like somebody playing an organ. It makes the most beautiful music you've ever heard in your life. It's spooky. Its like a chord organ. When it gets at a certain stage, it's beautiful."[67]

The Kentucky also speaks in other ways to those who take the time to listen. Wendell Berry has the poet's ear, and at floodtide he hears something different from Walters's assessment:

> But impressive as the sights may be, the river's wildness is most awesomely announced to the ear. Along the channel, the area of the most concentrated and the freest energy, there is silence. It is at the shore line, where obstructions are, that the currents find their voices. The river divides around the trunks of the trees, and sucks and slurs as it closes together again. . . . It is a storm of sound, changing as the shores change, increasing and diminishing, but never ceasing. And between the two storm-lines of commotion there is that silence of the middle, as though the quiet of the deep flowing rises into the air. Once it is recognized, listened to, that silence has the force of a voice.[68]

CHAPTER SEVEN

Don't Step in a Shadow

Working on the Kentucky

"Don't step in a shadow," warned longtime Kentucky River towboat captain John Donaldson in an interview. "More than one has done it." The work lights at night throw "awful shadows." This admonition comes from the danger of lockmen and towboat personnel being blinded by lights at night, stepping off a lock, boat, or barge into dangerous waters. "A boy walked off the lock," the daughter of a lockmaster recalled, "the light blinded him." Even today, "'Don't step in a shadow' is probably the most important thing you can tell a new deck hand," explained modern-day Ohio River towboat captain Butch Shearer, whose family has roots on the Kentucky near Boonesborough. Such were and are the dangers of working on the Kentucky.[1]

But working on the Kentucky also has its rewards. For the lockkeepers and their families, life could be very good indeed, particularly during the Great Depression. Originally, each of the fourteen locks on the Kentucky had two keepers—a lockmaster, who always lived in the upriver house, and the lockman, who lived in the lower though identical house. Lockkeeping became a tradition for many families like the Walters at Lock 10 at Boonesborough. Most of the lockmen came from river families in the early days. That tradition began to break up after World War II. Earl Gulley Jr., who supervises the Kentucky River Authority's locking operations today went to work on the Kentucky in 1958. "One of the first things Pete Hardin asked me was 'How in the hell did a foreigner like you get a job with the Corps of Engineers?'" Towboating also tended to become a family tradition. The Leitches of Henry County, the Prestons of Mercer County, and the Shearers of Clark County sent several generations onto the Kentucky and other rivers. Clyde Young Sr. and his brother and brother-in-law worked on the locks. The Dees brothers, their uncle Estill Thomas, and cousin

James C. Thomas kept the locks active for many years. Woodie Walden Jr., himself the son of a Kentucky River lockmaster born at College Hill in Madison County at Lock 11, went on to become a legendary lockman on the Ohio. He began his career working on the old Corps boat *Kentucky* as a deckhand. In 1990 the Corps of Engineers named a derrick boat in his honor. Perhaps there really is something to the old adage that "this river gets into your blood."[2]

Though doomed to mediocrity in the nineteenth century and then to obsolescence in the twentieth, the Kentucky River navigation is important to the economic, political, and cultural history of the Commonwealth. Construction of the locks and dams, particularly at Valley View and Boonesborough, can provide insight into the human story of the valley. Working on the Kentucky illustrates much about the lives of Americans everywhere.[3]

By the time acquisition of land and construction began at Locks 9 and 10, the Kentucky River navigation had already begun declining, logging being particularly hindered; no amount of Corps of Engineers rationalizing and local chambers of commerce cheerleading could help. The expenditures kept increasing each year, with $49,084.83 being spent in 1898 for lock operations and payroll, as well as sundry items such as supplies of ice and toilet seats. With the 1912 Corps report, lockages had decreased to the point of no longer being recorded individually by lock number in the annual report. The Kentucky did receive the honor of having Corps workboats named in its honor. The first, an 1891 snagboat at 136.6 x 30 with a 4.6-foot draft and weighing 330 tons, was the largest boat on the river. After scrapping that craft, a new steam-powered, paddle-wheeled *Kentucky* was built at the Howard Shipyards in Jeffersonville, Indiana, and commissioned in 1909. By now maintenance on such vessels could be done at the extensive "ways" and shops at Lock 4 in Frankfort. At 148 feet long, like the steamer *Falls City II*, the *Kentucky* had to turn sideways, "kind of cockeyed," to fit into the lower locks. Any wider and it would have been too bulky to fit in even the wider upper locks. Its 5.6-foot draft scraped the bottom during low water in some places, it being very difficult to keep the 6-foot minimum depth throughout the river basin. At several dams it proved to be almost impossible to keep a 6-foot depth on the lower miter sill of the lock.[4]

Only below Frankfort along the Monterey-Gratz area did the Kentucky River navigational system have a beneficial effect after the turn of the twentieth century. Ironically, perhaps even characteristically, at the same time most people recognized this, the Corps began studying construction of a lock and dam on the South Fork in 1915. (I have never found a copy of this report.) By 1929 the Corps no longer listed "steamer" on their reports as plying the Kentucky. The system limped into the modern era with a mimimum of two lock personnel at each of the fourteen locks along with relief workers. Several more men worked at the maintenance facility in Frankfort. Each spring, a Corps workboat, laden with machines to keep the river open, would slowly make its way to Beattyville, lifting out snags, casting sand and gravel out of the channel, refurbishing the locks, and performing other duties.[5]

Surveys for Locks 9 and 10 began in 1898, with benchmarks established every mile for the length of the proposed pools. Land acquisition created the usual problems. "The prices quoted were generally extortionate," the Chief of Engineers lamented in 1899, "and sites have been recommended for condemnation." Owners contested every square foot of land submerged by the rising waters when the pool filled. Subsequent surveys had to be made in lawsuits when farmers complained of good farmland inundated by "progress." The Corps surveyors made sure to differentiate between uncultivated and cultivated land, the latter being the most valuable to Kentucky River farmers. The Sheridan-Kirk Contract Company got the contract for Lock 9; Mason and Hoge contractors won the contract for Lock 10.[6]

The Corps appointed an inspector for each site, with C.W. Mann in 1902 at Lock 9 "hereby directed, until further instructions to assume charge of all operations then in progress or that may be required from time to time at that place; also to take charge of all office records, and to watch, care for, and preserve all engineer property at that point." The sites were prepared with steam-powered equipment, quite primitive by modern standards. Coffer dams, earthworks that locals called "coffee" dams, had to be built up with steam shovels during the low water months of summer and fall, high enough so that work could proceed on the lockwalls and dam. Wood needed for platforms and stone for lockwalls was produced locally or came from nearby sources. Cement, sand, and gravel had to be transported to the site. Photographs were taken as work proceeded, giving some idea of what the scenes looked like. Heavy cables were strung across the river valley, and with the use of steam power and pulleys, materials including concrete were moved to the worksite. A simple "A-frame," an upright wooden or metal post stabilized by cables, from which an arm and pulley mechanism was suspended, moved heavy stone and concrete into place. The site was alive with men working and steam boilers roaring from daylight until dark. Workboats nudged against the working areas

Above, Old construction method showing rock-filled crib works being sheathed with wooden planks at Lock and Dam 3 during rebuilding in the 1880s. Note the coffer dam in front of the workmen. *Below*, Workmen pause for picture taking inside the excavation for Lock 7 on 21 September 1896. (Both from National Archives)

or were tied up to the bank. Pumps powered by steam engines were constantly humming at Locks 9 and 10 to keep the work areas dry. Derrick boats moved river sand, gravel, and mud out of the way in preparation for the foundations of the lockwalls and dam on bedrock. The more dredging the construction company had to do, the less profit it made. A crew of dozens of men might be working at any one time during good weather, but a sudden rise in the river would bring work to a halt and threaten the uncompleted job. Contract laborers like the stonecutters made the best wages, twenty-five cents an hour. The men who labored in the pits, moving dirt, sand, and concrete by shovel, were usually poor black and white men. In photographs, they appear serious in their floppy wide-brimmed felt or straw hats, making fifteen cents an hour up to $40 a month. The men had to be fed, and cooks, quite often African American men, worked long hours over woodstoves even in the hottest weather.[7]

Lock 9 at Valley View was the first dam to be constructed entirely by pouring concrete in cells without the use of timber and rock cribs. The dam was not solid concrete, having open chambers within so that the concrete would cure properly. The apron on the lower side was backfilled with rock in order to help stabilize the dam. Locks were finished first so that navigation could proceed up and downriver while the coffer dam held back the river to create a pool. Although Corps records indicate that Lock 9 opened on 3 December 1903 and Lock 10 on 12 January 1905, the construction and repair was never finished. While Lock 9 was being constructed, it was nearly battered down by ice and logs, with the latter gouging out 6-inch to 12-inch slabs of concrete. Of course all of this had to be repaired. Alas, the improvement of dams made entirely of concrete failed at Locks 9 and 10 when washouts occurred during flooding, necessitating the rapid building of concrete auxiliary dams on rock and timber crib foundations. On 12 and 13 March 1905, floodwaters raced around the lockwalls, ending navigation as the pools rapidly lost water. Again more work was needed to get the system back into working order, this time with the auxiliary dam now connecting the lock with the bank. During this inundation, one of the lockhouses at Lock 10 washed away. Construction crews used oxen to pull what remained of the house above the floodplain, where it is today, and construct a replica nearby. Even with the restoring of the pools, the river system needed constant work to keep it operable. For example, to maintain the new pool from Lock 8 to 9 at Valley View, the Corps expended a total of $2,328.95; $1,852.11 of that amount was for labor for a ten-man crew, from 22 October 1899 to 17 May

New method using concrete cell construction at Lock and Dam 10 at Boonesborough. Twin lock houses are nearing completion in December 1903. (National Archives)

1900, with time off for the worst winter weather and tides. Winching the barge upriver, the crew used a small steam engine and an A-frame to hoist snags from the Kentucky. They cast off the timber they cut, to be carried away by the tides.[8]

Construction of houses for the lockmaster and the lockman kept pace with building of the lock and dam. The houses were always identical in every detail, following very specific drawings. Corps requirements were as rigid for this construction as for any of the locks and dams. Two-story houses at the locks were the norm, and those at Numbers 9 and 10 were no exception. The plan included a kitchen, dining room, and sitting room on the first floor and three bedrooms on the upper. Even the outhouses were meticulously designed, and barns and other outbuildings for equipment were included in the government "reservation," as it was officially known. All in all, the lockkeepers' houses were far better than most in the valley; only a very prosperous farmer in the community would have had something larger or more refined. At Lock 9 at Valley View one family even constructed a tennis court, where they could enjoy a spirited match on a lazy Sunday afternoon. "They were quite a showplace," recalled a lockman born at Lock 11 about his home.[9]

Lock operations required both the lockmaster and lockman, often supplemented by deckhands on a towboat. A boat would signal by two short blasts of a horn or whistle or by ringing a bell on the bank. Lockmen, on duty were not required to be on the lockwall, and they avoided the hot concrete of the lock and dam in summertime. Boaters, after having "to walk up there and get us, they didn't like that and next time they would buy a horn," one somewhat obstreperous lockman

The completed Lock and Dam 9 at Valley View in 1921. Two coal barges are already locked through and awaiting their towboat. In the background is the Riney-B Railroad bridge. Upriver is the Valley View Ferry. (National Archives)

recalled. While it might take as little as 15 minutes for a small boat to be locked through, it took at least an hour and a half for a towboat with three barges. Some lockages would take as long as 3 hours, particularly during high water or bad weather. Originally the valve mechanisms had to be turned by hand, but in later years electric devices were added, making the work somewhat easier. Although most families were grateful for the lockkeeping work, one man quit as a lockman when the price of tobacco went up because of the New Deal price support system. Another lockman railed against the Corps, believing that he should have gotten a settlement because of the loss of an eye on the job.[10]

But for most on the reservation, particularly for children of lockkeeping families, life was joyful. There was always activity around and something to keep children interested and happy. "It was always a pretty place," recalled a lockkeeper's son, wistfully. When he moved with his family from Lock 6 to 1, their "old jersey cow" made the trip on a barge. He found Lock 6 to be too isolated, much preferring the activity on the lower river. While one man discovered the lock at High Bridge to be too open to the public, another declared Lock 8 to be "almost like in the boondocks," eventually transferring to Lock 4 at

Frankfort in order to keep his children from making exceptionally long school bus rides. But there was a tradeoff. He often had to lock through a sand barge at 4:00 A.M. in bad weather. While the daughter of a lockkeeper at Lock 3 at Monterey recalled their house being without electricity, telephone, or indoor plumbing, her family got by during the Great Depression quite well on a meager salary. When the opportunity arose, the family moved to a lock that had electricity. Corps regulations required that all trees be whitewashed to a certain height, that grass and weeds be kept cut, and that all buildings receive a coat of paint when needed. Until World War II the district engineer, always a colonel, made an annual inspection of each reservation. Rufus L. Moberly recalled that the officer always rode in a "fancy boat." Lockkeepers' pay increased slightly just before the Depression, when the National Federation of Federal Employees tried to organize the river's workers in 1929. Lockmasters' pay increased from $1,140 to $1,200 a year and lockmen from $1,080 to $1,140. After World War II, lockkeepers and their families, like all Americans, wanted modern conveniences, and the Corps updated all of the houses. There could be tension at the lockwall between lockmaster and lockman. One lockman took early retirement after such a conflict of wills, taking a lower annual retirement pay. Humorously rationalizing the situation, he said: "I figured I could make $150 by matching pennies."[11]

Lockkeepers realized the locks were "antique" but fulfilled their responsibilities. The old locks took longer to drain than to fill, and those pleasure boaters waiting for service did not always do so patiently. One man recalled staying "out on that lockwall fourteen and fifteen hours a day" in the summertime. When on duty, lockmen were required to keep the locks working 24 hours a day. However, eventually most rebelled against the required 24-hour duty schedules, five days on and two days off, cooperating in a lawsuit against the Corps. One of the lock employees at Lock 12, having heard about a successful case against the government in Ohio, talked about the problem with Irvine lawyer Billy L. Wilson. Lockmen received regular pay for an 8-hour day, and if they worked an extra 4 hours, they got overtime; but if they worked longer, or were on the reservation, they got no further compensation for that day. Wilson found a precedent where a federal employee on the west coast had been required to be on call longer than a regular workday and won the case. Although not all of the lockmen joined in the lawsuit, most did. After getting no hint of compensation from the Corps of Engineers, the case of *Ralph Conway, et. al.* proceeded through the General Accounting Office, and finding no satisfaction there, Wilson filed suit in the U.S. District Court in Washington, D.C., in 1973. The court eventually ruled in favor of the lockmen in 1976, but the monetary settlement was not forthcoming until the next year, after the government decided to, in effect, settle out of court. More legal and financial wrangling ensued. According to Wilson, "In essence, if they require you to be on the premises, that is part of your employment, because using the theory they can hire you to do nothing as well as hire you to do something."[12]

While the lawsuit took years for settlement in favor of the lockmen, they did not always feel that they had won. Unfortunately, the Corps of Engineers decided to cut hours of lock operations and to require only one person on site. Moreover, after the original group won their lawsuit, the remaining lock personnel also filed, creating some bitterness. The highest award was nearly $120,000. One lockman told Wilson, "I don't care if it's a dollar, it beats a snowball." Taxes and legal fees ate into the settlements. One man complained about getting only $40,000. And he believed the Corps had retaliated against the lockmen and the Kentucky. "I never understand why the Louisville District was so dead against the Kentucky River," he said. Delphia R. Walters, the wife of lockmaster John A. "J." Walters Jr., recalled him saying to his co-workers, prophetically, because he died before the suit was settled, "'Well, boys, I tell you this much, we'll win the suit but we'll lose.' And they did. The jobs were abolished, the places are going to wrack and ruin, and there's somebody down there [Lock 10] maybe on the weekend but that's all. And it's a shame."[13]

Mrs. Walters's words and those of her husband sum up the current state of the Kentucky River navigation system. Locks 5–14 have been taken over by the state, operating only on weekends in the summertime, and the first four will soon be absorbed into the state system. The lock personnel live off the reservation, the once proud houses have fallen into ruin, many have been torn down. Reservation sites have been vandalized because there are no watchmen. Even at Lock and Dam 10 at Fort Boonesborough, where the Kentucky Department of Parks is making a slow but sure effort to return a reservation to what it looked like in its heyday of operations, there is a sadness about the loss of a key part of the Kentucky River's heritage.[14]

But most lockmen and their families recall the old days with a sense of nostalgia and well-being. Notwithstanding their squabbles with the Corps of Engineers, they had a job to do and they did it to the best of their abilities. Lock 10 at Boonesborough and Lock 4 at Frankfort usually had the most activity and lockages because of the wider use of powered pleasure boats after World War II. Born at Lock 10, J. Walters, with time out for service in World War II, lived there almost all of his life. He died shortly after retiring and moving to Richmond. Walters kept a meticulous diary of his time on the river, including weather conditions, water levels, and general comments about the work of the lockkeeping family. The Kentucky Historical Society houses seventy-five volumes of his observations. "He loved the river," recalled his wife. "The one thing I'm sorry is I didn't have him cremated and bring his ashes back to Boonesborough. I wish I had."[15]

Such is the attachment river people have, their sense of place strong even in the face of modernization as we rush into the twenty-first century. Other lockkeepers and their families reacted much the same as the Walterses. Young men on the river felt the tug of a lifestyle working there. Estill Thomas was working on the beach at Lockport when a friend got him a job working on the *Chenoka*, a Corps boat that often worked the Kentucky. "I made $120 and [was] just a kid," Thomas recalled. "Man, you talk about getting the girls. Every time we came up the river, they would see the boat and come down to the river." James B. Gordon had a similar experience, going to work on the *Lucien S. Johnson* under Capt. Curt Leitch, who "hired all of his people off the Kentucky River." He recalled many pilots who came from the Kentucky and went on to work the Ohio and Mississippi Rivers. Ernest Ashcraft went to work on the *Kentucky* at age 13 and ended his career as a lockkeeper. James C. Thomas, born at Gest near Lock 3, had a similar experience, beginning as a cook's helper at the age of 17. Becoming captain of a Corps workboat, he memorized the entire length of the Kentucky after his many trips upriver in the spring. In later years he labored mostly on the Ohio, once working 39 straight hours during one crisis. However, the interviewer could tell that Thomas's heart and mind were still on the Kentucky, it being a smaller, more personal stream. Delvia A. Hopper, also born at Gest, went on the river at an early age, working on the old *Kentucky*. He became expert at running and cleaning, or "scaling," the steam engine on that boat, revealing in an interview that only wool clothing could be worn in the engine room. "One time I went in there with a pair of overalls with them brass brads in them," he said, laughing. "Why, it was just like you struck a match to my legs and hips." Naval architect Alan L. Bates described cleaning the boilers as "a hell of a job" that was necessary at all times of the year. "Once every week to ten days you literally had to tie up the boat, cool down, and clean the boilers."[16]

Brothers Charles and Russell Dees were born at Lockport and

grew up on the Kentucky River near their cousin James C. Thomas and Uncle Estill. Their grandfather, a Syrian immigrant, ran a store at Lockport for many years and had his own wharf for the busy river traffic in the 1920s and 1930s. A 1932 fire that wiped out much of Lockport forced the rebuilding of the store. Work on the river was not easy. "Back in the fifties," Charles recalled, "you'd walk approximately three-quarters of a mile to make a lockage, turning everything by hand, walking around and opening and closing your gates and everything." The Dees brothers became very safety conscious after their father, also a lockkeeper, suffered a serious injury at Lock 2. "I want it safe; safety comes first with me," Charles said, while still working part-time at Lock 7 for the state of Kentucky. "I want to do it the easiest way, the safest way, and the quickest way possible. I've been lucky. I've never had anyone hurt."[17]

The Prestons of Oregon in Mercer County have a Kentucky River family tradition going back to steamboating days. "Squire" Jordan Preston, a "taskmaster," ran boats in the nineteenth century all the way to New Orleans. The same Uncle Millard who shot the sycamore stump prided himself on his footboats, which he claimed to be unsinkable. He would "put enough water over into the footboat, until just the oarlocks were sticking out and then row downriver, sit in it on the seat, and everything slightly below water, rowing with no sign of a boat under him. He liked to do things like that for effect." The Leitches of Henry County also placed several men on Kentucky and other rivers, even having Leitch's Landing named for them across from Gratz.[18]

Towboating, of course, has never been a very profitable enterprise on the Kentucky, because of the many bends and the small locks and slow lockages. For some years, just after World War I, oil and gasoline were towed from the Lee County field downriver. Kentucky Towing Company, a subsidiary of Aetna Refining Company, began towing oil in wooden barges to Louisville. Other companies like Stoll Oil also made plans to use the Kentucky for shipping. On 6 April 1919, the steamer *Advance* struck a snag, puncturing an oil barge. "Within a few minutes the entire fleet was in flames and was entirely destroyed," the Corps of Engineers reported, the company losing $60,000. These shipments continued sporadically until a pipeline ended the need for Kentucky River transportation and the river lost another source of income.[19]

After World War II, some efforts were made to barge coal shipments being made from coal tipples at Beattyville and Heidelberg. The new East Kentucky Power generating station at Ford received shipments of coal by river from about 1954 to 1964 in barges owned by

Charles W. Gilley. A coal port was also built at Clay's Ferry from which the black mineral was trucked to suppliers in Lexington and other parts of central Kentucky. Hargiss McQueen piloted boats for Gilley, using either the *Shamrock* or the *Zephyr*, both diesel-powered boats. Although McQueen could boast, "I never sunk no barge," he did admit to getting stuck on a sandbar once. The *John J. Kelley* towed gasoline upriver to Camp Nelson for some years. But later efforts to tow cargo on the Kentucky proved fruitless for some. "They didn't know what they was doing," according to a retired lockmaster. Barges ended up in cornfields, bringing to mind the old adage of an incompetent river pilot being known as a "cornfield sailor."[20]

But from time to time some people did well such as John Donaldson. Going to work for the Greene Line out of Cincinnati as a freight clerk in the mid-1930s, Donaldson moved up, earning his pilot's license in the early 1940s. After employment with several other companies, he began towing out of Frankfort on the Kentucky for Sam Dreyer and Lyne Goedecke. Along the way a boat called the *Sam Dreyer* was built specifically for the Kentucky River lockages, short enough so that it could lock through with one barge. But the life of a riverman often changes, depending on the fluctuating economy of the nation. Sometimes Donaldson and others got work towing for the highway and bridge building on the Kentucky, but any regular towboating above Frankfort has been dead for over two decades now. A lockmaster recalled that Donaldson succeeded where others failed because "he was smart. We'd be locking him and he had a pocket watch, and he'd always be looking at it. He'd get that watch after you."[21]

Donaldson was also author of a continuing part of Kentucky River lore. In partnership with some other river entrepreneurs, Donaldson refurbished a sternwheel diesel boat known as *Emma II*, renaming it the *Brooklyn*, because they docked at a sand pit at that site just below Lock 7 at Shakertown. "She was 99 x 22 in the hull," Donaldson recalled, "120 feet overall. Two full decks, pilot house on top, all steel. She had been built as the *Helen H.* at the Howard Shipyard in 1929." Like many boats, the name of the vessel changed over the years and it was modified from time to time, including having the hull cut in two and adding 14 feet after it burned in 1942. Donaldson ran the boat towing sand from Milton, Kentucky, on the Ohio. But the boat was too long and too slow for really making money in the Kentucky River trade and against the competing railroads. After being stripped of its engine and machinery, it lay for years just below Boonesborough Beach near the old U.S. 627 bridge on the Clark County side of the river. Hoping

The *Brooklyn*, about a mile past Hall's Restaurant. (Author's photo, Eastern Kentucky University)

to refurbish the boat as a tourist attraction or restaurant, the last owner refloated the *Brooklyn*, pushing it to where it is today, about a mile upriver in a sharp bend of the Kentucky near Hall's Restaurant. John Donaldson predicted in 1986 that the Coast Guard would never relicense the *Brooklyn*, because of the loosening of rivets in its hull. So far he has been correct and the old boat rests in the mud of the Kentucky, quite likely its final resting place. Most people passing it by water or sighting it from the nearby roadway know nothing of its history, this last vestige of the old towboating days on the Kentucky.[22]

As long as the lower four locks are operational, the towing of sand to Frankfort will continue into the foreseeable future. The day I interviewed David Strohmeier on the Kentucky upriver of Frankfort was beautiful. I experienced, vicariously, a hint of what it is to work on the river. After the interview, I drove down to the riverbank, and faintly hearing a towboat, the only one still operating on the Kentucky towing a load of sand to Frankfort, turned off my engine and sat there. As the boat wound around the river's bends, the sound of the powerful diesel

Roustabouts shooting "craps" on the *Falls City II*, ca. 1905. (Hibben Collection, Kentucky Historical Society)

engine changed volume and pitch. I was like the children who waited for the showboat at the turn of the twentieth century, anticipating a genuine Kentucky River experience. Then the towboat rounded a bend and passed me, churning up the river, so close I could see the pilot clearly. On a wider river like the Ohio, I would have missed the sight. The pilot had the most joyous look on his face, the smile of a man who was not only working but completely enjoying every minute of it.

But work on the Kentucky could be hard in the old days, particularly for deckhands and shore workers. Marine architect Alan L. Bates well described the hard life of the African American stevedore on the Louisville wharf in the late 1930s.

I used to watch them load and unload the Greene Line boats here in Louisville, and a big shipper was the Standard Sanitary Company. They'd bring a truckload of bathtubs down to the boat. They would have two roustabouts at the tailgate of the truck and two more on the boat. And all the rest of them carried the bathtubs. A man would run up the tailgate of the truck—they ran all day long, they never walked—and the two men there would put a bathtub on his back. He'd run to the boat with it and the two men there would take it off his back. If the bathtub had not been so delicate, they'd had him pick it up and dump it on the boat. They were all black. They worked for very low wages. Maybe for a couple of dollars a day in the late 1930s. And immediately after the boat departed, the roustabouts got paid off. They were paid off in cash on the spot. And immediately the watchboat captain would start a crap game and take it all away from them. That's the colorful old life. They just worked you to death on those things.

The life of the Kentucky river roustabout could not have been much better in the old days.[23]

The Shearers are the last old Kentucky River families still working, not on the Kentucky, but on the Ohio and its larger tributaries. O.F. Shearer grew up at the turn of the twentieth century "under the bridge" just below Lock 10 at Boonesborough. After working at the Burt and Babb sawmill at Ford, he bought a small 12-horsepower gasoline-powered towboat in 1908, renaming it the *Belle*. His young wife bore three children on the boat. When one was knocked off the vessel one day, the father deftly leaned over the deck and pulled him to safety. Four of his sons became pilots, and the fifth an engineer. Shearer towed coal from Beattyville and even operated a party barge for a brief spell in the 1920s. However, he and his sons soon expanded onto the Ohio and the lucrative business of carrying coal for power plants. From the little *Belle*, O.F. Shearer and Sons River Transportation boats grew to giant 4400-horsepower diesels before selling out in 1973 to American Electric Power, a major utility that operates twenty-one powerplants on the Ohio River. Today, two of O.F.'s grandsons still make their living towboating on the Ohio, "30 on and 30 off," referring to the number of days piloting and not working the river. Among the many boats the company built, the *Leila C. Shearer*, a sleek 3200-horsepower vessel, named in honor of O.F.'s wife, still works the Ohio. "I pass her every time I'm on the river," recalled Oliver Franklin "Butch" Shearer, with a sense of pride, nostalgia, and attachment to the river that still fills the hearts of Kentucky River families. But, like many Kentucky River traditions, there will not likely be other Shearers to carry on this three-generation tradition.[24]

CHAPTER EIGHT

Whither the Kentucky?
The River, the People, the Future

"There is probably no more important planning item facing the region than how to use the vast resource that is the Kentucky River," *The Mountain Eagle* of Whitesburg editorialized in 1989. "It is in many respects a much-maligned river," explained an environmental advocate, "and one that has been very much taken for granted." Who does the Kentucky River belong to? Who is responsible for it? What will happen to this vital river and watershed as we face the population, economic, cultural, and ecological crises of the twenty-first century? In microcosm and macrocosm, isn't the fate of the Kentucky symbolic for many of the problems of our world?[1]

Thomas D. Clark best summed up the historical context of the Kentucky River's importance in the lifeblood of the Commonwealth:

> I sometimes have crossed the river down at Frankfort, walked over what they call the Singing Bridge. I stop and look down at that stream, and I try to conjure up in my mind's eye what kind of society, what kind of human history that water flows off from. I see an awful lot of poverty. At one time there was a pretty stable, subsistence farming way of life, an isolated, rural country, a trapped civilization. And now it runs off of a civilization that's falling behind in every way you can imagine, educationally, tax-wise. It runs off of strip-mined land that never should have been touched. It's bringing down pollution. The Kentucky River is an artery, a life artery. If the Kentucky River ever got out of commission, the Bluegrass area would be a disaster of major proportions. I look at the river and think, this is not a river, this is a river that's segmented into chapters of history of the western movement of

Kentucky and of central, rural America. It means more than just a simple drinking system. It's a civilization, it's tied together with threads of water, but sometimes those threads can be pretty wayward in behavior.[2]

In the larger Ohio and Mississippi River drainage systems, the Kentucky is a small though important part of the present and future of this massive eastern watershed. From the beginning of white settlement, the Kentucky has been exploited, abused, misused, misread, and now, neglected. Although water quality appears to be crucial for Lexington and the Bluegrass region, it is just as important, perhaps more so, for the Three Forks. Even the climate forecasts for the future appear ominous as more violent weather may be with us for the foreseeable future. Higher than normal averages of rainfall will place even more stress on old dams that have long outlived their practical usefulness. Moreover, the rain may come excessively in short periods, threatening life and property as never before.[3]

And there is another part of the equation. We can never return the Kentucky to anything like what Daniel Boone and other white pioneers experienced in the later eighteenth century. Nor should we. We should not partake in "faking nature," any more than we can continue to pollute and desecrate this precious resource. We can only approximate a rear guard action that will save the Kentucky and other watersheds of the Commonwealth. We know how to do it, we only lack the collective will and initiative to do so. There will be many obstacles. Shortsighted entrepreneurs will try to sell us on the economic panaceas of unrestrained development. They must be balanced against those who would go too far in the other direction, implicitly limiting access to the Kentucky as if it were a monument of the past. The ancient paddlefish will never return to the upper Kentucky, but would it not be wonderful to be able to catch less exotic fish and swim in the river without fear of disease? Former Commissioner of Natural Resources William H. Martin succinctly summed up the fate of the Kentucky and other resources of the Commonwealth: "There must be a major effort to save them to the greatest extent possible." Important choices must be made soon, and the problems seem to be increasing. Now the river faces an added challenge from the faraway Black and Caspian Seas via the Great Lakes and the Ohio River—the zebra mussel. These tiny bivalve mollusks multiply by the millions and threaten to engulf water intakes and other structures on the Kentucky.[4]

So the crisis of the Kentucky continues, existing somewhere between the debilitated Pigeon River of Tennessee and North Carolina (which one writer describes as "an environmental nightmare, an eerie, earthly version of the hellish Styx,") and a pristine western mountain stream. The Kentucky River has never caught on fire, as did the Grand Calumet River at Gary, Indiana, it being so heavily laced with volatile chemicals. However, Kentucky seer Harry Caudill once warned, in his own inimitable way, about the connection between the Kentucky, the mountains, and the Bluegrass: "If the people of Lexington care for the future of their city, let them look to the hills that will provide the future's water. Unless these hills are saved, are kept green with timber and flowing with pure water, future generations will find themselves bound inseparably to a vast legacy of mud, slime, flood, and thirst. Economic decline will shrink it to an inconsequential town, dozing an hour's drive from a range of mountains that a new generation of insensate cupidity calmly murdered." An observer of America's rivers, Charles Kuralt, took a larger, longer view: "America is a great story, and there is a river on every page of it. If we want that story to continue, prosperously if possible, we must take care of this vital resource." Whither the Kentucky?[5]

The first question that begs answering concerns the fate of the locks and dams. Should the old navigational system be kept in repair for recreational use throughout the length of the river or for only towboating from Frankfort to the Ohio River? There is growing "anti-dam" movement in America proposing decertification and deconstruction of obsolete, dangerously undermined, or unnecessary dams. Could such pressures build along the Kentucky sometime in the twenty-first century? Almost since it assumed control of navigation on the Kentucky in 1880, the U.S. Army Corps of Engineers has tried to get out of its obligation for the Kentucky. Obviously, the Corps' commitments to rivers and harbors all over America, enforced by Congressional action insisted upon by local and state pressures, has created a classical catch-22. Just enough money is appropriated to keep the system barely operating without capital outlay for major improvements. Particularly since World War II, the Corps has retrenched its efforts, either privatizing or turning over facilities to local and state entities. The efforts of such groups as the Kentucky River Development Association of the 1950s, which pushed for improved navigation on the premise of opening up more coal deposits, have gone for naught.[6]

An Environmental Impact Statement by the Corps of Engineers in 1975 suggested keeping up the entire Kentucky River system. However, the Corps began a process of "Selective Discontinuation," even welding together the lockgates for two boating seasons in the early

1980s. In effect, the Corps has often simply abandoned the locks above Frankfort from time to time. Pleasure boaters and recreational business interests lobbied with the state and federal governments for keeping the locks operating, particularly on weekends during the warmer months of the year. Without deeper channels of at least 9 feet or more, the efficacy of towboating the Kentucky simply made no sense, and the Corps did little if any dredging above Frankfort. Depths of less than 3 feet have become the norm during low water along many isolated stretches of the river, and without removing snags, some boaters are fearful of using the river during high water.[7]

In the early 1980s old issues came to a head. New groups like the Kentucky River Task Force, formed by the General Assembly in 1982, protested the sealing of locks at that time. A flotilla of fifty boats motored from Lock 4 at Frankfort to Lock 7. Papers like the *Frankfort State Journal*, citing the "River's Great Potential," began editorializing in favor of action. House of Representatives Speaker Bill Kenton asked the Legislative Research Commission to take action in keeping the locks open. Vic Hellard, the executive director of the LRC and a lover of the Kentucky, more than willingly began to work on a solution. Central Kentucky U.S. Representative Larry Hopkins realistically noted that someone, either the federal government or the state, would have to pay. As early as 1965, Spindletop Research of Lexington suggested the General Assembly create the Kentucky Riverlands Development Authority. The Commonwealth of Kentucky responded to this increasing pressure in 1986 and passed a bill sponsored by Representative Tom Jones of Lawrenceburg, creating the Kentucky River Authority, ostensibly to handle the passing of the Corps of Engineers locks and dams to the state. Hellard, who headed the LRC until his death in 1996, should be credited for propounding the idea for this new state agency. "Vic loved the river," eulogized Andy Mead, a *Lexington Herald-Leader* reporter who covers the Kentucky River. "He loved talking about it. He loved being on it." When a federal water bill finally permitted the Corps of Engineers to get rid of the upper ten locks on the Kentucky, the KRA faced its first big challenge. However, the KRA was little more than a paper tiger as the Kentucky suffered from neglect.[8]

Before anything of substance could be done, the entire basin got a wake-up call—the terrible drought of 1988. Indeed, the drought of that year was recently described as "the deadliest and costliest U.S. weather disaster ever." The entire decade of the 1980s had been drier than normal, quite unlike the generally well-watered 1990s, until 1999. At a time when central Kentucky was already outstripping its water supply, the summer of 1988 hit. Although Kentucky-American Water Company argued for a more regularized water supply, there was enough water coming to their plant. As a matter of fact, Kentucky-American simply could not process water fast enough to keep up with demand. The *Lexington Herald-Leader* included a photograph one hot July day of a large leak in the dam at Valley View. It was estimated that more water leaked through the dam than was being drawn from Kentucky-American Water intakes for its customers. The Fayette Urban County Council and Mayor Scotty Baesler took special notice and announced minor water restrictions in mid-July. Meanwhile, the state of Kentucky wrangled with federal authorities over responsibility and, more importantly, the cost of repairs for maintenance of the river above Frankfort. At the time, the federal government still owned the system. "I view the Kentucky River as the lifeblood of the Bluegrass," declared a Lexington planner, "and it has been ignored."[9]

On the Kentucky River proper, Beattyville, Irvine, South-East Coal (since dissolved), Richmond, East Kentucky Power, Winchester, Kentucky-American Water Company, Nicholasville, Lancaster, Harrodsburg, Wilmore, Versailles, Austin Nichols Distilling, Lawrenceburg, Frankfort, and Ancient Age Distilling all drew from the Kentucky as its flow decreased. Over 600,000 people in the counties adjoining the Kentucky depended on it for their drinking water. The *Lexington Herald-Leader* editorialized emphatically: "Stop the quibbling; it's time to get serious about the river." In particular, the largest newspaper in the middle of the region most dependent on the constant flow of the Kentucky called on state and federal authorities to cooperate immediately. Fortunately, amid all the tumult and shouting and wringing of hands, the Kentucky kept timidly flowing during the summer of 1988, and fall rains lessened the fears of disasters like that of 1930 or 1954. However, the drought of 1988, coupled with the Corps of Engineers' insistence on leaving the Kentucky's basin, galvanized public and governmental concern about the future of the region's water supply.[10]

Even before the drought of 1988, plans were afoot to find solutions to the problems of the Kentucky. With the Red River Dam apparently a dead issue by the mid-1970s, other studies suggested ways for alleviating the water problems of central Kentucky. In a 135-page report in 1976, the Corps of Engineers concluded that a dam should be constructed on Station Camp Creek in Estill County at a cost of just over $6 million. Most important to the plan was the continued maintenance of the dams above Lexington, Locks 8–14. Environmentalist

Wendell Berry championed saving the Red River in *The Unforeseen Wilderness: Kentucky's Red River Gorge* in 1971 and in later writings. But if not a reservoir on the Red River or Station Camp Creek, what other solutions could there be?[11]

Many suggestions were made for alleviating the problems that so badly frightened central Kentuckians in 1988. "Build more dams," argued some; "Enforce sewage treatment in the Three Forks area," demanded others. Moreover, the number of players in the debates increased. In the *Lexington Herald-Leader,* Bill Bishop argued for a "self-funded regional authority." When the Kentucky River Authority appeared slow to react, not being quite sure of its mandate and with little power, Mayor Scotty Baesler became one of the important figures in the fate of the Kentucky, spearheading and chairing a study group called the Kentucky River Steering Committee. The Kentucky-American Water Company put $125,000 into the committee's efforts, and the Lexington-Fayette Urban County Government added $100,000. Baesler already had in hand a report prepared by the Department of Public Works of Lexington-Fayette County. This report urged construction of "an impoundment near Bowman's Bend in Pool 7 and ending near Boonesborough State Park in Pool 9."[12]

The composition of the steering committee represented several constituencies, including environmental sources and upper Kentucky political figures, thirty-one members in all. Reports and suggestions came from all directions. Virgil Proctor, a Lexington engineer, suggested rebuilding Locks and Dams 5–14, dredging silt to create deeper pools, and installing pumps on Locks 1–9 to pump water upstream from the Ohio River in times of low water in central Kentucky. Already in use in Europe, the pumps could generate electricity when there was a high enough waterhead. The *Lexington Herald-Leader* and *The Lane Report* of Lexington editorialized frequently on the subject and opened their pages for discussion and debate. In the end, the steering committee raised more questions than it answered, and Baesler's ardor for action cooled as wetter years alleviated pressures for a quick fix for the Kentucky River. After considering twenty-seven alternatives, the steering committee forwarded a lengthy report to the Kentucky River Authority in July 1991. This plan proposed building two or three dams, making needed repairs to the old dams and eventually replacing several. Estimated cost would be over $250 million.[13]

In 1990, Kentucky River supporters in the General Assembly, including Tom Jones, Eck Rose, Harry Moberly, and Joe Barrows, with Vic Hellard "behind the scenes," according to former KRA chairman

Tom Dorman, "quietly" pushed through broader powers for KRA, including the right to sell bonds and charge for water usage. Dorman recalled that Gov. Wallace Wilkinson initially thought of vetoing the legislation, then reconsidered, appointing Dorman to the authority to "watch out for" the governor. Dorman ran for chair of the group and won. Amid charges of political cronyism, the composition of the authority would change in the mid-1990s to have a slightly less political face than earlier. Moreover, new powers would be given to the authority, even the ability to set higher water quality standards than for the rest of the state. After getting off to such a slow start, the KRA finally began to stir. In 1991 Harza Engineering of Chicago recommended to KRA two higher dams on the Kentucky, citing in its weighty "10-pound report" a 7-billion-gallon water deficit in case of a 1930 type drought. KRA chairman Tom Dorman reported that he and his ten-member group had enough to "chew on this for some time." Estimates for repairs and construction costs extended into the hundreds of millions of dollars. Work and planning proceeded slowly. By 1993 Harza had changed its mind, now proposing the repair of all fourteen existing dams and building splashboards on 12 and 13, which would raise the river level 2 to 3 feet in these pools.[14]

Meanwhile, the Corps of Engineers and the Commonwealth of Kentucky continued their sparring over who should pay for repair of the decrepit locks and dams. With navigation still possible from Frankfort to Carrollton, the Corps promised to repair Locks and Dams 5–14 thoroughly before turning them over to the state. For the first time in decades, the Corps concentrated its efforts on the Kentucky. Sen. Wendell Ford diligently labored to get $5 million added to an Energy and Water Development Appropriations Bill to work on the ancient dams as well as getting $500,000 for the south Frankfort floodwall. The work continued for the next several years. Lock 5 on the Anderson-Woodford County line, thought by some about to be breached, received the first attention. With the old timbers of the dam visible in places, contractors reinforced the structure with a new concrete facing.[15]

As recreational boaters publicly argued for keeping the locks open, particularly during the summer months, the pressures built on the Corps and Commonwealth to arrive at a final solution to the navigational plight of the Kentucky. All through the 1990s, as the system was being transferred to the state, repair work continued. The old system broke down often. Locks would be opened only to have to be closed for costly and necessary repairs. Old lock gates leaked. It became increasingly difficult to find seasoned white oak for the miter sills and lock gates.

Some of the older dams appeared near collapse, but work proceeded as people along the Kentucky pushed for solutions. Boating clubs at Frankfort and Boonesborough worked hard for continued lock operations.[16]

Although given a stronger mandate by the 1990 General Assembly as well as the means to support itself, the KRA faced a daunting task: how to develop water policies in the turbulent climate of Kentucky politics. Moreover, Kentucky-American Water Company and other users of the river's resources clamored for solutions. Fear of a repetition of a 1988 type of drought or worse compelled board member Joe Mellen to say that KRA had "studied it to death and so far we've done nothing." To get a handle on the situation, the authority proposed a time bomb: Collect fees for all entities that take water from the Kentucky River. Monies from withdrawal fees would be used to fund repairs of dams and support other KRA needs. Fees from as little as five cents to as much as $4.47/per month were proposed in a late 1992 study prepared by the Public Service Commission. Citizens in the Three Forks area cried foul, not relishing the idea of paying for dams that would basically benefit central Kentucky. "Taxation without representation," proclaimed the editor of the Citizen Voice & Times of Irvine. The city of Danville, drawing its water from Herrington Lake, fed by Dix River, a tributary of the Kentucky, also voiced its disapproval of paying fees.[17]

Danville challenged KRA in the courts as the fees went into effect: averaging about fourteen cents per household on the forks and tributaries and about twenty-two cents per household on the main river. (As of mid-1999, I was paying a small Kentucky River Authority Assessment ranging from twelve cents to thirty-five cents on my monthly water bill.) Another plan was worked out for power plants and distilleries taking water from the river. Meanwhile, the KRA organized by developing an annual budget, hiring staff, and establishing its headquarters in Frankfort. It continues to be one of the smallest of dozens of state agencies, depending on contracts for much of its work. In early 1996 the Court of Appeals ruled in favor of KRA over the Danville lawsuit. In a two-to-one decision, the court reversed a Boyle County ruling that fees were unconstitutional. The settling of the lawsuit now allowed KRA to proceed with installing release valves in some of the central Kentucky dams.[18]

New leadership came on board KRA in 1995 when Hugh Archer became the first permanent executive director. A former state director of the Kentucky chapter of the Nature Conservancy, Archer came to the authority after working with a company that advised governments and utilities on mapping systems. Work continued on repairing dams, and by late 1998, 5–14 had been repaired sufficiently for about twenty-five years of service. However, as Archer said in an August 1998 interview, "The lock is the weak link in maintaining the pool." The KRA appeared committed to refurbishing Locks 5–9, making it possible to boat as far as Boonesborough. Longtime lockman Earl Gulley Jr. stated in August 1998 that the locks were near collapse, "None are in good shape."[19]

Public accountability for the authority's work first became widespread in its 1995 annual report. Subcommittees on locks and dams, legal affairs, clean-up, parks, water quality, and finance reported progress on resolving the crises of the Kentucky River. The Department of Natural Resources created a Lock and Dam Section to oversee the repair of the locks and dams and operation of the locks. Proposed raising of dams on the Kentucky with crest gates and other long-term solutions to the perceived water problems of central Kentucky only increased debate into the late 1990s.[20]

In the late nineties the most controversial issue before KRA continued to be Harza Engineering Company's idea of constructing crest gates on the dams at 9, 10, 13, and 14 that could be raised and lowered by hydraulic cylinders, depending on the water needs of the moment. The idea became an alternative to building higher dams, either on the Kentucky or its tributaries, which would cost many millions of dollars more. Just when KRA would appear to be settled on policy, another idea would emerge. State geologist and KRA member Donald Haney proposed building a new 30 to 36 foot high dam near the present site of Lock 8 on the Jessamine-Garrard County line. At an estimated cost of $100 million, a 36-mile reservoir with vast recreational possibilities would be created. "I'm really adamant about my dam," Haney declared, "I preach on this all the time." Kentucky-American Water opposed the plan. Recreational boaters also opposed the higher dam, because a lock was not included in the plan, thereby terminating their access to the upper river. But the KRA opted for a simpler plan, building crest gates at 9, 10, 13 and 14, raising the river about 4 feet in each pool. As of the late 1990s, none of the gates had been added. Gates at 11 and 12 were never considered after river bottom farmers in Estill and Lee Counties complained that higher water levels would flood their fields, which had been protected by expensive drainage systems built with federal funds.[21]

In the midst of this controversy, Kentucky-American Water Company touted its claim that a pipeline to Louisville, first broached in

1993, could alleviate its problems of supplying its central Kentucky customers in dry times. The 55-mile pipeline would cost an estimated $48 million according to company president Robert Gallo. Permission from the Public Service Commission would be necessary to construct the pipeline and promised to touch political nerves at several levels. Opponents argued that the pipeline would only be needed for a drought every one hundred years or so. With a computerized system of monitoring everything from intake at the Kentucky River to distribution to its 250,000 customers, Kentucky-American represented a growing state-of-the-art system. Pipeline critic William H. Martin believed Kentucky-American desired "strictly to increase its customers" and maintained that the company really needed to increase its plant capacity. State Geologist Haney seconded opposition to the pipeline, claiming that in the end it would cost twice as much for Kentucky-American rate-payers than publicly estimated. Moreover, if federal and state monies could pay for water projects all over the state, why not for the citizens of eastern and central Kentucky? But even its critics admitted that Kentucky-American needed a steady supply of water.[22]

Amid charges of a "covert pipeline campaign" made by the *Lexington Herald-Leader*, Kentucky-American pushed its pipeline before the Public Service Commission. Nevertheless, at a packed PSC meeting some zealots wore "I Support the Pipeline" buttons, and Kentucky-American released a poll demonstrating that the Lexington-Fayette County public trusted them on this subject. Democratic Party officials and supporters split over the issue. While "political insider" Terry McBrayer worked to get public support for the pipeline, Attorney General Ben Chandler became a spokesman for those opposing the pipeline, claiming it would bring unwanted rapid growth to Woodford County. Other Woodford County residents promised to fight the pipeline, fearing that it would disrupt natural springs at their farms. When the PSC tentatively approved the pipeline, to be paid for with costs passed on to Kentucky-American rate-payers, the debate raged on. Letters for and against the pipeline often appeared in the *Lexington Herald-Leader*, which continued to question the company's motives. Opponents held rallies. In early 1999 Kentucky-American agreed to move the pipeline route away from Old Frankfort Pike at the behest of Lexington-Frankfort Scenic Corridor Incorporated.[23]

Reason seemed to be on the side of Kentucky-American. The municipal water company in Jefferson County had overbuilt its purification capacity and could easily supply central Kentucky. Moreover, even in time of great drought the Ohio River always had a steady flow of water. Kentucky-American "has argued altruistically," maintained Andy Mead, longtime Kentucky River watcher and reporter for the *Lexington Herald-Leader*, "that they are protecting their customers, but they will also become a much bigger company." Other critics like State Geologist Haney and former Commissioner of Natural Resources Martin are more blunt, viewing the pipeline as a simple power play by a big utility, in this case a subsidiary of American Water Works System. Environmentalists such as Tom Fitzgerald, director of the Kentucky Resources Council, believed that construction of the pipeline would remove a large constituency of Kentucky-American customers who now are at least cognizant of the Kentucky River's importance to their lives.[24]

By mid-1998, Executive Director Hugh Archer reported that the 42-inch relief, or "mining," valves inserted at Locks 11–14, would, in the short term, provide enough water for the Kentucky River Valley and all its patrons through the year 2020. There is always the unexpected. Vandalism soon occurred at Lock 13, where a fisherman broke through several locks and devices, opening the valve, fully aware that small fish would congregate there and draw larger ones. The isolated, unguarded site may have to be supplemented with security. The KRA continued plans for building the crest gates as a simple method of assuring a plentiful water supply even for the 100-year drought that some pundits predicted would occur sometime early in the twenty-first century. Kentucky-American Water Company promised not to give up on the dreams of a pipeline to the Ohio River.[25]

A flurry of activity characterized Archer's two and one-half years at KRA, where he developed a small but efficient staff. Overseeing the daily activities of the authority proved crucial during difficult times. From installing relief valves to reconstructing dams to planning water quality initiatives, Archer's vision coincided with the growing sense of the board that the Kentucky River Authority could be a springboard for such groups across the Commonwealth. "Helping turn things around in the mountains," he recalled in an interview, could be the greatest legacy of his leadership, as well as being a continuing quest for the Kentucky River Authority. Archer left the authority in mid-1998 to become Commissioner of Natural Resources as Dorman continued his longtime chairmanship.[26]

The political nature of the authority could not help but intrude in the choice of a new executive director. The late June 1998 appointment of Jack Hall, who acted as a major fund-raiser for Gov. Brereton Jones when he ran for lieutenant governor and for governor, touched a few political nerves. Some critics asked if Hall was being appointed so that he could not become a major player in the 1999 gubernatorial plans of Jones, in which Gov. Paul Patton intended to run for reelection. Questions regarding Hall's longtime association with Kentucky-American lobbyist Terry McBrayer also raised a few eyebrows. Dorman touted Hall's administrative experience at the University of Kentucky and other public positions. None of these scenarios had time for testing, because Hall died suddenly two days after his appointment. Three weeks later the board of KRA appointed Stephen Reeder from a list of eleven finalists.[27]

"This river could die," a 1970 *Courier-Journal* article warned, citing "ominous symptoms" in the Kentucky headwaters region. But the times are changing. Besides the fledgling Kentucky River Authority, the river has other friends, giving promise for much-needed support for clean water and rehabilitation of this valuable resource. From national groups such as American Rivers, a Washington lobbying organization that seeks wild rivers and lessening dependence on dams as part of its agenda, to local volunteers who participate in trash collections and water quality studies, there is hope that the corner had been turned in recovering the Kentucky. American Rivers publishes an annual "Ten Most Endangered Rivers" series. Fortunately, the Kentucky is not on that list, but Tennessee's namesake river is. The Sierra Club's Kentucky River Watershed Watch Program employs dozens of volunteers in an ongoing effort to test the waters of the river and its tributaries for pollutants. Although there has been progress in cleaning up America's rivers, streams like the Ohio will need rehabilitation well into the next century.[28]

There have already been major victories. The protection afforded the Kentucky River Palisades, that wondrous region between Boonesborough and Frankfort, is testimony to what public and private efforts can do to preserve something irreplaceable. The Kentucky Chapter of the Nature Conservancy completed a monumental 1979 study, *The Kentucky River Palisades*, documenting the flora and vegetation of the region. In 1997 the Conservancy published a 112-page book of pictures and text, *The Palisades of the Kentucky River*. In early 1998 the same group dedicated a 500-acre nature preserve, named for environmentalist Sally Brown, at one of a growing number of such sites along the Kentucky. Another avid defender of wild things, Mary Wharton of Lexington, longtime chair of the Department of Biology at Georgetown College, also championed such refuges, willing her special place on Jessamine Creek and the Kentucky River to future generations of Kentuckians.[29]

Kentucky River watchers must constantly be on guard. Periodic problems attest to the fragility of the Kentucky River watershed. There are past reports of many fish kills in the headwaters from "black water," the runoff of coal dust from underground and strip mines. Even rock dust, used in coal mines to "deaden coal dust," can cause a fish kill when mixed with water and pumped into a tributary of the Kentucky. Salt water or brine, a consequence of oil and gas exploration and exploitation, often finds its way into the Kentucky and its tributaries, disrupting ecosystems. Moreover, logging in Daniel Boone National Forest continues to pit making a living in an economically depressed area against environmentalists with legitimate concerns about the future of Appalachia. In the nineteenth century, railroads were notorious for dumping "spoil" into the Kentucky River as they built their way into the mountains. Now, construction companies building highways that supply the lifeblood for economic development often do the same.[30]

The North Fork of the Kentucky, where Letcher County's six thousand "straight pipes," a euphemism for dumping raw household sewage into the headwater's watershed, has created special problems. Often cited by the Kentucky Division of Water as containing high levels of coliform bacteria from fecal contamination, the 163-mile long North Fork from Beattyville to Whitesburg, has frequently been called off-limits for summertime swimming in the 1990s. In 1992 twenty-two small sewage plants failed to pass muster, with Troublesome Creek more than living up to its name and its storied past.[31]

Initiatives by U.S. Representative Hal Rogers, whose Fifth Congressional District includes the headwaters of the Kentucky, Cumberland, and Big Sandy Rivers, KRA, and other state and federal agencies, offer some hope for the headwaters of the Kentucky and the entire mountain region. The Division of Water has cracked down on the most obvious polluters, but has faced increasing problems where there is little in the way of local initiative and resources. With the help of several agencies, Letcher County has created a countywide water and sewage district, something unheard of in the supercharged atmosphere of mountain politics. KRA and the Division of Water have proposed many alternatives for headwaters sewage problems, including hooking on to existing sewage plants, using composting toilets in some areas, building septic systems, and even using wetland or marsh treatment at a small site at Blackey. Representative Rogers and Natural Resources Secretary James Bickford initiated "the Eastern Kentucky PRIDE, or Personal Responsibility in a Desirable Environment." The Corps of Engineers has even been pressed into service by Rogers with $10 million for sewage projects. Grants to homeowners for building septic systems is only one approach. For example, grants from the Abandoned Mine Land Fund can be used to complete water lines to communities if a case can be made that drinking water had been damaged by mining before 1982.[32]

If the struggle to improve water quality by cleaning up sewage is receiving much belated effort now, addressing the trash, or solid waste, problem in the Kentucky basin is just as crucial. In order for natural places to receive protection, not only must pollution be cleaned up, but public attitudes about trashing the environment must change. If there are hundreds of volunteers willing to get their feet wet and their hands dirty pulling trash during the annual Kentucky "River Sweep," there are many others who think not at all about dumping anything imaginable into the river and its tributaries. "Kentucky River ducks," a euphemism for plastic milk jugs, are only the most visible of the detritus—human, industrial, and commercial—that finds it way into Appalachian streams. The Kentucky River Authority supplements volunteer efforts with small grants to clean up steep banks along the upper Kentucky, but there is never enough money. Moreover, some county officials have begun to crack down on solid waste polluters. In the end, however, it will be a change of attitude that will spell the difference in a blighted environment, a sadly polluted one. Psychologist Robert Adams suggests using the "carrot" more so than the "stick" approach, with monetary rewards for cleaning up dump sites. People tend to keep piling on trash at dump sites dating back many years. Prompt removal discourages such behavior, as do fines. The problem is not just in the Kentucky River basin. It is so pervasive that the *Kentucky Journal*, published by the Kentucky Center for Public Issues, devoted much of a 1997 publication to this issue. As with other problems facing the Kentucky, there is hope, but only if a sustained effort is made well into the twenty-first century. Fitzgerald argued in 1998 that as the river is cleansed and more people use the river, more individuals will become Kentucky River advocates.[33]

If Kentucky River residents are to keep their focus on the river and its problems, what better way to encourage that emphasis than the creation of a Kentucky River Museum, or even a series of historic sites. Beginning in 1993, several agencies, including the Department of Parks, the Kentucky Heritage Council, and the Department of Tourism, began cooperating with the Kentucky River Authority in creating such sites along the river. KRA created the Kentucky River Historical Advisory Committee in 1993, inviting individuals from state government, counties and towns along the river, and private agencies. Historians and an anthropologist lent their expertise. (Having recently completed the "Living and Working on the Kentucky River Oral History Project," I also added my perspective.) Two projects—a Frankfort River Park and museum at Boonesborough—drew the immediate attention of the advisory committee, which varied in membership from a dozen or more. Several meetings were held where some members presented well-thought-out exhibit themes about what could and should be included in a river museum. Although one member proposed tearing down the two early twentieth century lockhouses at Boonesborough and replacing them with a modern structure, others, including Thomas D. Clark, accepted the historical significance of the original structures and the need to conserve them into the twenty-first century.[34]

In the offing was an $800,000 Intermodal Surface Transportation Efficiency Act, or ISTEA, grant from federal coffers to be matched with $200,000 from KRA for construction of a museum at Boonesborough. Argabrite Associates Architects of Louisville won the contract to plan for the "Museum of the Kentucky River," incorporating the two lockhouses at Boonesborough. Nathalie Taft Andrews, director of the Portland Museum in Louisville, prepared an elaborate "Preliminary Interpretative Plan" under contract to Argabrite. The plan included extensive renovation of the lockhouses as well as construction of a "new gateway building" that would serve as an introduction to the entire river experience at Lock and Dam Number 10. "The Orientation Center," another report from Argabrite stated, "would be a new structure designed of concrete, wood and glass that would echo the physical elements of the lock." Unfortunately, plans for opening the museum before the end of the administration of Gov. Brereton Jones or for the fall of 1996 never materialized.[35]

Someone in state government should have known that ISTEA grant money cannot be used for new construction and that there should never have been any planning for such a structure. Then, lead on the lockhouses and in the surrounding ground had to be removed before the Commonwealth of Kentucky would take possession of the property. Negotiations between the state and the Corps of Engineers "took forever and a day," recalled William H. Martin, Commissioner of Natural Resources from 1992 to 1998. Lead mitigation on the houses included an incongruous combination of modern science and old-fashioned know-how. Wearing "plastic suits and respirators," an observer recalled workers "took duct tape and pulled it off and put it in plastic bags." Jerry Lee Raisor, brought on as curator of the River Museum "too late" after plans had already been made, complained about the lack of evidence about interior design "because they didn't save anything." Therefore, Raisor has had little to go on to replicate such things as wallpaper for interior reconstruction. Moreover, Argabrite took an inordinate amount of time with final interior drawings. "We are dealing with the lowest bidder here" Raisor added, humorously, "and it's one of those unfortunate circumstances." The Kentucky River Museum at Lock 10 at Boonesborough has moved slowly. Apparently it will not be in full operation until well into the next millennium. Former Commissioner Martin perhaps best expressed the frustration of many of those who had input on the project: "There is ineptitude in it as well as incompetency."[36]

The Kentucky River View Park in Frankfort has been completed at a price of over $1 million, with opening ceremonies on 19 September 1997 highlighted by remarks from Tom Clark. The park has an open pavilion, walking trails and wayside exhibits, picnic and parking areas, a boat ramp, Benson Creek Bridge restoration, and native plants. It is being used by the people of the Commonwealth, but has not received much publicity.[37]

The debate over central Kentucky's water supply appears to have no end. A jam-packed Fayette County Water Supply Planning Council meeting on 4 March 1999 illustrated the adamant stands taken by protagonists. Pipeline, crest gates, conservation, or what? Far behind the rest of the state in developing a mandated water supply program, Fayette County struggled to meet a 15 July 1999 deadline. Meanwhile, Kentucky-American continued to push for a pipeline, using a $200,000 media campaign to push its cause, while Neighbors Opposing Pipeline Extravagance, or NOPE, voiced its disapproval. The *Lexington Herald-Leader* finally came out in opposition to the pipeline, one columnist even proposing that the county buy out Kentucky-American and arguing for a stronger Kentucky River Authority. On the other hand, the president and CEO of the Greater Lexington Chamber of Commerce sided with the water company's proposal. More people began to question the quality of the Ohio River water that would be pumped to central Kentucky through the proposed pipeline. Ironically, the Louisville Water Company now plans to build a number of deep wells on the Ohio's riverbanks in order to pull cleaner water into its purification plants.[38]

The debate over the pipeline and other possible solutions to the water problems of central Kentucky intensified into the summer of 1999. Then a drought hit most of Kentucky, with the central part of the state suffering the most. The Kentucky-American Water Company continued to tout their pipeline idea as the politics of water became nearly as heated as the often 100-degree weather. The Water Supply Planning Council recommended the pipeline to the Lexington-Fayette County Urban County Council, only to be rebuffed by the latter. Then the public debate shifted to a buyout of Kentucky-American by the council and development of a municipal operation.[39]

As the drought worsened, Roy V. Mundy II, president of Kentucky-American, citing a lack of "consensus," announced that his company would "put on hold" its request for the pipeline before the Public Service Commission. Foes of the pipeline applauded. The *Courier-Journal* and the *Lexington Herald-Leader* praised the company's restraint and the time afforded for more discussion about the future of water resources. No amount of words could bring much-needed rainfall. As central Kentucky, indeed all of the state entered the normally dry months of fall, water restrictions went into effect in many counties. Officially, the drought became severe. When water stopped flowing over Dams 8 and 9, upriver of water-thirsty Lexington, the Kentucky River Authority in consultation with the Kentucky Division of Water allowed valves to be opened for the first time in dams above the Kentucky-American water intake system near Clay's Ferry. It was estimated that by allowing more water to flow through the dams on the upper river a fifty-day cushion would be achieved. But would that be enough combined with conservation measures to get central Kentucky through the dry times? The worsening condition surpassed that of 1988, then a few days later became more severe than 1954. As Kentuckians faced the remainder of 1999 they feared a return of the terrible droughts of the Great Depression years.[40]

The crisis of the Kentucky River persists. Water, trash, pollution—the human dimension—have all combined with natural causes to stress the Kentucky beyond reasonable limits. The Kentucky River Authority and other state agencies have their jobs cut out for them in the twenty-first century. They must be public "watchdogs" in the fullest sense. Politicians must be held accountable and constantly reminded to keep them from forgetting the needs of the Kentucky River basin. In late 1997, the Kentucky River Watershed Protection Conference, sponsored by the Kentucky River Watershed Watch, highlighted the basin and its promise and perils. There must be more such conferences to keep the plight as well as the promise of the Kentucky River on the public agenda.

Whither the Kentucky River? It is in the hands of its people. Perhaps the best hope lies in the young people who are much better educated environmentally than their forebears, but all Kentuckians must do what we can to protect this valuable, irreplaceable resource. One modern Kentucky River watcher believes the river is neglected because "most people today only see the river with a sideways glance as they drive over it on a high speed bridge," if they notice it at all. They should pay better attention, and it is the duty of the media and all lovers of the Kentucky River to keep its fate before the public. The Kentucky River Authority has, so far, brought attention to the problems of the river as well as taking the first steps toward alleviating many of the problems, the crises, that the basin has faced for many years. However, it must walk a political tightrope, working quietly and persistently, but not antagonizing political and regional forces that could bring it down.[41]

Taking the geologist's long view in a 1945 publication, Willard Rouse Jillson perhaps best described the primal nature of the Kentucky, the timelessness, that we should not forget, "when man and his civilization, . . . has, like many another once dominant form of life on this earth, passed entirely away, the Kentucky river still governed by immutable geologic laws, again unappreciated and unknown, will continue to sweep on in its ever changing valley!"[42]

NOTES

1. THE KENTUCKY

1. Robert M. Rennick, "Place Names," *Kentucky Encyclopedia*, ed. John Kleber, 725–26; Henderson, "Dispelling the Myth," 1–4.

2. William E. Ellis, "Kentucky River," *Kentucky Encyclopedia*, ed. John Kleber, 510–11.

3. *Ibid.*

4. Wharton and Barbour, *Bluegrass*, 15.

5. *Lexington Herald*, 10 Jan. 1965.

6. Wharton and Barbour, *Bluegrass*, 15–17.

7. *Lexington Herald-Leader*, 4 Jul. 1997; Rick Gore, "The Most Ancient Americans," *National Geographic* 192 (Oct. 1997): 93–98; Sharp and Henderson, *Mute Stones Speak*, 3; for an imaginative interpretation of life among Native Americans, see Henderson, *Kentuckians before Boone*.

8. Sharp and Henderson, *Mute Stones Speak*, 3; Lewis, *Kentucky Archaeology*, 15–20. The latter book deals extensively with the Kentucky River region and is of inestimable value to anyone reading for greater depth in the archaeological heritage of the Commonwealth. Unknown to many Kentuckians, there is also a wealth of ancient Native American rock art, as described in Fred E. Coy Jr. et. al., *Rock Art in Kentucky* (Lexington: Univ. Press of Kentucky, 1997).

9. Charles E. Parrish, "Big Bones and Salt at the 'Watering Hole,'" *Falls City Engineer* (Jan.–Feb. 1992), 8; R. Berle Clay, "Prehistoric Peoples," *Kentucky Encyclopedia*, 734–36.

10. Clay, "Prehistoric Peoples," 734–36.

11. *Ibid.*

12. *Ibid.*

13. *Ibid.*; Nancy O'Malley interview, 29 Nov. 1988. All oral history interviews are housed in Special Collections and Archives, Eastern Kentucky University Library. For an excellent discussion of the Woodland, Adena, and other peoples see Lewis, *Kentucky Archaeology*, chapters 4 and 6.

14. Clay, "Prehistoric Peoples," 734–36; *Lexington Herald-Leader*, 31 Mar. 1997.

15. Kentucky River Locks and Dams, U.S. Army Engineer District Louisville pamphlet, n.d.; Robert W. Kingsolver, "Buffalo," *Kentucky Encyclopedia*, 138; J. Allen Singleton, "Highway Development," *Kentucky Encyclopedia*, 429–30.

16. Kentucky River Locks and Dams; see Clark, *Historic Maps*, no. 1, and pages 10, 25–26.

17. Johnson, *Falls City Engineers* (1974), 1–2; Baker, *Report*, 6–8.

18. James O. Luken, "Cane," *Kentucky Encyclopedia*, 159.

19. Harrison and Klotter, *New History*, 24–30; O'Malley interview.

20. Gerald Griffin, "It's a Water Highway Once Again," *Courier-Journal Magazine*, 5 Apr. 1953, 8–10.

21. Clark, *History of Kentucky*, 41–60; O'Malley interview.

22. *Lexington Herald-Leader*, 27 Dec. 1992.

23. Kramer, *Capital on the Kentucky*, 12–20.

24. *Lexington Herald*, 20 Nov. 1970; *Courier-Journal*, 30 Aug. 1953; Verhoeff, *Kentucky River Navigation*, 50–51.

25. Clark, *History of Kentucky*, 82; Verhoeff, *Kentucky River Navigation*, 58, 61; *Frankfort State Journal*, 12 Oct. 1965; Ulack, *Atlas of Kentucky*, 66. Thankfully, Wilkinson's shenanigans were for naught; see Harrison and Klotter, *New History*, 58–64, 85–86, for a description of Wilkinson's efforts to take Kentucky out of the Union and carve out his own kingdom.

26. *Frankfort State Journal*, 12 Oct. 1965; Verhoeff, *Kentucky River Navigation*, 70; Enclosure from Charles E. Parrish, Corps of Engineers historian, 28 Oct. 1987; Gail King, "Flatboats," 324, and "Keelboats," 483–84, *Kentucky Encyclopedia*; Alan L. Bates interview, 30 Aug. 1988; Ulack, *Atlas of Kentucky*, 66. See Neal O. Hammon, "Research Note: Is the Spelling of Dix River a Little Lite?," *Filson Club History Quarterly* 72 (Oct. 1998), 419–22, for an interesting story on the changing of the name from Dick's to Dix River.

27. Mathew Carey, "Some Notices of Kentucky, Particularly of Its Chief Town, Lexington," 23 Aug. 1828, Mathew Carey, MSS, The Filson Club, Louisville, Kentucky; *Frankfort State Journal*, 15 Oct. 1965; Clark, *The Kentucky*, 324–25, 337.

28. Clark and Ham, *Pleasant Hill* 7–9; Susan Matarese and James C. Thomas, "Shaker Communities," *Kentucky Encyclopedia*, 810–13.

29. Clark and Ham, *Pleasant Hill*, 10–11, 27; F. W. Kephart interview, 21 Jan. 1988.

30. Clark and Ham, *Pleasant Hill*, 35.

31. *Ibid.*, 60–61, 76–77; Kephart interview; William E. Ellis, "High Bridge," *Kentucky Encyclopedia*, 428–29.

32. Parrish enclosure; Leland R. Johnson, *Falls City Engineers*, 1984, 242; Verhoeff, *Kentucky River Navigation*, 20; Kramer, *Capital on the Kentucky*, 50.

33. Parrish enclosure; Verhoeff, *Kentucky River Navigation*, 21.

34. "Edward West," *Kentucky Encyclopedia*, 941; Louis C. Hunter, *Steamboats*, 36–38; Verhoeff, *Kentucky River Navigation*, 95–96, 109; Bates interview; Dixie Hibbs, "John Fitch," *Kentucky Encyclopedia*, 322; John B. Briley and Leonard P. Curry, "Steamboats," *Kentucky Encyclopedia*, 852–53.

35. Johnson, *Falls City Engineers*, 1974, 147; *Frankfort State Journal*, 14 Oct. 1965; Verhoeff, *Kentucky River Navigation*, 96; Bates interview. For a wonderful description of the construction of steamboats, complete with diagrams, see Alan L. Bates, *The Western Waters Steamboat Cyclopoedium* (Leonia, New Jersey: Hustle Press, 1968).

36. "1829 Surveys of the Kentucky River," Inland Rivers Library, Hamilton County Public Library, Cincinnati; Verhoeff, *Kentucky River Navigation*, 24–26, 100; Johnson, *Falls City Engineers*, 1984, 244.

37. *Frankfort State Journal*, 14 Oct. 1965; John Owen Suter Collection, University of Kentucky Library, Special Collections; Bates interview.

38. Hunter, *Steamboats*, 523; Suter Collection.

39. Kramer, *Capital on the Kentucky*, 193–94; Suter Collection; *Frankfort State Journal*, 14 Oct. 1965; *Kentucky Ancestors*, 28 (Summer 1992), 2; Parrish and Johnson, "J. Stoddard Johnston . . . ," *Filson Club History Quarterly*, 72 (Jan. 1998), 8.

40. Johnson, *Falls City Engineers*, 1984, 244; R.P. Baker, *Report*, 23 Feb. 1836; Harrison and Klotter, *New History*, 113–15, 447.

41. Baker, *Report*, 1836, 3, 12–15, 23, 35–39, 42–46.

42. Johnson, *Falls City Engineers*, 1984, 245–47.

43. *Ibid.*, 248–49; Verhoeff, *Kentucky River Navigation*, 214–15.

44. Johnson, *Falls City Engineers*, 1984, 248–50; Suter Collection; *Frankfort State Journal*, 14 Oct. 1965; Record of Tolls, 90 SC28, #523, Steamboat Bills of Lading, 92 SC66, #900, Kentucky Historical Society, Manuscripts.

45. Johnson, *Falls City Engineers*, 1984, 248–49; Verhoeff, *Kentucky River Navigation*, 30–33.

46. *Frankfort State Journal*, 17 Oct. 1965.

47. *Ibid.*; Kramer, *Capital on the Kentucky*, 199–200; Bates interview.

48. Frankfort *Tri-Weekly Commonwealth*, 10 Nov. 1862; *Knoxville Sentinel*, 17 Dec. 1919; Verhoeff, *Kentucky River Navigation*, 148–150; Thomas D. Clark and Tom Pack, "Salt Making," *Kentucky Encyclopedia*, 793–94.

49. Verhoeff, *Kentucky River Navigation*, 157–64; J. Winston Coleman Jr., *Historic Kentucky*, 30; Michael Hudson and Charles D. Howes, "Iron Industry," *Kentucky Encyclopedia*, 455–57; Nancye J. Kirk, *Travels Through Kentucky History* (Louisville: Data Courier, Inc., 1976), 86–87.

50. *Frankfort State Journal*, 13, 17 Oct. 1965, 18 May 1969; *Courier-Journal*, 28 Sept. 1941.

51. *Frankfort State Journal*, 13 Oct. 1965, 1 Jul. 1975, 10 Jan. 1971, 26 Oct. 1981; Louis A. Stivers interview, 7 Dec. 1992.

52. *Courier-Journal*, 28 Sept. 1941; Burt and Babb Lumber Company Papers, University of Kentucky Library, Special Collections.

53. Hunter, *Steamboats*, 192; Verhoeff, *Kentucky River Navigation*, 33–34; Johnson, *Falls City Engineers*, 1984, note 279; *Report*, 1879, Part II, 1398–1437.

54. *Report*, 1879, Part II, 1399–1410; Johnson, *Falls City Engineers*, 1984, 251; "Josiah Stoddard Johnston, Sr.," *Kentucky Encyclopedia*, 478.

55. *Report*, 1880, Part II, 1825–1827; Johnson, *Falls City Engineers*, 1984, 251–54; Parrish and Johnson, "J. Stoddard Johnston . . . ," 3–23.

56. Suter Collection; *Report*, 1886, Part III, 1604, 1614–16; J. Stoddard Johnston and Basil W. Duke, *Transportation Systems together with a Review of Transportation Problems and Opportunities to be Solved, Part II* (Frankfort: Capital Printing Company, 1887), 51–65; Verhoeff, *Kentucky River Navigation*, 35–36.

57. *Report*, 1886, 1604–05; Verhoeff, *Kentucky River Navigation*, 36–38; Parrish and Johnson, "Engineering the Kentucky . . . ," 380–89.

58. Johnson, *Falls City Engineers*, 1974, 149; C.W. Kutz, "Advances made in the study and construction of dams and in the deposition of the apparatus of the intake of water and of the adjoining navigation works," 1926, Southeast Archives, Atlanta, Georgia, Corps of Engineers, Maintenance File, Box 7; *Engineering Construction: Canalization*, Vol. I (Fort Belvoir, Virginia: The Engineer School, 1940), 10, 25, 27. Ironically, beartrap type structures have been used on the Ohio River quite successfully toward the end of the twentieth century. Janiece French, "A Tribute to our folks at Smithland, 52, 53, and Olmstead locks and dams," *Falls City Engineer*, 19 (Dec. 1994/Jan. 1995), 10–11.

59. Johnson, *Falls City Engineers*, 1974, 149; Parrish and Johnson, "Engineering the Kentucky . . . ," 385–89; *Report*, 1887, Part II, 1873–85; *Ibid.*, 1888, 1770–71; *Ibid.*, 1889, 1971; *Ibid.*, 1890, 2262–64.

Although boosters wanted a system of twelve locks and dams constructed on the Big Sandy River in far eastern Kentucky, railroads soon tapped the coalfields in the

1880s. Carol Crowe-Carraco, *The Big Sandy Valley* (Lexington: The Univ. Press of Kentucky, 1979), 54–55.

60. William E. Ellis, "Tenement House Reform: Another Episode in Kentucky Progressivism," *Filson Club History Quarterly*, 55 (October 1981), 375–82.

61. Johnson, *Falls City Engineers*, 1984, 257–78; Verhoeff, *Kentucky River Navigation*, 36; *Report*, 1902, Part III, 1959; 1905, Part II, 1919–20.

62. *Report*, 1906, Part I, 492; *Ibid.*, 1906, Part I, 542; *Ibid.*, 1907, Part II, 1786; *Ibid.*, 1908, Part II,1853–54; *Ibid.*, 1909, Part I, 643; *Ibid.*, 1910, Part I, 718.

63. Verhoeff, *Kentucky River Navigation*, 120–21; *Report*, 1910, Part II, 1996, 2008; *Ibid.*, 1911, Part I, 771; *Ibid.*, 1916, Part I, 1266–67; Johnson, *Falls City Engineers*, 1984, 270–71.

64. *Report*, 1917, Part I, 1311–14.

65. Smither family papers; Suter Collection; Bates interview.

66. Smither family papers; Suter Collection; Young E. Allison, "The City of Louisville and a Glimpse of Kentucky," pamphlet, (Committee on Industrial and Commercial Improvement of the Louisville Board of Trade, 1887), 32–38.

67. Smither family papers; Suter Collection.

68. *Courier-Journal*, 23 Apr. 1927; Coleman, *Historic Kentucky*, 8, 113; See also Jillson Collection, Berea College; Robert W. Rowe interview, 18 Dec. 1987; Sallie F. Fullen interview 6 Jun. 1990.

69. *Ibid.*, 27; *Frankfort State Journal*, 1 Jul. 1975; Suter Collection; Smither family papers; "Estill Springs Resort, Irvine, Estill County, 1894," *Kentucky Ancestors*, V32–3, 1997, 149; "Estill Springs," *Kentucky Encyclopedia*, 299.

70. Suter Collection; Smither family papers.

71. *Frankfort State Journal*, 22 Dec. 1975; Verhoeff, *Kentucky River Navigation*, 199; *Courier-Journal*, 14–17 Feb. 1905; *Report*, 1918, Part I, 1355, Part II, 3067; Harrison and Klotter, *New History of Kentucky*, 290.

72. Verhoeff, *Kentucky River Navigation*, 129, 192–93, 205–06.

73. *Courier-Journal*, 6–7 Jul. 1939; *The Lexington Herald*, 6 July 1939; *The Jackson Times*, 9 Jul. 1992; Clark, *The Kentucky*, 18; Dorothy Spencer interview, 21 Aug. 1992.

74. *Courier-Journal*, 22–24 Jan., 7 Feb. 1957; Johnson, *Falls City Engineers*, 1974, 264; Johnson, *Falls City Engineers*, 1984, 98–99; "Flood of 1937," *Kentucky Encyclopedia*, 327–28.

75. *Courier-Journal*, 11, 13 Sept., 13 Oct. 1925, 29 Jan. 1926; Johnson, *Falls City Engineers*, 1984, 95–98; Colonel Roger G. Powell, "Exhibits Accompanying Report on Kentucky River," 1 Jul. 1931, Corps of Engineers Files, Southeast Archives.

76. Verhoeff, *Kentucky River Navigation*, 115; *Kentucky Geological Survey*, Series 4, 1913, Vol. 1, 63; *Courier-Journal*, 17 Feb., 5 Apr. 1953.

77. Coleman, *Historic Kentucky*, 153; *Courier-Journal*, 21 Feb. 1926; Wendell Berry interview, 28 June 1987; Kramer, *Capital on the Kentucky*, 234–36; Ellis "High Bridge," *Kentucky Encyclopedia*, 428–29.

78. *Courier-Journal*, 18 Nov. 1928, 18 May, 20–22 June, 7, 14–16 Jul., 28 Dec. 1951, 4 Mar., 16 Apr. 1952, 23 Apr., 8 Aug., 11, 29 Dec. 1953; Verhoeff, *Kentucky River Navigation*, 112, 117, 205–06.

79. Todd Hornback, "District to transfer ownership of Kentucky River locks and dams 5 through 14 after repairs are completed," *Falls City Engineer*, 18 (Jul./Aug. 1993), 3; *Lexington Herald-Leader*, 5 Dec. 1988, 27 Nov. 1996; *Kentucky River Authority*, 1995, 1–20;

80. William E. Ellis, H.E. Everman, and Richard Sears, *Madison County: 200*

Years in Retrospect (Richmond: The Madison County Historical Society, 1985), 311–12; *Courier-Journal,* 11 Aug. 1939, 29 Aug., 4 Dec.1965, 28 June 1970; *Lexington Herald-Leader,* 9 Jan. 1994; Eric Howard Christianson, "Kentucky-American Water Company," *Kentucky Encyclopedia,* 490.

81. *Courier-Journal,* 18 Dec. 1927,19 Apr. 1963; Gene D. Tindall interview, 14 May 1990.

82. *Courier-Journal,* 29 Jan. 1928.

2. FOLDS, FAULTS, AND UPLIFTS

1. *Random House Encyclopedia, Third Edition* (New York: Random House, 1990), 246.
2. Ulack, *Atlas,* 18–20; *Random House Encyclopedia,* 247–49.
3. McFarlan, *Geology,* 152–53; W.C. MacQuown interview, 19 Jan. 1988; Jillson Collection, Berea College, Box 43, File 1; Garland R. Dever Jr., "Geology," *Kentucky Encyclopedia,* 371; *Lexington Herald-Leader,* 26 Apr. 1998; "Sandstone Secrets: Quartz Pebbles Reveal Ancient River System in Appalachia," *Odyssey: The Magazine of University of Kentucky Research and Graduate Studies,* XV (Spring 1998), 17–20.
4. *Lexington Herald-Leader,* 18 Jul. 1993; Greb, *Guide,* 6–7; Frank R. Ettensohn, "Fossils," *Kentucky Encyclopedia,* 348–49.
5. Greb, *Guide,* 12.
6. *Ibid.,* 21; Preston McGrain, *Geologic Story,* 6.
7. Greb, *Guide,* 30.
8. *Ibid.,* 31–35.
9. McGrain, *Geologic Story,* 12–13; Greb, *Guide,* 2; Dever, "Geology," 370.
10. McGrain, *Geologic Story,* 12–13, 32; William A. Withington, "Knobs," *Kentucky Encyclopedia,* 521–22.
11. Wharton and Barbour, *Bluegrass,* 15–16; Jillson, *Kentucky River,* 10; Mary E. Wharton interview, 14 Jan. 1988; Ivan L. Zabilka, "Willard Rouse Jillson," *Kentucky Encyclopedia,* 471; Dever, "Geology," 369–71.
12. James T. Teller, "Preglacial (Teays) and Early Glacial Drainage . . . ," 3677.
13. W.C. Swadley, "The Preglacial Kentucky River of Northern Kentucky," *Geological Survey Research,* (1971), D127–D131; Jillson, *Geology,* 95–97; Eugene J. Amaral, "Glaciers," *Kentucky Encyclopedia,* 376; Garland R. Dever Jr. interview, 1 Mar. 1988.
14. Jillson, *Kentucky River,* 13–15; *Random House Encyclopedia,* 250–51; Dever, "Geology," 369; Dever interview; Ulack, *Atlas,* 20.
15. Dever interview; Lexington *Sunday Herald-Leader,* 10 Jan. 1965; McFarlan, *Geology,* 145–49; *Lexington Herald-Leader,* 25 Feb. 1998; Jillson, *Kentucky River,* 26–28; Dever, "Geology," 371; personal interview with E.B. Estes, 19 Aug. 1998; Donald C. Haney interview, 27 Aug. 1998; Ulack, *Atlas,* 38–39; "Clay's Ferry Bridge," *Kentucky Encyclopedia,* 205–06.
16. Jillson, *Kentucky River,* 21–30.
17. *Ibid.,* 39–40; Jillson, *Geology,* 47; *Ibid., Elkhorn Abandoned Channel of the Kentucky River* (Frankfort: Roberts Printing 1944), 5–15; *Ibid., Nonesuch Abandoned Channel of the Kentucky River* (Frankfort: Roberts Printing 1946), 5–12; *Ibid., Hickman Abandoned Channel of the Kentucky River* (Frankfort: Roberts Printing 1948), 5–13; *Ibid., Geology,* 47; John L. Donaldson interview, 10 Nov. 1986; Ed Land Jr. interview, 1 Aug. 1988.
18. Verhoeff, *Kentucky River Navigation,* 78; Jillson, *Kentucky River,* 41–45; *Frankfort State Journal,* 10 Oct. 1965.

19. William H. Martin, *Kentucky River Palisades*, passim; William S. Bryant interview, 7 Jul. 1988; J. Dan Pittillo interview, 30 Sept. 1988.

20. Emil Napier interview, 24 Mar. 1988; Jillson, *Kentucky River*, 6; Verhoeff, *Kentucky River Navigation*, 213; Jillson Collection, Photo; *Report*, 1879, Part II, 1404, 1413; *Kentucky Atlas and Gazetteer* (DeLorme, 1997), 54, 55, 70, 71.

21. Homer D. Allen interview, 9 Mar. 1990; Samuel W. Thomas, *Dawn Comes*, 109; *Report*, 1879 Part II, 1413-15; Napier interview; Ulack, *Atlas*, 144-45.

22. *Kentucky River Navigation Charts*, Charts 34-37C; Benny Powell interview, 15 Dec. 1987; McFarlan, *Geology*, 170-72; Wharton and Barbour, *Bluegrass*, 7-8; Keith Allen interview, 22 Jul. 1988.

23. *Kentucky River Navigation Charts*, Charts 24-27; McFarlan, *Geology*, 172-74; Ulack, *Atlas*, 21.

24. *Kentucky River Navigation Charts*, 21-23; McFarlan, *Geology*, 172-76; Enclosure from W.C. MacQuown, 12; "Fishing & Boating Chart of the Kentucky River and Surrounding Facilities, Chart No. 1, From Valley View to Irvine," Angler Graphics, Lexington, Kentucky, 1991.

25. *Kentucky River Navigation Charts*, 17-20; Jillson Collection, Boxes 15, 25; MacQuown interview and enclosure; Jones and Taylor, *Palisades of the Kentucky River*, 7, 59.

26. McFarlan, *Geology*, 167-74; *Kentucky River Navigation Charts*, 8-15; MacQuown interview; Kramer, *Capital on the Kentucky*, 345, 348; Keith Allen interview.

27. *Kentucky River Navigation Charts*, 1-7; Powell interview; Willie C. Hawkins interview, 3 Jul. 1991; Robert M. Rennick, *Kentucky Place Names* (Lexington: Univ. Press of Kentucky, 1984), 201, 230.

28. Jones and Taylor, *Palisades of the Kentucky River*, 52; *Kentucky River Navigation Charts*, 1-37C; Powell interview; Bates interview; *Report*, 1920, Part II, 2758.

29. McGrain, *Geologic Story*, 52-53; Wharton and Barbour, *Bluegrass*, 16-18; "Georgetown," *Kentucky Encyclopedia*, 317; Ulack, *Atlas*, 23-24; *Lexington Herald-Leader*, 9 May 1998.

30. MacQuown interview and enclosure, 6-10; Dever interview; J.C. Dykes Jr. interview, 29 June 1989; Keith Allen interview; "Bybee Pottery," *Kentucky Encyclopedia*, 147.

31. Jillson Collection, Box 33; Dever interview; MacQuown interview and enclosure, 8-9; Joe Nickell, "Swift's Silver Mines," *Kentucky Encyclopedia*, 863-64.

32. MacQuown interview and enclosure, 9-10; Dever interview; Jillson Collection, Boxes 15 and 25; McFarlan, *Geology*, 387-91.

33. MacQuown enclosure, 8; Jillson Collection, Boxes 15 and 25; Preston McGrain, "Fluorspar," *Kentucky Encyclopedia*, 331-32; McFarlan, *Geology*, 387.

34. Dever interview; McFarlan, *Geology*, 388-89; MacQuown interview and enclosure, 7-8; Jillson, *Geology*, 129-42; Ruby Stewart interview, 26 Jul. 1990.

35. Ulack, *Atlas*, 20; Dennis L. Spetz, "Geography," *Kentucky Encyclopedia*, 367-69.

3. RIDING THE TIDE

1. Harrison and Klotter, *New History* 300-301.

2. Clark, *Kentucky*, 331-33; Thomas D. Clark interview, 26 May 1987.

3. Mary Verhoeff, *Kentucky River Navigation*, 167, 172-73; *Frankfort State Journal*, 10 Jan. 1971; Harry M. Caudill, "John Caldwell Calhoun Mayo," *Kentucky Encyclopedia*, 620-21.

4. Ben H. Robinson interview, 25 June 1989; Everett Byrd interview, 6 June

1989; Harrison and Klotter, *New History*, 300; Arnold Hurd interview, 28 Jun. 1989; Ernest Robinson interview, 16 Feb. 1989; Steven A. Schulman, "Rafting Logs . . . ," 24; Willis H. Wagner and Clois E. Kicklighter, *Modern Woodworking: Tools, Materials, and Processes* (South Holland, Illinois: Goodheart–Willcox, 1986), 4.

5. Byrd interview; Ernest Robinson interview; Ike Short interview, 10 Sept. 1987.

6. Picture in *The Bulletin*, Kentucky Historical Society, 15 (Feb. 1989), 6; Verhoeff, *Kentucky River Navigation*, 214; *Report*, 1907, Part II, 1796; 1905, Part I, 492, Part II, 1920; *Ibid.*, 1913, Part I, 1034–37; Byrd interview; Gary P. Garrison interview, 17 Jul. 1989.

7. Homer D. Allen interview, 9 Mar. 1990; Billy Robinson, Manuscript on rafting, possession of Ernest Robinson, Oneida, Ken.

8. Homer D. Allen interview; Homer D. Allen to the author, 27 Feb. 1990.

9. Robinson Ms; Short interview; Nevyle Shackelford interview, 22 Feb. 1988; Herbert C. Marcum interview, 20 Jun. 1989.

10. Pole Road Article, Kentucky Historical Society; Verhoeff, *Kentucky River Navigation*, 198; Herbert Marcum interview; Short interview; Sam Wilson interview, 24 Mar. 1988.

11. Samuel W. Thomas, *Dawn Comes*, 108; Verhoeff, *Kentucky River Navigation*, 191–92; Drawing of Log Boom by Robert Wilson Rowe, Frankfort, Kentucky; Tom R. Walters, "Logging By Splash Dam," *Appalachian Heritage*, 5 (Winter 1977), 28–34.

12. Schulman, "Rafting Logs . . . ,"19; Verhoeff, *Kentucky River Navigation*, 192; John W. Irvin interview, 19 Aug. 1989; Robinson Ms; Byrd interview; Ed Combs interview, 4 Nov. 1991; Robert Wilson Rowe interview, 18 Dec. 1987.

13. Clark, *Kentucky*, 331–48; Clark interview.

14. Edward Campbell interview, 7 Jul. 1989; Hurd interview; Napier interview, 24 Mar. 1988; Sam Wilson interview.

15. Schulman, "Rafting Logs . . . ," 16–17; Robinson Ms.; Ernest Robinson interview; Charles Edwin Hopkins manuscript, Kentucky Historical Society, 3; Byrd interview; Ed Combs interview.

16. Verhoeff, *Kentucky River Navigation*, 184–85; Robinson Ms.; Ernest Robinson interview; Homer D. Allen interview; Herbert Marcum interview; Thomas A. Combs interview, 5 Mar. 1987.

17. Robinson Ms.; Homer D. Allen interview; Ernest Robinson interview; Herbert Marcum interview.

18. Robert Callahan interview, 13 May 1989; *Courier-Journal*, 10 Aug. 1981.

19. Ed Combs interview; Robinson Ms.; *Frankfort State Journal*, 17 Oct. 1965.

20. Thomas, *Dawn Comes, 109*.

21. Ed Combs interview; Schulman, "Rafting Logs . . . ," 21.

22. Robinson Ms.; J. Gordon Combs interview, 5 Mar. 1987.

23. J. Gordon Combs interview; Thomas A. Combs interview.

24. Robinson Ms.; Schulman, "Rafting Logs . . . ," 21–22; J. Gordon Combs interview; Shackelford interview; Verhoeff, *Kentucky River Navigation*, 192; Vernon Alcorn interview, 8 Aug. 1988.

25. Logan Adams interview, 29 Mar. 1991; S.B. and Mary Kelley interview, 9 Sept. 1988; J. Gordon Combs interview; Ida Dell Mackey interview, 25 Mar. 1991; Bessie Martin Perkins interview, 10 Jul. 1988; Byrd interview.

26. Harrison Broce interview, 26 Jul. 1989; W.M. Fint interviews, 16 Sept. 1988, 11 Aug. 1989; Avery Imel interview, 23 June 1990.

27. Ed Combs interview; Short interview; Walker Wilson interview, 21 June 1989; J.W.F. Williams, "The Peavine, On the Kentucky River," *Lee County Historical and Genealogical Society Newsletter*, (Oct.-Dec. 1992), n.p.; Myrtle Hoskins Ware to the author, 27 Feb. 1990; Maggie Wolfinbarger interview, 2 June 1989; Shackelford interview.

28. J.N. Sewall interview, 13 June 1988; Thomas D. Clark, "The Kentucky River in a Turbulent Tide," *Courier-Journal Magazine*, 28 Sept. 1941, 1–2; Alcorn interview.

29. Hopkins Ms.; Joe Helton interview, 27 Jul. 1988.

30. Irvin interview; Preston Johnson interview, 2 Aug. 1989; Hargiss McQueen interview, 12 Sept. 1988; Schulman, "Rafting Logs . . . ,"15.

31. Schulman, "Rafting Logs . . . ," 15; Marvin Hawkins interview, 30 Jun. 1989; Wolfinbarger interview; Thomas Combs interview; Alcorn interview.

32. Clark, *Kentucky*, 345; Carl E. Kramer, *Capital on the Kentucky*, 179, 337, 365–67.

33. *Twenty-Five Kentucky Folk Ballads*, Vol. I (Lexington: Transylvania Printing Company, 1936), 5, 12, 16–17; Charles E. Parrish, "Looking Backward," *Falls City Engineer*, (Apr.-May, 1990), 10.

34. John Fox Jr., *The Little Shepherd*, 54–83; Wade Hall, "John Fox Jr.," *Kentucky Encyclopedia*, 351–52.

35. Robert Cogswell, "Tie Hacking," 17–19; Verhoeff, *Kentucky River Navigation*, 193–94; Homer D. Allen interview; Ed Combs interview.

36. Herbert Marcum interview; Verhoeff, *Kentucky River Navigation*, 197–98; Ed Combs interview.

37. Chester Finney interview, 5 Aug. 1988; Ralph E. McClanahan, *Kentucky's Miniature Nile*, 7–10; Rena Niles, "Salvaging the Logs of Long Lost Rafts," *Courier-Journal Magazine*, 25 Feb. 1940, 13; Hugh Reece interview, 1 June 1989; Hawkins interview.

38. Garrison interview; Clark interview; Louis A. Stivers interview, 7 Dec. 1992.

39. *Report*, 1887, Part III, 1894; *Ibid.*, 1896, Part I, 297; *Ibid.*, 1904, Part II, 2650; *Ibid.*, 1905, Part I, 492, Part II, 1920; *Ibid.*, 1916, Part III, 2920; *Ibid.*, 1918, Part II, 3066–67; *Ibid.*, 1940, Part II, 874; Verhoeff, *Kentucky River Navigation*, 199; Bill Broadus interview, 6 May 1989.

40. Verhoeff, *Kentucky River Navigation*, 192; *Valley View Argent*, n.d., Eastern Kentucky University, Special Collections.

41. *Frankfort State Journal*, 17 Oct. 1965, 1 Jul. 1975; Verhoeff, *Kentucky River Navigation*, 199–200; Rowe interview; *Report*, 1899, Part III, 2533; *Valley View Argent*.

42. Alcorn interview; Rowe interview.

43. J.B. Thomas to W.H. Beckner, 9 Aug. 1894, University of Kentucky Special Collections; Burt and Babb Papers, University of Kentucky Special Collections; *Report*, 1913, Part I, 1035–36.

44. *Courier-Journal*, 14–16 Feb. 1905; *Louisville Evening Post*, 14 Mar. 1905; Broadus interview; James Hubert Tuttle interview, 18 Jun. 1990.

45. Harrison and Klotter, *New History*, 301; Charles Hays, "Breathitt County," *Kentucky Encyclopedia*, 116; Verhoeff, *Kentucky River Navigation*, 188–90; *Report*, 1902, Part I, 589; Nevyle Shackelford, *Robinson Substation: A Short History* (Lexington: U.K. College of Agriculture), 5–12.

46. Reece Interview; E.C. Park, "History of Irvine and Estill County," ca. 1900, n.p.; *Irvine Citizen Voice & Times*, 18 June 1981; *Irvine Times-Herald*, 25 Sept. 1975; Margaret Stevens Embry to the author, 6 Mar. 1990.

47. Helen Stevens Witt interview, 20 June 1990; Reece interview; Charles W. Stevens interview, 27 June 1990; Margaret Lee Embry interview, 6 Jul. 1990.

48. Hawkins interview; Claude Horn interview, 11 June 1987; Witt interview; Stevens interview.

49. Tuttle interview; Stevens interview; Reece interview.

50. Stevens interview; Witt interview; Embry interview.

51. Harrison and Klotter, *New History*, 301.

4. HARNESSING THE RIVER

1. J. Allen Singleton, "Ferries," *Kentucky Encyclopedia*, 314; Transfer of Ferry, 13 Oct. 1800, 90 SC08, #455, Kentucky Historical Society, Manuscripts.

2. *Ibid.*; Broce interview; *Report*, 1906, Part II, 1656; RA912.7693qv58 Microfilm, Southeast Archives, Atlanta, Georgia.

3. Dorothy White interview, 20 Aug. 1989; Sherman Estes interview, 27 June 1989; Zelphia Denham Kearns interview, 15 Sept. 1989; Walker Covington interview, 13 Aug. 1989; John S. Parks interview, 13 Aug. 1989; Marvin Wall interview, 14 Aug. 1989; Preston Johnson interview.

4. *Courier-Journal*, 11 Sept. 1925, 30 Aug. 1953; Maurice D. Flynn interview, 14 June 1990; *Lexington Herald-Leader*, 28 May 1993, 24 Apr. 1994; *Richmond Register*, 3, 12 Jul. 1993, 28 Mar. 1999.

5. *Courier-Journal*, 2 Aug. 1925, 30 Aug. 1953; *Richmond Register*, 1 Jul. 1988, 8 June 1996, 29 Mar. 1998; *Lexington Herald*, 20 Nov. 1970; *Lexington Herald-Leader*, 20 Apr. 1989, 3 Oct. 1990, 28 Jul. 1991, 17 Jan. 1996, 7 Mar. 1998; Claude Howard interview, 7 Jul. 1988.

6. Land interview.

7. *Ibid.*

8. *Ibid.*

9. *Ibid.*

10. *Ibid.*

11. *Ibid.*

12. *Ibid.*

13. Howard interview.

14. Johnson interview; "Information Guide and Map to the Valley View Ferry," Richmond Tourism and Main Street Development, n.d., n.p.

15. *Kentucky River Navigation Charts*, Charts 1–37.

16. Wendell C. Thomas, "Covered Bridges," *Kentucky Encyclopedia*, 235–36; L. Martin Perry, "Louis Wernwag," *Kentucky Encyclopedia*, 941; Correspondence, 86 SC43, #1045, Kentucky Historical Society, Manuscripts; *Courier-Journal*, 14 Dec. 1925, 21 Feb., 1 Mar. 1926; *Lexington Herald-Leader*, 4 Sept. 1997; Coleman, *Historic Kentucky*, 153.

17. *Courier-Journal*, 14 Dec. 1924; Coleman, *Historic Kentucky*, 104.

18. *Courier-Journal*, 6 Dec. 1928, 29 Jul. 1943, 25 Mar. 1945, 3 Jan., 17 Feb. 1952; "J. Lyter Donaldson," *Kentucky Encyclopedia*, 268–69; *Richmond Register*, 8 Dec. 1995, 7 Apr. 1998.

19. Tuttle interview; Witt interview; J. Allen Singleton, "Highway Development," *Kentucky Encyclopedia*, 429–30; *Lexington Herald*, 28 Nov. 1939.

20. *Frankfort State Journal*, 16 May, 15 Oct. 1965; "Kentucky River View Park," Frankfort pamphlet, n.d., n.p.; Kramer, *Capital on the Kentucky*, 132, 219, 234–36.

21. *Courier-Journal,* 9 Feb. 1928, 1 Sept., 10, 16 Nov. 1935, 21 Oct. 1965; *Frankfort State Journal,* 21 Oct. 1965; Kramer, *Capital on the Kentucky,* 336–37.

22. *Kentucky River Navigation Charts,* Chart Number 17; William E. Ellis, "High Bridge," *Kentucky Encyclopedia,* 428–29.

23. Ellis, "High Bridge," 428–29; Smith, *Nomination for Designation,* n.p.; Eddie B. Smith interview, 20 Jul. 1988; Howard Curry interview, 21 Jul. 1987; Paul A. Tenkotte, "Roebling Suspension Bridge," *Kentucky Encyclopedia,* 779–80.

24. Ellis, "High Bridge," 428–29.

25. Harrison and Klotter, *New History,* 246–48; Steven A. Channing, *Kentucky: A History,* 146–51.

26. Howard Curry, *High Bridge,* 21–22; Smith interview.

27. Smith interview; Curry, *High Bridge,* 19–32; Smith, *Nomination for Designation,* n.p.; Martin Hayden, *The Book of Bridges* (New York: Galahad Press, 1976), 112–16.

28. Thomas Curtis Clark and Theodore Voorhees, *The American Railway* (New York: Bramhall House, 1888), 89–91; Henry Grattan Tyrrell, *History of Bridge Engineering* (Chicago, 1911), 263.

29. J.A.L. Waddell, *Bridge Engineering* (New York: John Wiley and Sons, Inc., 1916), I: 25–29; Smith, *Nomination for Designation,* n.p.; Curry, *High Bridge,* 30; Henry Petroski, *Engineers of Dreams: Great Bridge Builders and the Spanning of America* (New York: Knopf, 1995), 79–80.

30. Curry, *High Bridge,* 30–33, 36–37; Smith interview; Curry interview.

31. Smith interview; Smith, *Nomination for Designation,* n.p.

32. Smith, *Nomination for Designation,* n.p.; Curry, *High Bridge,* 83–106.

33. *Engineering Record,* 62 (26 Nov. 1910), 618; *Ibid.,* (31 Dec. 1910), 774–76; Smith, *Nomination for Designation,* n.p.

34. *Lexington Herald,* 6 Sept. 1911.

35. Smith interview; *Lexington Herald-Leader,* 8 Sept. 1999.

36. William Ison interview, 1 Apr. 1988; Curry interview.

37. Michael E. Walters, "Dix River," *Kentucky Encyclopedia,* 268; Jillson Collection, Berea College, Box 8; *Courier-Journal,* 30 Jan. 1924, 2 Feb., 13 Oct. 1925, 29 Jan., 11 Oct. 1926; James C. Klotter, *Kentucky: Portrait in Paradox,* 291–92; Clyde Hayslett interview, 7 Feb. 1988.

38. "Dix River Dam and Hydro-Electric Station," pamphlet, Jillson Collection, Box 8.

39. *Kentucky Utilities Company: A Pictorial History* (Lexington: Kentucky Utilities, n.d.), 3–7.

40. *Ibid.* 8; "Dix Dam Hydro-Electric Station," Kentucky Utilities brochure, an enclosure from Robert Lykins, 16 Dec. 1987; *Courier-Journal,* 27 Sept. 1924, 11, 13 Sept. 1935; R.H. Freising to Willard Rouse Jillson, 13 Feb. 1925, Jillson Collection.

41. *Lexington Herald,* 6 Dec. 1925; *Kentucky Utilities News,* #42, May 1928, n.p.; Major R.G. Powell, "Report on Flood Control Reservoirs, Appendix VII, Dix River, 1927," Southeast Archives, Atlanta, Georgia, Operations and Maintenance File, HN 77T5 NA-1110; Harrison and Klotter, *New History,* 357; Alex P. Herrington interviews, 31 Mar., 5 Apr. 1988; *Courier-Journal,* 8 Aug. 1925.

42. *Lexington Herald,* 22 Nov. 1924; George C. Wright, "The Forced Removal . . . ," 6–7.

43. Wright, "The Forced Removal . . . ," 7; *The Harrodsburg Herald,* 20 Feb. 1925, 19 Feb. 1926; Hayslett interview; For racial antagonisms during construction of

Kentucky Dam, see Eric L. Rowsey, "The Worker's Life at Kentucky Dam, 1938–1945," *Filson Club History Quarterly*, 71 (Jul. 1997), 355–64.

44. Hayslett interview; *Lexington Herald-Leader*, 14 Nov. 1991; Gilbert H. Britton interview, 14 Aug. 1989; William D. Yount interview, 15 Aug. 1989.

45. Robert Burns, "To a Mouse," 1875, Seventh Stanza.

46. James C. Thomas interview, 26 June 1987; McQueen interview; Jesse Boyd Dalton interview, 17 Aug. 1988.

47. Lt. Col. R.G. Powell, "Report on the Kentucky River," Southeast Archives, Operations and Maintenance Files, HN 77T5 NA-1110.

48. *Report*, 1879, Part I, 146, *Ibid.*, 1887, Part II, 1873–74, 1881; Verhoeff, *Kentucky River Navigation*, 214; *Kentucky River Desk Maps*; Inland Rivers Library, Hamilton County Public Library.

49. Verhoeff, *Kentucky River Navigation*, 117, 120; David F. Ross, "Mary Verhoeff Versus the Army Engineers on Canalization of the Kentucky River," *Filson Club History Quarterly*, 65 (Apr. 1991), 275–76.

50. Ross, "Mary Verhoeff . . . ," 276–80; Parrish and Johnson, "J. Stoddard Johnston . . . ," 20–23.

51. *Report*, 1881, Part II, Appendix AA, 1979; *Ibid.*, 1890, Part III, 2263–66. For more information see Parrish and Johnson, "Engineering the Kentucky River . . . ," 369–94.

52. *Courier-Journal*, 5 Sept. 1948; *Report*, 1899, Part III, 2540.

53. *Report*, 1904, Part I, 482; *Ibid.*, 1910, Part I, 718; *Ibid.*, 1911, Part I, 771; Johnson, *Falls City Engineers*, 1974, 153–54; Parrish and Johnson, "Engineering the Kentucky River . . . ," 390–94.

54. *Lexington Herald-Leader*, 8 Dec. 1995, 7 Apr. 1998.

55. Leola B. Bush interview, 1 Aug. 1989.

5. THE RIVER ALWAYS WINS

1. *Lexington Herald-Leader*, 26 Jul. 1993; Sam Wilson interview; Aileen Suter interview, 21 May 1990.

2. *Courier-Journal*, 24 Apr. 1927; John M. Barry, *Rising Tide: The Great Mississippi Flood of 1927 and How It Changed America* (New York: Simon and Schuster, 1997), *passim*.

3. "Frank Wurtz's Report on the High Tides in the Kentucky River," 17 Sept. 1886, ms. in the Kentucky Historical Society.

4. *Courier-Journal*, 2 Jan., 2 Nov. 1919, 5, 10 Jan. 1920, 27 Dec. 1926; R. Harris, "Record of the Kentucky Flood, 30 May 1927," *Newsletter: Lee County Historical and Genealogical Society*, (April-May-June, 1993), 7–17.

5. "The Great '37 Flood: A Fifty-Year Remembrance," *Bulletin of the Kentucky Historical Society*, 13 (Feb. 1987), 1; "Flood of 1937," *Kentucky Encyclopedia*, 326–27.

6. T. Kyle Ellison, "Prisons," *Kentucky Encyclopedia*, 742–43; *Courier-Journal*, 22, 24 Jan. 1937; *Richmond Register*, 24 Feb. 1987.

7. *Frankfort State Journal*, 22 Jan. 1937; Kramer, *Capital on the Kentucky*, 339–41; Stivers interview; Floyd Hahn interview, 7 Aug. 1989; Andrew J. Palmer interview, 2 Sept. 1989; Charles W. Douthitt interviews, 1 Dec. 1988, 27 Apr. 1989.

8. Amalie Preston interview, 28 Jul. 1989; Lonnie W. Atha interview, 12 Jul. 1990; Horn interview; Charles Dees interview, 22 Jul. 1987.

9. Donaldson interview, 1986; Imel interview; Allen L. Gillock interview, 15 May 1990; James B. Roberts interview, 5 Jul. 1990.

10. *Richmond Register*, 24 Feb. 1987; *Richmond Daily Register*, 13, 17, 25–28 Jan. 1937.

11. Stivers interview; Rufus L. Moberly interview, 13 Aug. 1988; T.C. Dedman Jr. interview, 22 Dec. 1987; *Sunday Herald-Leader*, 2 Aug. 1970; Homer D. Allen interview; Elmer K. Lee interview, 12 Aug. 1989; Bush interview.

12. *Courier-Journal*, 8 Feb. 1939, 8 Mar. 1945, 15, 16 Feb. 1948; James Hubert Tuttle interview, 18 June 1990; Moberly interview.

13. Johnson, *Falls City Engineers*, 1974, 207–08; Charles E. Parrish, "Flood Control," *Kentucky Encyclopedia*, 327.

14. Willard Rouse Jillson, Ms., 1 May 1925, Jillson Collection, Berea College; *Courier-Journal*, 19 Mar. 1925, 13 Aug. 1939, 8 June 1954; *Report*, 1942, Part I, Vol. 2, 1235; *Ibid.*, 1944, Part I, Vol. 2, 1170; Monroe Barrett interview, 7 June 1989.

15. Napier interview; *Courier-Journal*, 27 Jan., 4, 7, Feb. 1957; Homer D. Allen interview; Johnson, *Falls City Engineers*, 1974, 264; Jane Furnas, "Water, Water, Everywhere," 3–8.

16. *Courier-Journal*, 18 Feb. 1962, 29 Aug. 1965; Johnson, *Falls City Engineers*, 1974, 264; Johnson, *Falls City Engineers*, 1984, 48–50, 61–62, 95–98, 120, 162; *Report*, 1951, Part I, 1498; *Ibid.*, 1952, Part I, 1461; *Ibid.*, 1953, Part I, 946; *Ibid.*, 1955, Part I, 903; *Ibid.*, 1957, Part I, 1042; *Ibid.*, 1958, Part I, 988–89, 1011; *Ibid*, 1963, Part I, 1007; *Ibid.*, 1984, Part I, 24–25.

17. Johnson, *Falls City Engineers*, 1984, 98.

18. John Lambert interview, 5 Jul. 1989; John M. Sparks interview, 18 Jan. 1988; Grant Richardson interview, 24 July 1988; Dalton interview.

19. Covington interview; Kearns interview; Dykes interview.

20. Jane Early Snyder interview, 1 Sept. 1988; Florence G. Tudor interview, 17 June 1987; *Lexington Herald-Leader*, 26 Dec. 1988; Kelley interview.

21. Hayslett interview; Scott Barbour interview, 15 Aug. 1989; Lee interview; Yount interview; *Lexington Herald-Leader*, 26 Dec. 1988; Powell interview.

22. Johnson, *Falls City Engineers*, 1984, 98; Kramer, *Capital on the Kentucky*, 394–95; David L. Strohmeier interview, 11 Oct. 1988; Ann G. Shepherd interview, 28 Jan. 1988; Opal Tillett interview, 6 Oct. 1988; Douthitt interview.

23. George O. Moore interview, 14 June 1988; Preston interview; Broce interview; Britton interview; Dedman interview; Marion Mershon interview, 15 Aug. 1989.

24. Tindall interview; Stewart interview.

25. Johnson, *Falls City Engineers*, 1984, 99–101; Kramer, *Capital on the Kentucky*, 395; *Courier-Journal*, 31 Mar. 1997; *Lexington Herald-Leader*, 16 Feb. 1990, 7 Nov. 1992; *Frankfort State-Journal*, 6 Apr. 1992.

26. *Richmond Register*, 27 Jul. 1992; *Country*, Premier, Collector's Edition 14, 62; *Lexington Herald-Leader*, 8 Mar. 1997; Thomas D. Clark, *Kentucky*, 28; Lowell H. Harrison, "Bert T. Combs," *Kentucky Encyclopedia*, 218.

27. Stanley Taulbee interview, 18 May 1990.

28. *Courier-Journal*, 6–8 Jul. 1939.

29. *Lexington Herald*, 6 Jul. 1939; William H. Garrett interview, 6 June 1991; Lorene Rose interview, 30 Aug. 1992; Kentucky Mountain Holiness Association, brochure, 1966, n.p.; Spencer interview.

30. *The Jackson Times*, 1 Nov. 1990, 9 Jul. 1992; Spencer interview; Rose

interview; Lela G. McConnell, *Faith Victorious in the Kentucky Mountains* (Winona Lake, Indiana: Light and Life Press, 1946), 142–47.

31. Spencer interview; *Courier-Journal*, 8 Jul. 1939; Rose interview; *The Jackson Times*, 1 Nov. 1990; Lela G. McConnell, *The Pauline Ministry in the Kentucky Mountains* (Berne, Indiana: Economy Printing, 1942), 114–18.

32. "Kentucky River and Tributaries Kentucky, Letter from the Secretary of War, 20 Mar. 1944," Operations and Maintenance File, 4N 77T5 NA7110, Southeast Archives, 61.

33. Preston Johnson interview; Homer Renfro interview, 20 June 1988; Eva Perkins Sams interview, 5 Jul. 1988; Howard interview.

34. Land interview; Christine Ashcraft interview, 1 Jul. 1988; *Richmond Register*, "Reflections," 24 Feb. 1987; Ivan M. Tribe, *The Stonemans: An Appalachian Family and the Music That Shaped Their Lives* (Urbana: Univ. of Illinois Press, 1993), 39–40.

35. *Sunday Herald-Leader*, 25 June 1967; *Lexington Leader*, 25 May 1971; Ernest Ashcraft interview, 6 June 1989.

36. O.H. Gullette interview, 7 Jul. 1989; Dalton interview; James C. Thomas interview.

37. Estill Thomas interview, 14 Feb. 1988; Moberly interview; Hardin interview; Frank C. Marcum interview, 25 Jul. 1988; Richardson interview.

38. James N. Floyd Jr. interview, 22 May 1990; Charlie R. Gibson interview, 23 Jul. 1990; Douthitt interview, 1 Dec. 1988.

39. Sparks interview.

40. Howard interview; Sherman Estes interview; Eleanor L. Elder interview, 12 Jul. 1989.

41. Eunice Perkins interview, 25 June 1987; Bessie Martin Perkins interview; Land interview; *Richmond Daily Register*, 22 Dec. 1926.

42. Land interview.

43. *Ibid.*

44. *Ibid.*

45. Howard interview; Lonnie Ashcraft interview; Eunice Perkins interview; *Richmond Daily Register*, 22 Dec. 1926.

46. *Lexington Herald-Leader*, 18 Oct. 1988.

47. Fint interview, 11 Aug. 1989; Stivers interview; Irene M. Rucker interview, 16 Aug. 1989.

48. Ulack, *Atlas*, 34; Glen Conner, "Climate," *Kentucky Encyclopedia*, 207; *Lexington Herald-Leader*, 7 Sept. 1997; *Courier-Journal*, 4 Dec. 1965.

49. Clyde Young Sr. interview, 22 June 1989; Lonnie Ashcraft interview; Covington interview; Broadus interview; Bush interview; Sherman Estes interview.

50. Mary Walters McCauley interview, 11 Sept. 1988; White interview; Parks interview; Sams interview; Richardson interview; Lee interview; Renfro interview.

51. *Courier-Journal*, 4 Dec. 1965, 28 June 1970; Strohmeier interview.

52. McCauley interview; Young interview; Sparks interview; Estill Thomas interview.

53. Suter interview.

6. MY MIND ON THE RIVER

1. Preston interview; Tillett interview; Garrison interview; Preston Johnson interview; Bryant interview.

2. John G. Stuart Journal, Kentucky Historical Society.

3. Horn interview.

4. Garrett interview; Glynn Welsh interview, 11 Jul. 1990; Atha interview; Marvin Hawkins interview; Hahn interview; Stivers interview.

5. Picture of the *Falls City II*, Kentucky Historical Society; Reece interview.

6. Roberts interview; Broce interview; Yount interview.

7. Suter interview; Stewart interview; Preston interview; McCauley interview.

8. Susie B. Lair interview, 14 June 1990; Zelma L. Filson interview, 15 May 1990.

9. *Courier-Journal*, 18 Dec. 1927, 12 Oct. 1952; *Eminence Patriot-Statesman*, 9 Aug. 1973; "Drennon Springs," *Kentucky Encyclopedia*, 271; "Western Military Institute," *Kentucky Encyclopedia*, 944; Roberts interview; Lair interview; Britton interview.

10. Preston interview; Coleman, *Historic Kentucky*, 161; Britton interview; Delphia Walters interview, 1 Sept. 1988.

11. McCauley interview; Walters interview.

12. McCauley interview; Coleman, *Historic Kentucky*, 27; Thomas B. Ripy interview, 6 Jul. 1989; Bessie Martin Perkins interview; Margaret H. True interview, 8 June 1988; Betty Bryant, *Here Comes the Showboat!* (Lexington: Univ. Press of Kentucky, 1994), 121–22.

13. Coleman, *Historic Kentucky*, 27; Coleman, *Steamboats*, 37; Lonnie Ashcraft interview; Rowe interview; *Richmond Register*, 19 Sept. 1988; Bryant, *Here Comes the Showboat!* 122.

14. Thomas B. Ripy interview; Filson interview; Coleman, *Historic Kentucky*, 27; Philip Graham, *Showboats* (Austin: Univ. of Texas Press, 1951), 125–27, 201.

15. Sewall interview.

16. Tudor interview; Preston Johnson interview; Ernest Ripy Jr. interview, 6 Jul. 1989; Sams interview.

17. Tudor interview; Sams interview; Witt interview; Perkins interview.

18. Tudor interview; Thomas B. Ripy interview; James Young interview, 7 May 1989; Ernest Ripy Jr. interview; Strohmeier interview; Snyder interview; William E. Hall interview, 17 Aug. 1989; *Lexington Herald-Leader*, 23 Sept. 1990; 1941 Jessamine County Highway Map, Willard Rouse Jillson Collection, Berea College; *Courier-Journal Rotogravure*, 18 Aug. 1946; Carolyn Terry Bashaw, "Sarah Gibson Blanding," *Kentucky Encyclopedia*, 87.

19. Estill Thomas interview.

20. Napier interview; Palmer interview; Sparks interview.

21. Imel interview.

22. Roberts interview; Renfro interview; Sams interview; Stivers interview; Clark interview; Sallie Fullen interview, 6 June 1990; Bernie Hackett interview, 14 Aug. 1989; *Frankfort State Journal*, 12 Jul. 1981; David A. New interview, 6 Jul. 1988.

23. Sam Wilson interview.

24. Napier interview; Homer D. Allen interview; Ernest Robinson interview.

25. Reece interview; Parks interview; Bush interview; Kearns interview; Covington interview.

26. Johnson interview; Perkins interview; Sams interview; Elizabeth Saylor interview, 3 Dec. 1986; Jesse Newby interview, 3 Dec. 1986; Saylor interview; Tudor interview; *Richmond Register*, 12 Sept. 1992; Elmer G. Sulzer, *Ghost Railroads of Kentucky*

(Indianapolis: Vane A. Jones, 1967), 33–41; *Valley View Argent,* copies in the Eastern Kentucky University Special Collections; Mrs. Leonard Harned to the author, 27 Feb. 1990.

27. Fullen interview; Dedman interview; Marion Mershon interview, 15 Aug. 1988; Suter interview; Sidney R. Clements and F.E. Webster interview, 13 Apr. 1989; Flora Dawson interview, 6 Apr. 1989; S.F. Spurr interview, 28 Mar. 1989; Fint interview; Map, Jillson Collection, Box 16, Berea College; *Lexington Herald-Leader,* 30 Oct. 1996, 23 May 1997.

28. Barrett interview; Homer D. Allen interview; Imel interview; Dykes, interview; Alcorn interview; Floyd interview; Ed Combs interview; Welsh interview; *Lexington Herald-Leader,* 15 Sept. 1996.

29. Lonnie Ashcraft interview; Spurr interview; Roberts interview; Shackelford interview; James B. Roberts to the author, 1 Mar. 1990.

30. Jeffrey Norman, "How to Run a Trotline," *Southern Magazine,* (Apr. 1989), 80; Imel interview; Callahan interview; Stewart interview; Wolfinbarger interview. For more about commercial fishing methods see Jens Lund, *Flatheads and Spooneys: Fishing for a Living in the Ohio River Valley* (Lexington: Univ. Press of Kentucky, 1995).

31. R.E. Nightingale interview, 29 Jan. 1988; Preston interview; Moore interview.

32. Fint interview; Douthitt interview; Gibson interview; *Lexington Herald-Leader,* 3 Jul. 1988.

33. Campbell interview.

34. Moore interview; Estill Thomas interview; Dalton interview.

35. Clements and Webster interview; Coleman, *Steamboats,* 34; Rachel Maupin to the author, 26 Feb. 1990.

36. Dalton interview.

37. Elder interview; Hackett interview; *Courier-Journal,* 19 Apr. 1963.

38. New interview; *Richmond Register,* 21 Nov. 1994; Russell T. Dees interview.

39. John A. Lee, *Shiner Slattery* (Auckland, New Zealand: Collins, Fontana Silver Fern, 1964).

40. Atha interview; New interview; Tindall interview.

41. Victor Bourne interview, 10 Nov. 1988; Atha interview.

42. James Clark Hudson interview, 5 Jul. 1988; Bourne interview; New interview; Charles Hudson to the author, 13 Mar. 1990.

43. Hudson interview; Atha interview; New interview; Tindall interview; Bourne interview.

44. Land interview.

45. Shackelford interview; Sewall interview.

46. Campbell interview; Sherman Estes interview; Helton interview; Garrett interview; Ed Combs interview.

47. Elder interview; Imel interview; Flynn interview; Suter interview; Christine Ashcraft interview.

48. Young interview; Short interview. For an interesting explanation of the differences between "killing" and "murder," in the southern context, see William Lynwood Montell, *Killings: Folk Justice in the Upper South* (Lexington: Univ. Press of Kentucky, 1986).

49. Harrison and Klotter, *New History,* 434; Klotter, *Kentucky: Portrait in Paradox,* 65–72; White interview; Seldon L. Brewer interview, 23 May 1988; Roberts interview;

Snyder interview; Bessie Martin Perkins interview; Mayme Seale interview, 3 Nov. 1988; Lair interview.

50. William E. Hall interview; Lair interview.

51. William E. Hall interview; *Richmond Daily Register*, 12–15 Mar. 1923; Frances Sweat interview, 19 Jul. 1989.

52. Hall interview.

53. "Paul Sawyier," *Kentucky Encyclopedia*, 798; Jones, *The Art of Paul Sawyier*, 3–14; Willard Rouse Jillson, *Paul Sawyier: American Artist* (Frankfort: Blue Grass Press, 1961), 1–15.

54. "Paul Sawyier," *Kentucky Encyclopedia*, 798; *Lexington Herald-Leader*, 22 June 1992; Billy L. Wilson interview, 14 Mar. 1989; Jillson, *Paul Sawyier*, 16–30.

55. "Paul Sawyier Galleries Status Report, June 1997"; Jones, *Art of Paul Sawyier*, 1, 86, 105; William H. Coffey interview, 7 June 1988; Rowe interview; Jillson, *Paul Sawyier*, 30–37.

56. *Frankfort State Journal*, 19 Oct. 1965; Jones, *Art of Paul Sawyier*, Plate 13, 104; True interview; Jillson, *Paul Sawyier*, 43–46.

57. *Lexington Herald-Leader*, 22 June 1992; Jones, *Art of Paul Sawyier*, Plate 64, 103; Jillson, Paul Sawyier, 47–50.

58. Jones, *Art of Paul Sawyier*, 87; Madeline Covi, "Madison Julius Cawein," *Kentucky Encyclopedia*, 176; William S. Ward, *A Literary History of Kentucky* (Knoxville: Univ. of Tennessee Press, 1988), 95–97; Madison Cawein II to the author, 15 March and 12 Apr. 1990.

59. Cawein to the author.

60. Cawein to the author.

61. Ed McClanahan, "Wendell Erdman Berry," *Kentucky Encyclopedia*, 73–74.

62. Berry interview.

63. Berry interview.

64. *Lexington Herald-Leader*, 18 Sept. 1987; *The Christian Science Monitor* 10 Jul. 1986; Berry interview; Wendell Berry, *The Rise* (Lexington: Univ. of Kentucky Library Press, 1968), 2–15; Berry, *The Kentucky River: Two Poems* (1976), 14; Ward, *Literary History*, 203–6.

65. Berry, *The Rise*, 6; Ward, *Literary History*, 208.

66. John Harrod interview, 28 June 1988; Charles K. Wolfe, *Kentucky Country*, 20–30; Harry Rice, "The Doc Roberts Collection," *Heritage Highlights* 3 (1999), 34–35.

67. Walters interview.

68. Berry, *The Rise*, 9–10.

7. DON'T STEP IN A SHADOW

1. Donaldson interview; Oliver F. Shearer interview, 17 Aug. 1998; McCauley interview.

2. Walters interview; Filson interview; Preston interview; *Lexington Herald-Leader*, 4 Aug. 1990; Enclosure from Betty Walden Secoy, 12 Jul. 1990; Shearer interview; Earl Gulley Jr. interviews, 20 May 1988, 11 Aug. 1998.

3. *Report*, 1882, Part I, 257–58; *Ibid.*, 1891, Part IV, 2461; *Ibid.*, 1898, Part III, 2025–30; *Ibid.*, 1909, Part I, 644, Part II, 1846; *Ibid.*, 1910, Part II, 2008; *Ibid.*, 1917, Part I, 1311.

4. *Report*, 1903, Part III, 1754; *Ibid.*, 1904, Part I, 482; *Ibid.*, 1905, Part I, 492;

Ibid., 1906, Part I, 542; *Ibid.*, 1912, Part II, 2395; Donaldson interview; Clyde Young Sr. interview.

5. *Report*, 1915, Part I, 1178,1180; *Ibid.*, 1916, Part I, 1266–67; *Ibid.*, 1920, Part I, 1389; *Ibid.*, 1922, Part I, 1411; *Ibid.*, 1927, Part I, 1227; *Ibid.*, 1929, Part II, 650.

6. "Survey of Kentucky River for Locks 9 and 10," Inland Rivers Library, Hamilton County Public Library, Cincinnati; *Report*, 1899, Part I, 438, Part III, 2522; *Ibid.*, 1901, Part IV, 2744; *Ibid.*, 1902, Part I, 420; Part III, 1954–55; RA912.7693.qv58 Microfilm, Inland Rivers Library.

7. *Report*, 1906, Part II, 1653; RA627.84q105 and Pictures, Inland Rivers Library; Pictures, Southeast Archives, Atlanta, Georgia; Russell T. Dees interview; Enclosure from Charles E. Parrish, S.F. Wood materials, 14 Apr. 1993.

8. Lock and Dam 9 and 10 diagrams, Inland Rivers Library; *Report*, 1904, Part III, 2650; *Ibid.*, 1905, Part II, 1915; *Ibid.*, 1906, Part I, 542; *Ibid.*, 1907, Part I, 569; *Ibid.*, Part II, 1786; *Ibid.*, 1917, Part I, 1313–14. *Louisville Evening Post*, 16 Mar. 1905; Jerry Lee Raisor interview, 14 Aug. 1998. The Corps report for the snagging expedition became the basis for the author's short story, "Snaggin' in Pool 8" in his book of short stories with a Kentucky River setting, *River Bends and Meanders* (Burnsville, North Carolina: Celo Valley Books, 1992).

9. Original Kentucky River House for Lock Keeper, Lock No. 10, diagrams and pictures, Inland Rivers Library and Southeast Archives; Moberly interview.

10. *Courier-Journal*, 5 Sept. 1948; Britton interview; Dalton interview; Gullette interview; Charles E. Parrish and John L. Donaldson, Talk aboard the *Dixie Belle*, Shakertown, 27 June 1987.

For all the idealization of the lockkeeper's life, they could not escape the violence that often struck in the Kentucky River Valley or a corrupt local judicial system. In one case, for example, only federal intervention kept the murderer of a lockmaster from escaping justice at the turn of the twentieth century. U.S. Attorney General to Secretary of War, 6 Jul. 1901, and reports, File 37957, General Correspondence, 1894–1923, Group 77, Records of the U.S. Army Corps of Engineers, National Archives, Southeast Region, Atlanta, Georgia.

11. Floyd interview; Sparks interview; Rucker interview; Moberly interview; Clyde Young Sr. interview; Cecil Hardin interview, 13 Aug. 1988; S.F. Wood letter, 10 Aug. 1929, enclosure from Charles E. Parrish.

12. Ernest Ashcraft interview, 6 June 1988; Billy L. Wilson interview; Sparks interview; Gulley interview.

13. Wilson interview; Dalton interview; Walters interview.

14. Walters interview.

15. Walters interview; *Richmond Register*, 29 Sept. 1988.

16. Estill Thomas interview; James B. Gordon interview, 22 June 1988; James C. Thomas interview; Delvia A. Hopper interview, 15 Sept. 1988; Ernest Ashcraft interview; Bates interview.

17. Russell T. Dees interview, 2 Feb. 1988; Charles Dees interview.

18. Preston interview; Myrtle Preston Carter interview, 11 Aug. 1989; Filson interview.

19. Ernest Ashcraft interview; *Report*, 1918, Part I, 1356; *Ibid.*, 1919, Part II, 3133; *Ibid.*, 1923, Part II, 1266.

20. Thomas E. Gravett, Joe Christian, and Hubert Bush interview, 7 Mar. 1989; *Courier-Journal*, 9, 15 Sept. 1952; Gerald Griffin, "It's a Water Highway Once Again,"

Courier-Journal Magazine, 5 Apr. 1953; Hardin interview; McQueen interview; Lambert interview; Land interview.

21. Donaldson interview; Shepherd interview; William J. and Patrick C. Lynch interview, 17 January 1988; Russell T. Dees interview.

22. Donaldson interview; *Lexington Leader*, 9 Jun. 1960; *Winchester Sun*, 30 Sept. 1986.

23. Bates interview.

24. Shearer interview.

8. WHITHER THE KENTUCKY?

1. *Lexington Herald Leader*, 26 May 1989; Thomas J. Fitzgerald interview, 16 Sept. 1998.

2. Clark interview.

3. William S. Ellis, "The Mississippi: River Under Siege," *National Geographic*, (Special Edition 1997), 90–115; Bill McKibben, "A Special Moment in History," *Atlantic Monthly*, 281 (May 1998), 68–72.

4. Ashley L. Preston, "Nature Conservation . . . ," 21–37; William H. Martin interview, 11 Aug. 1998; *Courier-Journal*, 7 Aug. 1997; *Lexington Herald-Leader*, 6 Aug. 1997.

5. Richard A. Bartlett, *Troubled Waters: Champion International and the Pigeon River Controversy* (Knoxville: Univ. of Tennessee Press, 1995), x; *Dams and Rivers: Primer on the Downstream Effects of Dams* (Denver: U.S. Geological Survey, 1996), Circular 1126; "Charles Kuralt, 1934–1997," *American Rivers*, XXV (Summer 1997), 12; *Lexington Herald-Leader*, 4 June 1972; *Courier-Journal*, 21 May 1997.

6. Patrick Joseph, "The Battle of the Dams," *Smithsonian*, 29 (November 1998), 48–61; *Frankfort State Journal*, 24 Oct. 1965; *Lakeland Boating*, June 1958, 17–19, 29; *Courier-Journal*, 3 February 1952, 10 June 1962; *Lexington Herald-Leader*, 14 Sept. 1986.

7. *The Harrodsburg Herald*, 6 Dec. 1984; *Courier-Journal*, 9 Dec. 1945; "Draft Environmental Impact Statement," Operations and Maintenance, Kentucky River Navigation Project, U.S. Army Corps of Engineers, Louisville District, June 1975, Summary; Thomas M. Dorman interview, 20 Aug. 1998; Gulley interview.

8. *Frankfort State Journal*, 20 Sept., 10 Oct. 1981, 19 July 1982; Dorman interview; Haney interview; Fitzgerald interview; *Madison County Post Advertiser*, 14 Nov. 1984; *Lexington Herald-Leader*, 14 Sept. 1986, 22 Sept. 1996; "Kentucky Riverlands Development Program," (Lexington: Spindletop Research, 1965), 10, Inland Rivers Collection; Andy Mead interview, 28 Aug. 1998.

9. Haney interview; *Courier-Journal*, 17 Jul. 1988; *Lexington Herald Leader*, 3, 4, 31 Jul., 5 Dec. 1988; Michael Parfit, "Living with Natural Hazards," *National Geographic*, 194 (Jul. 1998), 15; Glenn Connor, "Climate," *Kentucky Encyclopedia*, 207; Eric Howard Christianson, "Kentucky-American Water Company," *Kentucky Encyclopedia*, 490.

10. *Lexington Herald Leader*, 3, 15, 31 Jul. 1988.

11. *Special Report, Water Supply Alternatives to Red River Lake, Vol. I, Main Report, 1976*, (Louisville: U.S. Army Corps of Engineers, Rev. 1978), d-e, 135, Inland Rivers Library, Hamilton County Public Library, Cincinnati; *Courier-Journal*, 22 Jan., 16 May, 28 Jul. 1976; *Lexington Herald-Leader*, 23 June 1991; Wendell Berry, *The Unforeseen Wilderness* (republished by North Point Press, 1991).

12. Haney interview; Fitzgerald interview; *Lexington Herald-Leader*, 1 Dec. 1988, 20 Feb., 8, 15 Apr., 10 Jul. 1990; "Draft, A Multi-Purpose Surface Impoundment Proposal for the Kentucky River," Sept. 1987, U.S. Army Corps of Engineers, Inland Rivers Collection; *Richmond Register*, 11 Jul. 1990.

13. *Lexington Herald-Leader*, 2, 28 Jul. 1991, 5, 12 Nov., 4–6 Dec. 1998; J. Virgil Proctor interview, 15 Nov. 1988; J. Virgil Proctor to Hon. Scotty Baesler, Mayor, 31 Oct. 1988, 25 Apr. 1989, copies sent to author; Haney interview; Brian Malloy, "Watering the Bluegrass," *The Lane Report*, 5 (1st Quarter 1989), 1, 8–12.

14. *Lexington Herald-Leader*, 4 Dec. 1990, 2 Jul., 29 Aug., 28–29 Sept. 1991; *Richmond Register*, 14 Apr. 1993; *Frankfort State Journal*, 28 Apr. 1991; Dorman interview; Fitzgerald interview.

15. Todd Hornback, "District to transfer ownership of Kentucky River locks and dams 5–14 after repairs are completed," *Falls City Engineer*, 18 (Jul./Aug. 1993), 3; Hornback, "Fleet not just another chip off the old block," *Falls City Engineer*, 22 (Jul. 1997), 10; *Lexington Herald-Leader*, 17 Sept. 1992.

16. *Lexington Herald-Leader*, 27 May 1988, 18 Aug. 1990, 22 May 1992, 9 Mar., 28 May 1993, 5 May 1994; *Richmond Register*, 12 Mar., 6 Sept. 1991; Gulley interview; Dorman interview; Hugh Archer interview, 19 Aug. 1998.

17. *Lexington Herald-Leader*, 30 Jan., 1 Sept., 12 Oct., 18 Dec. 1992; Archer interview; Dorman interview; Martin interview; Haney interview.

18. Archer interview; Gulley interview; Martin interview; Haney interview; *Lexington Herald-Leader*, 13 Mar., 16 Apr., 12 June, 30 Oct., 18 Dec. 1993, 11 Feb. 1994, 17 Feb. 1996; Kentucky River Authority Meeting #56 Agenda, 20 Dec. 1996; Kentucky River Authority Meeting #63 Agenda, 21 Nov. 1997.

19. Archer interview; Gulley interview; *Lexington Herald-Leader*, 30 Oct., 17 Nov. 1995; *Richmond Register*, 23 June 1994.

20. *Kentucky River Authority Annual Report*, 1995, 1–20; Hugh Archer to Kentucky River Authority Constituents, 11 Mar. 1996.

21. *Lexington Herald-Leader*, 21 Feb., 16 Mar., 24 Aug. 1996, 15 Jan., 27 Sept. 1997; *Richmond Register*, 13 Jan. 1996; Haney interview; Archer interview; Dorman interview; see also David S. Devine, "The Trouble with Dams," *Atlantic Monthly*, 276 (Aug. 1995), 64–74.

22. *Lexington Herald-Leader*, 27 Jan., 3 Feb. 1993, 9 Jan. 1994, 1 Jul., 27–28 Sept. 1997; Martin interview; Dorman interview; Haney Interview; Fitzgerald interview; "Statement of the Kentucky Resources Council, Inc., Before the Kentucky River Authority, February 19, 1993," copy to the author; *Bluegrass Water Project Update*, Volume 1, Number 1, June 1998.

23. *Lexington Herald-Leader*, 10–11 June, 8 Jul., 22, 27 Aug., 1, 7, 20 Sept. 1997, 23 Aug. 1998; Dorman interview.

24. Archer interview; Martin interview; Mead interview; Fitzgerald interview; Haney interview.

25. *Lexington Herald-Leader*, 22 Mar. 1998; Gulley interview, 11 Aug. 1998; Dorman interview; Archer interview.

26. Archer interview; Haney interview.

27. *Lexington Herald-Leader*, 27, 29 June, 15 Aug. 1998; *Richmond Register*, 24 Aug. 1998.

28. *Courier-Journal*, 28 Jun. 1970: Rebecca R. Wodder, "Rivers Endangered and Restored," 2; *Lexington Herald-Leader*, 23 Mar., 24, 28 Apr., 28 Jul., 3 Aug., 23 Nov.

1997, 12 June, 30 July 1998; *Richmond Register*, 14 Apr., 3 Aug. 1998; Archer interview; Dorman interview; Martin interview.

29. *Lexington Herald-Leader*, 16 Dec. 1987, 30 Apr. 1989, 20 Oct. 1991, 2 Nov. 1992, 29 Oct. 1993, 15 Apr. 1996, 27 Apr., 20 May, 1998, 17 Jan. 1999; William H. Martin, et. al., *The Kentucky River Palisades;* Martin interview; Adam Jones and Richard Taylor, *The Palisades; Frankfort State Journal*, 23 Oct. 1992; Wharton interview; see also Mary E. Wharton and Roger W. Barbour, *Bluegrass.*

30. *Owensboro Messenger-Inquirer*, 13 June 1991; *Lexington Herald-Leader*, 11–12 Feb. 1989, 21 Jul. 1996, 23 Sept. 1997, 5 May 1998; *Richmond Register*, 28 Feb. 1990, 16 May 1991, 17 June 1997.

31. *Richmond Register*, 18 June 1992; Archer interview; *Lexington Herald-Leader*, 30 June 1990, 29 June 1991, 2 June 1992, 25 June 1993, 3 Jul. 1997, 23 May 1998; Dorman interview; Martin interview; Haney interview.

32. *Lexington Herald-Leader*, 26 Sept. 1992, 30 June, 1–2 Jul. 1997, 16 Aug. 1998; *Courier-Journal*, 1, 5 Jul. 1997; Dorman interview; Archer interview; Martin interview; see John P. Wiley Jr., "Wastewater Problem? Just Plant a Marsh," *Smithsonian*, 28 (Jul. 1997), 24, 26.

33. Martin interview; Archer interview; Dorman interview; Fitzgerald interview; *Lexington Herald-Leader*, 2 Mar. 1990, 12 Aug. 1992, 10 May 1993, 8 Aug. 1996, 24 Apr., 21 Sept., 1997, 15 May, 12 Jul. 1998; *Richmond Register*, 24 June, 1 Jul. 1992; *Eastern* (Kentucky University) *Progress*, 9 Jul. 1998; *The Kentucky Journal*, Aug. Sept., 1997, 1–2, 4, 11.

34. David L. Morgan, Director, Kentucky Heritage Council, to the author, 24 Mar. 1993; Daniel D. Bennett, Deputy Commissioner, Kentucky Department of Travel Development, to the author, 21 Jan. 1994; Kentucky River History Advisory Committee minutes, 14 Dec. 1993; Dorman interview; Thomas M. Dorman to the author, 30 Sept. 1993.

35. Raisor interview; the author to David L. Morgan, 19 Apr., 16 Aug. 1993; Dorman to the author, 23 Nov. 1993; "Kentucky Historic Resources for Lock and Dam No. 10, Kentucky River"; Kentucky River Museum Advisory Committee Minutes, 22 Feb., 22 Mar., 6 Dec. 1994; Nathalie Taft Andrews, "Museum of the Kentucky River, Preliminary Interpretative Plan," 28; "Museum of the Kentucky River, ISTEA Application," Kentucky Tourism Cabinet, Department of Parks; Nathalie Andrews, "Proposal: Kentucky River Museum, Preliminary Museum Design and Planning," 18 Apr. 1994; Preliminary Drawing, Kentucky River Museum, Argabrite Associates Architects, Inc.; John Lee, Departments of Parks, and Butch Hatcher, Architect, Division of Engineering, 7 Mar. 1996; Kentucky River Historical Advisory Committee Meeting Minutes, 22 Mar. 1994; Kentucky River Lock Museum, Fort Boonesborough State Park, 1993 Time Line.

36. Dorman interview; Martin interview; Raisor interview; *Lexington Herald-Leader*, 6 Mar. 1998.

37. Kentucky River View Park, Opening Ceremony, 19 Sept. 1997, program; "Proposal to Revise the Kentucky River Park Plan for Frankfort, Kentucky, 3 Dec. 1993," Kentucky Department of Travel Development.

38. *Lexington Herald-Leader*, 17 Jan., 3, 19, 21 Feb., 3, 5, 24, 28 Mar., 7, 16, 19 Apr., 14 May 1999; NOPE brochure; Author's notes from 4 Mar. 1999 Fayette County Water Supply Planning Council Public Meeting; *Louisville Courier-Journal*, 18 Apr. 1999; *Bluegrass Update*, Volume 2, Number 1, no date.

39. *Lexington Herald-Leader*, 11, 13 June, 23, 24, 27, 31 Jul., 8, 9, 12 Aug. 1999.

40. *Lexington Herald-Leader*, 24, 28, 29 Jul., 1, 11, 18, 22 Aug., 8, 11, 14, 18 Sept. 1999: *Courier Journal*, 1 Aug. 1999.

41. Mead interview; Fitzgerald interview.

42. Jillson, *Kentucky River*, 74.

SELECTED BIBLIOGRAPHY

PRIMARY AND SECONDARY SOURCES

Andrews, Nathalie Taft. "Museum of the Kentucky River, Preliminary Interpretative Plan." Louisville: Argabrite Associates Architects, 1 Dec. 1995.

Baker, R.P. *Report of the Principal Engineer to the Board of Internal Improvement in Relation to the Kentucky River.* 1836.

Berry, Wendell. *The Unforeseen Wilderness: Kentucky's Red River Gorge.* Lexington: Univ. Press of Kentucky, 1971.

Bryant, Betty. *Here Comes the Showboat!* Lexington: Univ. Press of Kentucky, 1994.

Carey, Mathew. Manuscripts. The Filson Club, Louisville, Ky.

Channing, Steven A. *Kentucky: A History.* New York: Norton, 1977.

Clark, Thomas D. *Historic Maps of Kentucky.* Lexington: Univ. Press of Kentucky, 1979.

———. *A History of Kentucky.* Lexington: Bradford, 1960.

———. *The Kentucky.* New York: Farrar and Rinehart, 1942. Bicentennial ed., Univ. Press of Kentucky, 1992.

Clark, Thomas D., and F. Gerald Ham. *Pleasant Hill and Its Shakers.* Shakertown at Pleasant Hill: Pleasant Hill Press, 1968.

Cogswell, Robert. "Tie Hacking." *Rural Kentuckian* 38 (Nov. 1984): 17–19.

Coleman, J. Winston Jr. *Historic Kentucky.* Lexington: Henry Clay, 1968.

———. *Steamboats on the Kentucky River.* Lexington: Winburn, 1960.

Corps of Engineers, Records. Louisville District and Southeast Archives, Atlanta, Ga.

Curry, Howard. *High Bridge: A Pictorial History.* Lexington: Feeback, 1983.

The Falls City Engineer. Corps of Engineers, Louisville District, 1990 to present.

Fox, John Jr. *The Little Shepherd of Kingdom Come.* New York: Charles Scribner's Sons, 1903.

Frankfort State Journal, 1930 to present.

Furnas, Jane. "Water, Water, Everywhere." *Quarterly Bulletin of the Frontier Nursing Service* 32 (winter 1957): 3–8.

Greb, Stephen F. *Guide to "Progression of Life."* Lexington: Kentucky Geological Survey, special publication 13, series 11, 1989.

Harrison, Lowell H., and James C. Klotter. *A New History of Kentucky.* Lexington: Univ. Press of Kentucky, 1997.

Henderson, A. Gwynn. "Dispelling the Myth: Seventeenth- and Eighteenth-Century Indian Life in Kentucky." *Register of the Kentucky Historical Society* 90 (Bicentennial issue 1992): 1–25.

———. *Kentuckians before Boone.* Lexington: Univ. Press of Kentucky, 1992.

Hunter, Louis C. *Steamboats on the Western Rivers.* New York: Dover, 1993.

Jillson, Willard Rouse. *The Kentucky River: An Outline of the Drainage of a Master Stream During Geologic Time.* Frankfort: The State Journal, 1945.

———. Collection. Berea College Library.

———. *Geology of Henry County.* Frankfort: Roberts, 1967.

Jones, Adam, and Richard Taylor. *The Palisades of the Kentucky River.* Englewood, Colo.: Westcliffe, 1997.

Jones, Arthur F. *The Art of Paul Sawyier.* Lexington: Univ. Press of Kentucky, 1976.

Johnson, Leland R. *The Falls City Engineers: A History of the Louisville District, Corps of Engineers, United States Army.* U.S. Army, Corps of Engineers, 1974.

———. *The Falls City Engineers: A History of the Louisville District, Corps of Engineers, Unites States Army, 1970–1983.* U.S. Army, Corps of Engineers, 1984.

Kentucky River Authority Annual Report, 1995. Frankfort.

Kentucky River Desk Maps. U.S. Army, Corps of Engineers, Cincinnati, Ohio, 1919.

Kentucky River History (Museum) Advisory Committee Minutes, 1993 to present.

Kentucky River Navigation Charts. U. S. Army, Corps of Engineers, Louisville District, Jul. 1987.

Kleber, John, ed. *The Kentucky Encyclopedia.* Lexington: Univ. Press of Kentucky, 1992.

Klotter, James C. *Kentucky: Portrait in Paradox: 1900–1950.* Frankfort: Kentucky Historical Society, 1996.

Kramer, Carl E. *Capital on the Kentucky.* Frankfort: Historic Frankfort, 1986.

Lewis, R. Barry, ed. *Kentucky Archaeology.* Lexington: Univ. Press of Kentucky, 1996.

Lexington Herald-Leader. 1880 to present.

Louisville Courier-Journal, 1880 to present.

Lund, Jens. *Flatheads and Spooneys: Fishing for a Living in the Ohio River Valley.* Lexington: Univ. Press of Kentucky, 1995.

Malloy, Brian. "Watering the Bluegrass." *The Lane Report* 5 (1st Quarter 1989): 1, 8–12.

Martin, William H., et. al. *The Kentucky River Palisades: Flora and Vegetation.* The Kentucky Chapter of the Nature Conservancy, 1979.

McClanahan, Ralph E. *"Kentucky's Miniature Nile": A Brief History of the Kentucky River.* Irvine: 1972.

McFarlan, Arthur C. *Geology of Kentucky.* Lexington: Univ. of Kentucky Press, 1943.

McGrain, Preston. *The Geologic Story of Kentucky.* Lexington: Kentucky Geological Survey, Special Publication 8, Series II, 1983.

Montell, William Lynwood. *Killings: Folk Justice in the Upper South.* Lexington: Univ. Press of Kentucky, 1986.

"Museum of the Kentucky River, ISTEA Application." Kentucky Tourism Cabinet, Department of Parks.

Norman, Jeffrey. "How to Run a Trotline." *Southern Magazine* (Apr. 1980), 80.

Parrish, Charles E. and Leland R. Johnson. "Engineering the Kentucky River: A Disastrous Debut." *The Register of the Kentucky Historical Society* 95 (Autumn 1997): 369–94.

———. "J. Stoddard Johnston Versus the Army Engineers on Canalization of the Kentucky River." *The Filson Club History Quarterly* 72 (Jan. 1998): 3–23.

Preston, Ashley L. "Nature Conservation in a Deconstructed World." *Humanities and Technology Review* 16 (Fall 1997): 21–37.

Report of the Chief of Engineers, Annual Report. U.S. Army, Corps of Engineers. 1873 to the present.

Robinson, Billy. Manuscript on Rafting. Possession of Ernest Robinson, Oneida, Kentucky.

Ross, David F. "Mary Verhoeff Versus the Army Engineers on Canalization of the Kentucky River," *The Filson Club History Quarterly* 65 (Apr. 1996): 268–80.

Schulman, Steven A. "Rafting Logs on the Upper Cumberland River." *Pioneer America* 6 (Jan. 1974): 14–24.

Sharp, William E., and A. Gwynn Henderson. *Mute Stones Speak.* Lexington: Kentucky Geological Survey, 1997.

Smith, Eddie B. Chairman. *Nomination for Designation as a National Historic Civil Engineering Landmark, Cincinnati Southern Railway, High Bridge.* Kentucky Section: American Society of Civil Engineers, 1985.

"Special Report, Water Supply Alternatives to Red River Lake, Vol. I, Main Report, 1976." Louisville, U.S. Army, Corps of Engineers, Rev. 1978.

Teller, James T. "Preglacial (Teays) and Early Glacial Drainage in the Cincinnati Area, Ohio, Kentucky, and Indiana." *Geological Society of America Bulletin* 84 (Nov. 1973), 3677–88.

Thomas, Samuel W. *Dawn Comes to the Mountains.* Louisville: George Rogers Clark, 1981.

Ulack, Richard. Ed.-in-Chief. *Atlas of Kentucky.* Lexington: Univ. Press of Kentucky, 1998.

Verhoeff, Mary. *The Kentucky River Navigation.* Louisville: The Filson Club, 1917.

Walters, Tom R. "Logging by Splash Dam." *Appalachian Heritage* 5 (Winter 1977): 28–34.

Wharton, Mary E, and Roger W. Barbour. *Bluegrass: Land and Life.* Lexington: Univ. Press of Kentucky, 1991.

Wodder, Rebecca R. "Rivers Endangered and Restored." *American Rivers* 25 (Fall 1997): 2.

Wolfe, Charles K. *Kentucky Country: Folk and Country Music of Kentucky.* Lexington: Univ. Press of Kentucky, 1982.

Wright, George C. "The Forced Removal of Afro-Americans from Rural Kentucky." *Reflections: Occasional Papers on Research in Kentucky Public Records* 1 (1990): 1–8.

ORAL HISTORY INTERVIEWS

All interviews are located in special collections, John Grant Crabbe Library, Eastern Kentucky University, and in the holdings of Kentucky Oral History Commissions.

Adams, Logan. 29 March 1991.

Alcorn, Vernon. 8 August 1988.

Allen, Homer D. 9 March 1990.

Allen, Keith. 22 July 1988.

Archer, Hugh. 19 August 1998.

Ashcraft, Christine. 1 July 1988.

Ashcraft, Ernest. 6 June 1988

Ashcraft, Lonnie, 2 July 1988.

Atha, Lonnie W. 12 July 1990.

Barbour, Scott. 15 August 1989.

Barrett, Monroe. 7 June 1989.

Bates, Alan L. 30 August 1988.

Berry, Wendell. 28 June 1987.

Bourne, Victor. 10 November 1988.

Brewer, Seldon L. 23 May 1988.

Britton, Gilbert H. 14 August 1989.

Broadus, Bill. 6 May 1989.

Broce, Harrison. 26 July 1989.

Bryant, William S. 7 July 1988.

Bush, Leola B. 1 August 1989.

Byrd, Everett. 6 June 1989.

Callahan, Robert. 13 May 1989.

Campbell, Edward. 25 July 1989.

Carter, Myrtle Preston. 11 August 1989.

Clark, Thomas D. 26 May 1987.

Clements, Sidney R. and F.E. Webster. 13 April 1989.

Coffey, William H. 7 June 1988.

Combs, Ed. 4 November 1991.

Combs, J. Gordon. 5 March 1987.

Combs, Thomas A. 5 March 1987.

Covington, Walker. 13 August 1989.

Curry, Howard. 21 July 1987.

Dalton, Jesse Boyd. 17 August 1988.

Dawson, Flora. 6 April 1989.

Dedman, T.C. Jr. 22 December 1987.

Dees, Charles. 22 July 1987.

Dees, Russell T. 2 February 1988.

Dever, Garland R. Jr. 1 March 1988.

Donaldson, John L. 10 November 1986.

Dorman, Thomas M. 20 August 1998.

Douthitt, Charles W. 1 December 1988, 27 April 1989.

Dykes, J.C. Jr. 29 June 1989.

Elder, Eleanor L. 12 July 1989.

Embry, Margaret Lee. 6 July 1990.

Estes, E.B. 19 August 1998.

Estes, Sherman. 27 June 1989.

Filson, Zelma L. 15 May 1990.

Finney, Chester. 5 August 1988.

Fint, W.M. 16 September 1988, 11 August 1989.

Fitzgerald, Thomas J. 16 September 1998.

Floyd, James N. Jr. 22 May 1990.

Flynn, Maurice D. 14 June 1990.

Fullen, Sallie. 6 June 1990.

Garrett, William H. 6 June 1990.

Garrison, Gary P. 17 July 1989.

Gibson, Charlie R. 23 July 1990.

Gillock, Allen L. 15 May 1990.

Gordon, James B. 22 June 1988.

Gravett, Thomas E., Joe Christian, and Hubert Bush. 7 March 1989.

Gullette, O.H. 7 July 1989.

Gulley, Earl Jr. 20 May 1988, 11 August 1998.

Hackett, Bernie. 14 August 1989.

Hall, Marvin. 14 August 1989.

Hall, William E. 17 August 1989.

Hahn, Floyd. 7 August 1989.

Haney, Donald C. 27 August 1998.

Hardin, Cecil. 13 August 1988.

Harrod, John. 28 June 1988.

Hawkins, Marvin. 30 June 1989.

Hawkins, Willie C. 3 July 1991.

Hayslett, Clyde. 7 February 1988.

Helton, Joe. 27 July 1988.

Herrington, Alex P. 31 March, 5 April 1988.

Hopper, Delvia A. 15 September 1988.

Horn, Claude. 11 June 1987.

Howard, Claude C. 7 July 1988.

Hudson, James Clark. 5 July 1988.

Hurd, Arnold. 25 June 1989.

Imel, Avery. 23 July 1990.

Irvin, John W. 19 August 1987.

Ison, William. 1 April 1988.

Johnson, Leland R. 4 February 1988.

Johnson, Preston. 2 August 1988.

Kearns, Zelphia Denham. 15 September 1989.

Kelley, S.B. and Mary. 8 September 1988.

Kephart, F.W. 21 January 1988.

Lair, Susie B. 14 June 1990.

Lambert, John. 5 July 1989.

Land, Ed Jr. 1 August 1988.

Lee, Elmer K. 12 August 1989.

Lynch, William J. and Patrick C. 17 January 1988.

MacQuown, W.C. 19 January 1988.

McCauley, Mary Walters. 18 September 1988.

McKinney, Elmer. 25 July 1988.

McQueen, Hargis. 12 September 1988.

Mackey, Ida Dell. 25 March 1991.

Marcum, Frank. 25 July 1988.

Marcum, Herbert. 20 June 1989.

Martin, William H. 11 August 1998.

Mead, Andy. 28 August 1998.

Mershon, Marion. 15 August 1988.

Miller, Dorothy. 20 August 1989.

Moberly, Rufus L. 13 August 1988.

Moore, George O. 14 June 1988.

Napier, Emil. 24 April 1988.

New, David A. 6 July 1988.

Newby, Jessie, Eunice Perkins, Elizabeth N. Saylor,
    and Eva Sams. 3 December 1986.

Nightingale, R.E. 29 January 1988.

O'Malley, Nancy. 29 November 1988.

Palmer, Andrew J. 2 September 1989.

Parks, John S. 13 August 1989.

Parrish, Charles E. 27 June, 27 November 1987.

Patrick, Elise and Hickman. 23 April 1989.

Perkins, Bessie Martin. 10 July 1988.

Perkins, Eunice. 25 July 1987.

Pittillo, J. Dan. 30 September 1988.

Preston, Amalie. 28 July 1989.

Proctor, J. Virgil. 15 November 1988.

Powell, Benny. 15 December 1987.

Raisor, Jerry Lee. 14 August 1998.

Reece, Hugh. 1 June 1989.

Renfro, Homer. 20 June 1988.

Richardson, Grant. 24 July 1988.

Ripy, Ernest Jr. 6 July 1989.

Ripy, Thomas B. 6 July 1989.

Roberts, James B. 5 July 1990.

Robinson, Ben H. 25 June 1989.

Robinson, Ernest. 16 February 1989.

Rose, Lorene. 30 August 1992.

Rowe, Robert W. 18 December 1987.

Rucker, Irene M. 16 August 1989.

Sams, Eva Perkins. 5 July 1988.

Seale, Mayme. 3 November 1988.

Sewall, J.N. 13 June 1988.

Shackelford, Nevyle. 22 February 1988.

Shearer, Oliver F. 17 August 1998.

Shepherd, Ann G. 28 January 1988.

Short, Ike. 10 September 1987.

Smith, Eddie B. 20 July 1988.

Snyder, Jane Early. 1 September 1988.

Sparks, John M. 18 January 1988.

Spencer, Dorothy. 21 August 1992.

Spurr, S.F. 28 March 1989.

Stevens, Charles W. 27 June 1990.

Stewart, Ruby. 26 July 1990.

Stivers, Louis A. 7 December 1992.

Strohmeier, David L. 11 October 1988.

Suter, Aileen. 21 May 1990.

Sweat, Frances H. 19 July 1989.

Taulbee, Stanley. 18 May 1990.

Thomas, Estill. 14 February 1988.

Thomas, James C. 26 June 1987.

Tillett, Opal. 6 October 1988.

Tindall, Gene D. 14 May 1990.

True, Margaret H. 8 June 1988.

Tudor, Florence G. 17 June 1987.

Tuttle, James Hubert. 5 June 1989, 18 June 1990.

Wall, Marvin. 14 August 1989.

Walters, Delphia R. 1 September 1988.

Welsh, Glynn. 11 July 1990.

Wharton, Mary E. 14 January 1988.

White, Dorothy. 20 August 1989.

Wilson, Billy L. 14 March 1989.

Wilson, Sam. 24 March 1988.

Wilson, Walker. 21 June 1989.

Witt, Helen Stevens. 20 June 1990.

Wolfinbarger, Maggie. 2 June 1989.
Young, Clyde, Sr. 22 June 1989.
Young, James. 7 May 1989.
Yount, William D. 15 August 1989.

INDEX